Class and Stratification

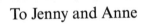
To Jenny and Anne

Class and Stratification

Third Edition

Rosemary Crompton

LEARNING RESOURCES
CENTRE
Havering College
of Further and Higher Education

Polity

First published in 2008 by Polity Press

Polity Press
65 Bridge Street
Cambridge CB2 1UR, UK

Polity Press
350 Main Street
Malden, MA 02148, USA

ISBN-13: 978-07456-3869-0
ISBN-13: 978-07456-3870-6 (pb)

A catalogue record for this book is available from the British Library.

Typeset in 10 on 12 pt Times NRMT
by Servis Filmsetting Ltd, Manchester
Printed and bound in Great Britain by MPG Books Ltd, Bodmin, Cornwall

For further information on Polity, visit our website: www.polity.co.uk

CONTENTS

FIGURES AND TABLES

Figures

Tables

INTRODUCTION TO THE FIRST EDITION

Introductions to books are usually the last thing to be written, and this one is no exception. I would like to take this opportunity, however, to describe some of the factors which led me to write this textbook, not least because many of the themes developed within it are rather different from positions taken up in my previous work – particularly *Economy and Class Structure* (Crompton and Gubbay 1977).

During the 1960s and 1970s, sociology underwent a period of rapid expansion as an academic subject. Within the social sciences, sociology had always been a critical discipline. During this period, therefore, one major focus of sociological criticisms was the ideas and hypotheses relating to the 'end of ideology' thesis. This thesis included arguments to the effect that industrial societies were characterized by a broad consensus on values and attitudes, and that conflicts relating to 'class' were rapidly becoming outdated in such societies. In contrast, sociological sceptics argued that, even in welfare capitalism, class conflicts persisted, and that class inequality and conflicts could not be eradicated or even 'managed' in capitalism. During the 1960s and 1970s, therefore, 'class theory' came to assume an increasingly important place within sociology. This was accompanied by a revival of interest in the classical theorists, especially the work of Marx. In particular, Braverman's *Labor and Monopoly Capital* (1974) provided a number of insights into how the divisions revealed by the Marxist analysis of the labour process might be mapped on to the structure of jobs and occupations. *Economy and Class Structure*, written during the 1970s, reflected these developments. It sought to provide a Marxist alternative to the predominantly Weberian mapping of social classes within sociology which had prevailed hitherto.

Theoretical ideas relating to social class in sociology had been grafted on to an existing approach to social stratification in which 'classes' were taken to be occupational aggregates. Other existing conventions were also carried forward into these new developments in 'class analysis' – most notably, the assumption that as the class of the household corresponded to that of the main breadwinner, and that as the 'head of the household' would usually be a man, then the 'class structure' could be reliably assumed to correspond to the structure of male employment. Without exception, therefore, in Britain all of the major surveys in the area of class and stratification had, until the 1970s, drawn upon men-only samples.

This practice came under increasing attack from the feminist critique within sociology which developed from the early 1970s. These criticisms, however, were directed not only at the exclusion of women from empirical investigations, but also at the underlying assumptions upon which the identification of a class structure within the structure of employment was predicated. That is, it was argued that the class (employment) structure was itself 'gendered'. Logically, therefore, the effects of 'class' and 'gender' could not be disentangled within the structure of employment. These feminist arguments were paralleled by developments in social theory, which, particularly in Giddens's account of 'structuration', argued that actions could not be separated from structure in sociological investigations – including investigations into 'social classes'.

As a consequence of these and other developments, 'class analysis' in sociology moved in a number of different directions. However, during the 1980s, debates within sociology itself were somewhat overshadowed by the crisis which sociology faced as an academic discipline in Britain, as departments were 'rationalized' and subject to increasing economic pressures, and sociologists themselves underwent the (often painful) process of adapting to 'new times'. Perhaps because of these developments, a number of key sociological concepts – in particular, class – came under increasing, and critical, scrutiny. The end – or, at least, the irrelevance – of class analysis in sociology was ever more frequently argued.

By the end of the 1980s, therefore, the empirical work of those pursuing a theoretical interest in class within sociology had fragmented into (at least) three areas: first, the macro-level analysis of large data sets, gathered by those who had developed theoretical, relational, approaches to 'social class' (Goldthorpe and Wright); second, socio-historical accounts of class formation (Lash and Urry 1987; McNall et al. 1991); and third, a growing interest in the *cultural* construction and reproduction of class associated with a developing 'sociology of consumption' and fuelled by the emphasis on consumerism which seemed, increasingly, to characterize contemporary societies (Bourdieu 1986). Those sociologists not directly concerned with these debates carried on doing what they had always done – that is, using convenient sociological shorthand whereby 'occupation' was taken to be a measure of 'class' without worrying too much about the finer details – even though, as we shall see, this assumption is highly problematic. It is one of the major arguments of this book that the largely unacknowledged fragmentation of approach within 'class analysis' in sociology is one of the reasons why its practitioners were not well placed to respond to the growing tide of criticisms of both the class concept and class analysis in general which had emerged by the end of the 1980s.

This book, therefore, was written with the aim of providing an overview of the field which would facilitate the moving forward of debate in an area which had, in my view, got somewhat bogged down in arguments between and within different schools of 'class analysis'. The unfortunate result was that many outsiders – even within the sociological community – had lost any real sense of what was going on. Despite claims to have provided an 'overview', however, there are a number of gaps in this text which I would freely acknowledge. As reflects my own interest, the question of gender is discussed reasonably thoroughly, but the important topic of race and ethnicity is discussed only in relation to the question of citizenship. Other crucial stratification issues – such as, for example, age – are not discussed at all. Nationalism, which following the break-up of the Eastern bloc is emerging as a central topic for the 1990s, is not considered. I can only apologize in advance for these and other deficiencies.

It would have been pleasant to record the fellowships, scholarships, and sabbatical leaves which had contributed to the writing of this book, but unfortunately there were none. Roger Burrows organized a debate on class at the 1990 British Sociological Association Conference, to which I contributed along with Ray Pahl and Gordon Marshall, and which was important in getting me started. Gordon Marshall was the first to suggest that I was writing a book, not an article, and has read the first draft of chapter 5. Communications with Mike Savage over the last few years have done much to clarify my thinking, as did conversations with Bob Holton in 1990. I would also like to thank David Held and Tony Giddens at Polity Press for their advice and comments, as well as an anonymous Polity reader for detailed comments on the first draft. Gerald Crompton has had to listen to far more monologues on class and stratification than an economic historian has any reasonable right to expect. Justine Clements has made the final alterations to my word-processed text, for which many thanks. Many others have contributed, directly and indirectly, to the writing of this book and I hope that a general acknowledgement will suffice – the good bits (if any) are theirs, and the faults are all mine.

Rosemary Crompton
University of Kent
September 1992

INTRODUCTION TO THE SECOND EDITION

The first edition of this book was written in order to provide an overview of an area of sociology which had become somewhat fragmented – with, I argued, somewhat negative consequences. This fragmentation continues to be reflected in the many books, commentaries and articles on the subject of class and stratification which have appeared since 1993, although a measure of clarification has been achieved as well. In Britain, an extended debate was stimulated by Goldthorpe and Marshall's (1992) defence of 'class analysis' as they saw it (Lee and Turner 1996). Further afield, Clark and Lipset's critical contribution was seen as having a particular significance given Lipset's historic role in establishing the centrality of 'class' within sociology (Bendix and Lipset 1967a). Two major cross-nationally comparative class projects have delivered their final reports (Erikson and Goldthorpe 1993; Wright 1997). If judged only by the number of publications with 'class' in the title, therefore, then within sociology class and stratification might still appear, relatively speaking, to be very much alive.

Nevertheless, the 'end of class' continues to be asserted with some regularity, and the postmodern and culturalist 'turn' in British sociology shows no sign of abating. A second edition of the book, therefore, seemed justified not only in relation to the volume of new and relevant work which had appeared on the scene, but also in order to restate the continuing significance of the topic within sociology (and indeed, the social sciences more generally).

In this second edition I have tended to concentrate on developments in the theoretical debates relating to class and stratification analysis, rather than providing a detailed empirical account of the various dimensions of class structures. This is in large part because there are a large number of recent books which do an excellent job of summarizing the empirical evidence (Devine 1997; Breen and Rottman 1995; Reid 1998). This does not mean, however, that I do not attach considerable importance to the need to justify statements with reference to empirical evidence, and this evidence is provided where necessary.

My own views have not radically changed, although there have been some shifts in emphasis which are reflected in the second edition. I am more convinced than ever that the way ahead in class and stratification analysis is to recognize the *de facto* plurality of conceptual frameworks and methodologies in the field. Thus I do not think it is particularly useful to argue about which class scheme is the 'best', for example – which is one reason why I have dropped 'Testing and refining measures of employment class' (1993: chapter 5) from this edition. In 1997, I would be even more cautious about laying an excessive emphasis on the unity of 'structure' and 'action' than I was in 1993. In sociological terms, structure and action are indeed interdependent, but as far as empirical research is concerned – and this is no more true than in the case of class analysis – an analytical separation has to be assumed (Layder 1990; Archer 1996).

The first edition of this book has been extensively revised and updated, but some chapters have been reworked more than others, and others have virtually disappeared. Chapters 1, 2 and 3 have probably changed least. Chapters 4 and 5 have been virtually rewritten. In chapter 4, I have taken out much of the emphasis on 'where to put people' (in line with my argument that there can be no single 'best' class scheme, then it is likely that different schemes will vary in their allocations of particular jobs, despite their broad similarities of purpose). Recent debates on 'class' have been incorporated, and the emerging convergence of Goldthorpe and Wright's recent work is emphasized. In chapter 5 I have systematically considered the implications of recent social theories (in particular, poststructuralism and postmodernism) for class and stratification analysis. I suggest that these debates remain a prime source of confusion and 'pseudo-debate' – that is, sociologists talking past, rather than to, each other.

In particular, I stress the need to distinguish between theoretical arguments relating to the possibility of a fundamental shift in the very nature of society itself (as is suggested in some versions of 'postmodernism' or 'reflexive modernity'), and the 'employment-aggregate' approach of Goldthorpe and Wright, which is largely concerned with the persisting consequences of job-related inequalities. These are two very different kinds of arguments, and should be seen as such.

The order of chapters 6 and 7 has been reversed from the first edition, although they still deal with the same broad topics. Chapter 6, on culture and consumption, has been extended to include a discussion of recent developments in employment and their likely implications for class consciousness and identity, as well as a section on gender and the middle classes. Chapter 7 is largely unchanged in outline, but the discussion of the 'underclass' debate has been extended and developed in order to provide a 'worked example' of the necessity of a multidimensional empirical approach. Chapter 8 has been completely rewritten. Rather than providing a descriptive outline of the 'class structure', as in the first edition, I have chosen to examine in some depth the related topics of social mobility, educational opportunity and social polarization. This is in part because it may be argued that the culturalist and postmodernist turn in sociology is in some danger of removing altogether any requirement that we systematically examine those structures and processes in society which repeatedly ensure that some are less equal than others – in other words, social class.

I conclude that although contemporary capitalist societies continue to be fundamentally stratified by systematic inequalities associated with access to property, jobs and 'life chances' in general, the fragmentation of being and experiences brought about by developments such as the flexibilization of employment, privatism and 'home-centredness', and the growth of insecurity – of jobs, of 'falling off the ladder' in an increasingly competitive and 'marketized' environment – make the development of a cohesive, collective, occupationally based 'class consciousness' of a 'Fordist', 'trade union' variety not very likely. Thus in this sense recent criticisms have some validity. Nevertheless, at the end of the millennium, the actual capacity of dominant economic interests to be realized shows little sign of being undermined. Class processes still count, even if the class interests of particular groups remain poorly articulated. It might be argued, therefore, that rather than sociologists continuing to argue for the 'end of class', together with a refocusing of interests away from the 'material' to the 'cultural', we should, rather, be going in the *opposite* direction.

Finally, I would like to thank the Research School of Social Sciences, the Australian National University for inviting me to take up a visiting scholarship, and the University of Leicester for giving me leave of absence to take it. I would never have achieved this rewrite without this assistance, which is gratefully acknowledged. Fiona Devine and Mike Savage read the first drafts of the manuscript, and Lisa Adkins the first draft of chapter 5. Many other people have helped in lots of different ways – from a willingness to tolerate a certain level of abstractedness (and lack of sweetness of temper) to answering specific academic enquiries. I really am very grateful to you all.

Rosemary Crompton
University of Leicester
December 1997

INTRODUCTION TO THE THIRD EDITION, AND ACKNOWLEDGEMENTS

This book has been very extensively revised and rewritten. Although much of the old chapter 1 remains (as chapter 2 in this edition), the discussion has been considerably extended with the objective of demonstrating just how thoroughly intertwined debates on 'class' have been with wider theoretical debates in sociology, and the consequences of this intertwining for our understanding of 'class analysis'. Chapter 3 (old chapter 2) will probably be the most recognizable to those familiar with the previous edition, although it has been revised and updated. Chapter 4, as in old chapter 3, has a major focus on the strategy of measuring (operationalizing) class by dividing up the employment structure – what I have described as the 'employment-aggregate' approach to class. This chapter now includes a discussion of the new class scheme introduced in the British Census of 2001 – the Office of National Statistics Socio-Economic Classification (ONS-SEC).

In previous editions, much space was devoted to the exposition and critique of the two major cross-national 'employment-aggregate' comparative research programmes that had dominated 'class analysis' in the 1980s and much of the 1990s, and which were led by John Goldthorpe and Erik Wright. These research programmes converged somewhat towards their endings, and have now been concluded. The discussion of these programmes in this edition, therefore, has been reduced. In previous editions, it also seemed necessary to devote considerable attention to a sustained defence of the complex project of 'class analysis', as, within sociology, class was so frequently argued to be at best irrelevant, or at worst completely useless as a concept and needing to be superseded by some 'new' approach, theory or whatever.

However (and I hope I am not mistaken here), class analysis still seems to be alive and flourishing, so I have accordingly devoted less space to its defence. This means that the arguments of chapters 4 and 5 in the second edition have been combined in a single chapter in this edition (chapter 5). However, this has not simply been a matter of 'cutting and pasting'. Besides extensive updating, the argument is also developed that the processes of 'individualization' and 'detraditionalization', which social theorists have argued to be characteristic of 'reflexive modernity', should rather be seen as being, at least in part, the consequences of the growing impact of political and economic neo-liberalism.

The revival of interest in 'class analysis' has been accompanied by an increasing interest in cultures of class and culturalist explanations more generally. Bourdieu's work has been of considerable importance in this regard, and chapter 6 (which includes some elements from chapter 6 of the second edition) has a major focus on Bourdieu's work and the cultural dimensions of class. Much new material has been added here. The previous chapter 7 has largely disappeared (although citizenship is discussed in relation to status in chapter 6 of this edition). Chapter 7 in this edition (on social mobility and education) is largely new, although a discussion of social mobility has been incorporated from chapter 8 of the second edition. Chapter 8 is also new, although incorporating (updated) discussions of the underclass from chapter 7 of the second edition, as well as similar updated discussions of social polarization from chapter 8.

As I revised the references of this third edition, I came to realize just how much had disappeared. These disappearances include summaries of feminist debates from the 1970s and 1980s, extended debates around citizenship, much of the literature on race, and extensive discussions of the service class and changes in employment. Given my own research interests, the discussion of the impact of changes in the gendered division of labour on debates within class analysis remains, so to speak, 'embedded' in the chapters of this third edition. My reasons for the absence of a specific focus on 'race' are explained in chapter 8 of this book – but nevertheless, this may still be counted as a weakness. Another absence in this book is a lack of any systematic data outlining changes in the occupational 'class structure', or descriptions of class-related inequalities. This is quite deliberate. Not only do such materials 'date' very rapidly, but more importantly, the relevant information is quickly and easily available (for free) via the Internet (for Britain, see www.statistics.gov.uk/; see *Social Trends* for regularly updated materials).

In general, my perspective on class and stratification analysis has not changed over the ten years since the second edition, although it has, of course, been brought up to date. I still hold to the view that what is required is a combination of different approaches to class and stratification rather than the development of a 'new' approach or perspective, even though the theoretical underpinnings of these different approaches might appear to be incompatible. I also still hold to the view that although it is essential to recognize the very real social and economic changes that have taken place over the last half century, it is important to exercise some caution in assuming that a fundamental 'societal shift' has occurred, requiring completely new or transformed analytical tools and methods.

Finally, I have to confess that I have found this second revision of *Class and Stratification* to be quite a difficult task, and I hope that the sweat does not drip too obviously off the pages. Thanks to Fiona Devine, Mike Savage, Andrew Sayer and John Scott for keeping my interest and engagement in class and stratification issues alive over the last decade. Any faults in this text are mine alone.

Rosemary Crompton
City University, London
July 2007

SETTING THE SCENE

1

Over the decade since the publication of the second edition of this book, political, economic and social change has continued apace. Not surprisingly, these changes have been reflected in debates and discussions within sociology and indeed, within the social sciences more generally. One of this book's objectives is to recognize the very real changes that have taken place, whilst simultaneously retaining our awareness of underlying societal continuities. It will be argued that largely on account of these continuities, the intertwined topics of class and stratification remain central to the sociological enterprise. This approach means that an historical perspective is essential – not only in relation to the events of the recent past, but also in relation to dominant ways (or 'theories') of thinking about them. As we shall see, many ideas, perspectives and sociological theories that are presented as 'new' or contemporary have their roots in much older debates. It will be argued that to recognize these origins will, at the very least, give us a better understanding of current discourses, and at best enable us to identify those which are most likely to carry our discussions forward.

The first part of this introductory chapter, therefore, will briefly review some of the relevant changes that have taken place over the last decade. The example of Association Football in Britain will be employed as a metaphor in order to illustrate the changes that have taken place in 'class' relations, as well as the social and economic consequences of the unleashing of 'market forces' as a consequence of the encouragement and application of 'neo-liberal' principles of economic and social organization. The second part of this introductory chapter summarizes the rest of this book.

Individualization, neo-liberalism and 'extreme capitalism'

The election of a 'New Labour' government in Britain in 1997, after eighteen years of Conservative rule, seemed to offer new possibilities for change and improvement, particularly for those concerned with addressing inequalities. However, although equality-directed New Labour policies (such as reducing child poverty) have been introduced, the New Labourite 'third way' (see p. 136) has to a large extent retained the neo-liberal economic policies developed under Thatcherism.

In brief, contemporary neo-liberalism builds on the foundations of nineteenth-century economic liberalism (that is, economic *laissez-faire*), and indeed, the majority of its principles are very similar to this older doctrine.[1] Neo-liberalism claims that society as a whole is best served by maximum market freedom and minimum intervention by the state. Thus the role of government should be limited to security, the defence of the realm and the protection of private property, together with the creation and maintenance of markets. Other functions, including the provision of essential services (such as transport, water, energy and even health and education), are best carried out by private enterprise. The profit motive will ensure rationality in decision-making and thus the 'best' outcome for society as a whole, whilst individual citizens remain free from the oppressive demands of the state.

In Britain (and the United States) the decades after the Second World War had been characterized by social and economic policies (often described as 'Keynesian'[2]) that had sought directly to restrain the impact of 'market forces'. These policies had included restraints on borrowing and lending and the use of taxation, interest rates, etc. to control demand, as well as the regulation of prices and incomes. These policies were redistributive (indeed, up until the 1970s, the extent of material inequalities declined). However, Keynesian policies were increasingly criticized, by neo-liberals, as contributing to economic decline. In Britain, the election of the Conservative government in 1979 marked a decisive shift to neo-liberal policies, and 'the market' was reintroduced as the preferred mechanism of economic and social organization. As documented in the chapters that follow (see chapter 5 in particular), state-owned assets (e.g. gas, electricity, transport, telecommunications) were privatized, wage controls and other labour market 'restrictions' were removed, financial services were deregulated, and 'quasi-markets' introduced in areas of public provision such as education and health.

'New Labour', despite its long period in office, has not substantially reversed these neo-liberal policies. Thus the labour market in Britain remains largely deregulated (although a minimum wage has been established) and the government continues to adopt a 'hands-off' policy as far as business interests, and market forces more generally, are concerned. Indeed, neo-liberal economic policies would seem to be gaining in influence worldwide and are particularly entrenched in the US (Harvey 2005). There has been no real change, therefore, in the broad structuring of economic class inequalities.

Nevertheless, other profound changes *have* taken place. In most 'Western' countries, the structure of employment is in a process of constant transformation. The proportion of those engaged in 'professional and managerial' employment continues to rise (although at a slower rate), and in England and Wales, nearly a third of the adult population were so classified in the 2001 Census. There has been a corresponding decline in the proportion of jobs requiring physical strength and a modicum of intelligence – that is, the 'good' working-class jobs (in mining, car assembly and steelworking, for example) once held by men.

Technological change means that this kind of labour has increasingly been replaced by machines (or computers). However, many of these kinds of jobs have been 'exported' to countries such as China and India, and in Britain, immigrant labour is increasingly recruited to carry out the jobs at the lower levels of the employment structure. In addition, the nature of jobs is constantly changing – in the 1990s, for example, call centres were considered as a 'new' form of employment; today, they are outsourced overseas.

In all 'Western' countries, women increasingly expect to be in employment for most of their adult lives, even when they have small children. Indeed, in Britain, the greatest growth in employment from the last decade of the twentieth century onwards has been amongst women with children under school age. Women who are well educated and in good jobs tend to enter into partnerships with similar men, and (besides the loss of 'good' working-class jobs and increasing wage disparities) this 'assortative mating' is another factor contributing to social polarization, as the gap widens between two-earner households and households in which no adult works at all (Gregg and Wadsworth 2001).

Despite this process of constant change, however, a number of underlying processes remain the same. Capitalism (and the capitalist state) continues to generate a diverse range of differentially rewarded jobs. Profitability remains a major concern for the capitalist enterprise. Great concentrations of wealth persist – and indeed, are on the increase. At the individual level, people still want to do the best they can for themselves and their families. Thus parents still work around the educational system as far as they can, and 'market'-inspired changes in the education system have increased opportunities for middle-class parents to ensure that their children are placed in academically successful schools (in Britain, social mobility is actually in decline). People still constantly compare themselves to others, and economic and social hierarchies are enduring.

It still makes sense, therefore, to describe Britain and other, similar societies as 'class' societies. What, however, of the explanatory value of the 'class' concept? As we shall see in the chapters that follow, there is no straightforward answer to this question, not least because of the variety of ways in which 'class' has been defined. In terms of 'class' relations, and perceptions of class, however, there is one important change (or rather, set of changes) that it would be best to acknowledge from the outset.

This is the fact that, although class divisions are persistent, the *idea* of 'class' has lost its importance as a central discourse, or political organizing principle, in contemporary societies. This is a consequence of changes in jobs, in employment and in localities, as well as quite deliberate and conscious changes in discursive frameworks. In respect of the latter, for example, in Britain, the Labour Party, for most of the twentieth century, defined itself as the party of the 'working class'. However, 'New Labour' has consciously distanced itself from 'class' connotations of any kind. Poverty is seen as a problem of 'social exclusion' rather than as an outcome of class processes. Thus government policies tend to be directed at equipping the individual with the capacities for inclusion (training, parenting classes, new skills) rather than at systematic structural or contextual changes that might reduce inequalities (increases in taxation, or employment regulation that would generate 'better' jobs, for example). An emphasis on the individual, of course, is one of the defining features of neo-liberalism.

It could be argued – and indeed, many social theorists have done so (Giddens 1991; Beck and Beck-Gernsheim 2002) – that an increasingly individualistic emphasis within society at large is an outcome of the kinds of structural economic and social changes that have been briefly reviewed above, rather than just a shift in ideas and dominant 'ways of thinking'. The decline – indeed disappearance – of traditional working-class communities has removed an important mechanism of socialization within which collectivist ideas and attitudes were once generated. Although, for most people, work as employment remains of central importance, changes in the nature of work itself, the employment relationship and management styles have all contributed to increasing individualism. In Western countries, increasing affluence has resulted in a greater emphasis on consumption and leisure. Moreover, opportunities to consume have been massively widened (cheap holidays overseas, for example), and information on these opportunities is widely available both in the media and in more recent developments such as the Internet.

In Britain, the example of Association Football may be used as a metaphor through which to illustrate some of the many different strands contributing to the growth of individualism and the decline of collectivism. Football was once the 'people's game' (Walvin 2001, although this did not usually include women). The majority of today's leading clubs began as an extension of their local community, linked to a workplace (Arsenal and West Ham), a working men's social club (Manchester United), a church (Everton) or educational institution (Tottenham Hotspur), and both supporters and players tended to be 'locals'. In a similar vein, financial support for these early ventures was drawn from the local community, and the major shareholders were local employers and businessmen. As with boxing, professional football was (and still is) a way in which working-class youths could achieve upward mobility and economic security – to a point.

Until the 1960s, the wages of football players were regulated at a level that certainly provided a good income, but not excessive riches. The major market in football was in the transfer (of players), and promising young players in the lower divisions were almost invariably sold on to the more successful clubs. Nevertheless, Association Football in Britain, even at the higher levels, retained strong local links until well into the second half of the twentieth century. This rootedness in local working-class communities meant that 'football's politics, such as they are, have tended to loiter on the left wing' (Ronay 2007). Even in the 1960s, 1970s and 1980s major figures in football, such as Bill Shankly and Brian Clough, identified themselves as socialists, and traced their beliefs back to childhoods spent in areas dominated by heavy industry and trade union influence.

The regulation of footballers' wages ended in the 1960s. Wages increased, but not dramatically, and were still restricted by the ability of clubs to pay. However, the nature of football in Britain was changing, as the more successful clubs opened up their shareholdings via stock market flotations. The erosion of the 'traditional' working-class fan base and football's growing attraction for the middle classes meant that the successful clubs became increasingly attractive in financial terms, grounds were improved, and ticket prices rose dramatically. The really big change, however, came in 1992 when the sale of television rights, at a stroke, massively increased the money available to the clubs, particularly the more successful clubs. The introduction of the Premiership (an elite 'super league', replacing the old First Division) hugely increased the financial polarization between the top and bottom clubs. The leading teams have become global brands, and local links have to a large extent disappeared. The clubs themselves are now up for grabs, either as the playthings of the international super-rich, or as sound commercial investments. Footballers' wages now average £12,300 a week and the top players have become multimillionaires. The international trade in the top players means that national, as well as local, links have been attenuated. Local heroes have been replaced by international celebrities.

As a recent commentary has argued (Ronay 2007):

in its own way modern British football is a deeply political affair. Just take a look at the Premiership to find out what 15 years of hot-housed free-market capitalism looks like . . . The players have come to represent an acme of consumption, a brutally linear expression of a certain way of living. In our footballers we see a funfair mirror reflection of the same forces working on the people watching them from the stands. We don't admire them, so much as aspire to their lifestyle . . . The top tier of British football stands as an extreme expression of a certain kind of politics, rampant capitalism with the volume turned up to 11.

This brief excursion into the recent history of British football has been made not in order to sentimentalize the past, or as a yearning for the 'good old days', but as a (hopefully) accessible illustration of the many different factors that have fed into the generation of an increasingly individualistic perspective in Britain and other countries. The erosion of local communities, the deregulation of the labour market, the growth of commercialism and the impact of the media have polarized the game and created in Britain a global leisure industry marked by a highly individualistic culture. The example of football may be seen as an extreme case of the processes that fuel increasing individualism in society at large.

However, in this book it will be argued that although it is pointless to attempt to deny, or ignore, this individualistic societal shift, this does not mean, as some have argued, that 'class is dead'. 'Class' still persists as systematically structured social and economic disadvantage, which is reproduced over the generations. With regard to the explanatory value of the concept of 'class', it will be argued that we should not attempt to cling on to old frameworks, but also that it is equally important not to discard approaches and techniques that are still relevant to the analysis of contemporary societies. Indeed, in this book it will be further suggested that at times, the pursuit of the currently fashionable within sociology (in particular, in respect of 'culture' and 'identity') has resulted in a loss of sociological 'cutting edge' as far as discussions of class inequalities are concerned (see Crompton and Scott 2005). A 'return to structures' is required. In this third edition, therefore, this imbalance will be redressed by focusing (particularly in chapters 7 and 8) on the impact of neo-liberal economic and social policies and thinking on social mobility, class differences in educational achievement, and social polarization. As Harvey (2005: 202) has argued:

progressives of all stripes seem to have caved in to neoliberal thinking since it is one of the primary fictions of neoliberalism that class is a fictional category that exists only in the imagination of socialists and crypto-communists . . . The first lesson we must learn . . . is that if it looks like class struggle and acts like class war then we have to name it unashamedly for what it is.

This is not a book about the 'one best way' of approaching the analysis of class and inequality. It will be argued that a variety of different approaches is required, depending on both the nature of the topic and the kinds of evidence available. This volume (chapter 3 in particular) may also be seen as a book about the history of 'class analysis', as I hold to the view that in order to understand the present, we have to understand the past. Moreover, as argued above, sorting through the numerous concepts, theories and analytical frameworks that have been developed in the study of class and stratification is an essential way of establishing what can be set aside, but more importantly, what should be retained. Another recurring theme of this book is that in order to grasp the totality of social inequality and its persistence, we have to be prepared to work *across* and with conflicting approaches and methods. Different approaches to class and stratification may often appear to be diametrically opposed to each other, but if we are prepared to work with both, we are able to see that they illuminate different parts of the whole.

Summary of chapters

The next chapter (chapter 2, 'Approaches to Class and Stratification Analysis') reviews the history of frameworks developed in order to understand (and explain) the persistence of social inequality. It is also concerned with conceptual clarification, emphasizing the many different ways in which class and stratification have been defined, and the very wide range of topics that have been incorporated within their scope. This discussion involves the 'embedding' of class and stratification debates within wider topics and issues in social theory. These debates have generated apparently irreconcilable 'positions' in relation to our understanding of the social world – and this would include our understanding of class and stratification. In chapter 3 ('Class Analysis: The Classic Inheritance and its Development in the Twentieth Century'), we carry further forward some of the issues and debates sketched out in chapter 2. Besides a more comprehensive examination of Marx's and Weber's ideas on 'class', we also explore their impact on sociology (and indeed, social science more generally), as well as on 'class analysis', since the Second World War. This history of 'class analysis' over the second half of the twentieth century illustrates the emergence of a persisting 'divide' between 'action' and 'structure' within the debates. However, as will be argued throughout this book, this should not be seen as a divide, but rather as an *interdependence*. It is not a case of 'either/or', but 'both/and'.

Chapter 4 ('Measuring the "Class Structure" ') focuses on 'structural' accounts of class, that is, the systematic attempts that have been made to operationalize (measure) the 'class structure' by dividing up the occupational structure (the 'employment-aggregate' approach). Both 'official' and 'sociological' class schemes are examined and reviewed, as well as those used by policy and market researchers. Chapter 5 ('An Untimely Prediction of Death and a Timely Renewal') begins with an account of the *de facto* convergence in the work of the two major protagonists of the 'employment-aggregate' approach – Goldthorpe and Wright. The major objective of this chapter, however, is to examine the extensive changes in contemporary societies, as well as theoretical accounts of these changes, that have led to assertions as to the 'death of class' and the rise of 'individualization'. It is argued that what we have witnessed in recent decades is not a 'societal shift' – that is, a fundamental transformation of 'modern' societies consequent on globalization and technological change – but rather, the intensification of neo-liberalism or 'extreme capitalism'. In the light of these arguments, recent attempts to develop updated, inclusive, overarching 'class theories' are critically examined.

Nevertheless, it is explicitly recognized that much in the established tradition of 'class analysis' might legitimately be criticized as economistic and overdeterminist. In chapter 6 ('Class and Culture: The Ethnography of Class'), therefore, we explore in some depth the cultural dimension of class and stratification, beginning with an exposition of the 'status' concept together with T. H. Marshall's influential conception of 'citizenship'. Bourdieu's approach to 'class' is examined in some detail, together with applications of his approach to the investigation of both the 'middle' and 'working' classes. It is argued that the investigation of class and stratification needs to draw upon both 'economic' and 'cultural' approaches, and in the conclusions, recent attempts to combine the two into a single approach are critiqued and reviewed. Again, it is suggested that 'combinatory' approaches have not been particularly successful; rather, we have to recognize inherent 'theoretical' contradictions, but at the same time work across them.

Both 'economic' and 'cultural' approaches to class, despite their differences, agree that the family plays a major role in the reproduction of class inequalities. Chapter 7 ('Families, Social Mobility and Educational Achievement') investigates the linked processes of social mobility and class differences in educational achievement. It is suggested that the development of a 'quasi-market' in education in Britain, associated with the increasing influence of neo-liberal policies, has enhanced the opportunities for the middle-class deployment of economic, cultural and social capital and is associated with declining rates of social mobility. In the conclusions, the *interdependence* (rather than opposition) of sociological 'binaries' in approaches to class and stratification is again emphasized.

In the final chapter (chapter 8, 'Widening Inequalities and Debates on "Class": Discussion and Conclusions'), we turn to the question of the widening of class inequalities. Debates on the 'underclass' are examined, together with contemporary discussions of poverty and 'social exclusion'. It is argued that, despite their very real differences from theories of the 'underclass', these contemporary debates still retain the focus on the individual that is characteristic of the 'underclass' theorists. Some of the reasons for widening inequalities, even in 'affluent' Western societies, are reviewed. It is argued that even though structural trends, such as deindustrialization and the shift of employment to the service sector, changes in the family, and globalization, have contributed to this widening, nevertheless, the shift to economic and political neo-liberalism has also been central to the growth of class inequality. 'Individualization', it is suggested, is not some unstoppable trend, but is linked to these changes in economic and social policies. Finally, the possibilities of 'countermovements' against neo-liberalism (or extreme capitalism) are briefly examined.

APPROACHES TO CLASS AND STRATIFICATION ANALYSIS

2

Introduction

All complex societies are characterized, to varying extents, by the unequal distribution of material and symbolic rewards. The study of the causes and consequences of these inequalities is the major focus of class and stratification theorists and researchers. As we shall see in this book, the range of issues and topics falling within this broad rubric is immense, and the concepts, theories and measures developed to address these topics have often been the subject of extended (and sometimes acrimonious) debates. Nevertheless, common to all sociological conceptions of class and stratification is the argument that social and economic inequalities are not 'natural' or divinely ordained, but rather, emerge as a consequence of human behaviours.

'Social stratification' describes the hierarchical ordering of social relationships, and is a general term which describes these systematic structures of inequality. The terms 'class' and 'stratification' are often used interchangeably. However, without drawing a hard and fast distinction between the two, it is useful to think of 'stratification' as the more general term. Hierarchical positioning in the social order, at both macro- and micro-levels, is all-pervasive. It can draw upon a number of different dimensions, both material and cultural. Thus positioning in a stratification order is an outcome of a wide range of factors including the extent of social recognitions and esteem, gender, age, ethnicity, income and other material resources, knowing how to behave (and the people you know) as well as other characteristics – religious affiliation, for example, might be crucial in some societies but not in others. In contrast, the term 'class' is often reserved for descriptions of material inequalities and their origins – and indeed, as we shall see in the following chapters, many sociologists insist on a sharp distinction between 'class' and 'status' (or hierarchy).

It has become commonplace to argue that there is no single, 'correct' definition of the class concept, nor any universally 'correct' measure of it, and this is the position that will be taken in this book. However, it *can* be argued that particular concepts, and measures, are more appropriate for the analysis of particular problems and topics than others are. For example, Wright (2005: 180) has recently argued that 'specific definitions and elaborations of the concept of class . . . are shaped by the diverse kinds of questions class is thought to answer'. Thus, for example, different 'class' concepts would be needed for an investigation of how inequalities in 'life chances' and material standards of living are to be explained, as compared to the exploration of how individuals and groups *subjectively* locate themselves within unequal 'class' structures (the question of class 'identity'). This 'horses for courses' approach is an eminently sensible one, and a useful way of avoiding 'pseudo-debates', in which class analysts talk past, rather than to, each other. Particular approaches to 'class' may be very different from each other, but if they have a focus on different things, then they are not necessarily incompatible. It might be suggested, therefore, that one appropriate strategy for a textbook on class and stratification might be to identify the broad range of topics with which 'class analysis' is concerned, and then describe the concepts and measures developed in relation to each topic. These would vary according to the topic under investigation.

Unfortunately, although there is a lot to be said for this argument, matters are not quite so straightforward. As we shall see in this book, even when class and stratification analysts are focusing on very similar topics, they have developed very different theories, concepts and measures, and these have often been endlessly contested. It will be suggested that these disputes frequently have their origins in fundamental (and probably non-resolvable) differences in methodological approaches to sociology as a discipline. The study of class and stratification has been profoundly affected by these debates.

Debating inequality

No persisting structure of economic and social inequality has existed in the absence of some kind of meaning system(s) which seek both to explain and to justify the unequal distribution of societal resources. In pre-industrial or traditional societies, inequalities and thus social stratification were widely held to be natural, and/or to reflect an aspect of a cosmology which provided an account of the society itself. Thus, for example, in ancient Greece Aristotle asserted that: 'It is thus clear that there are *by nature* free men and slaves, and that servitude is just and agreeable for the latter . . . Equally, the relation of the male to the female is *by nature* such that one is superior and the other inferior, one dominates and the other is dominated' (cited in Dahrendorf 1969: 18). A pre-established harmony is being asserted between things natural and things social. This is a view which effectively rules out any sociological treatment of the issue – if inequalities are 'natural', then nothing can be done about them and there is no need to investigate them further.

Besides this assumption of 'naturalness', inequalities have been viewed as deriving from the divinely ordained structuring of society, as in the Hindu caste system in classical India. In this system, social rank corresponded to religious (ritual) purity. Lower castes polluted the higher and, as a consequence, a series of restrictions was imposed on low-caste individuals and their families. Thus the caste system corresponded (although not precisely) to the overall structure of social inequality.[1] Two religious concepts, *karma* and *dharma*, sustained the system. Karma teaches a Hindu that he or she is born into a particular caste or sub-caste because he or she deserves to be there as a consequence of actions in a previous life. Dharma, which means 'existing according to that which is moral', teaches that living one's present life according to the rules (dharma) will result in rebirth into a higher caste and thus ultimate progression through the caste system. Both existing inequalities of caste, therefore, and any possibility of change in the future are related to universal religious truths and are thus beyond the reaches of systematic sociological examination.

The justification of material inequality as stemming from some 'natural' or divine ordinance, therefore, is a common feature of traditional or pre-industrial societies. Such accounts not only explain inequality, but also assert that it is part of the natural order of things that the 'best' should get the majority share of the rewards that society has to offer. In feudal Europe as in classical India, stratification was accompanied by religious and moral justifications. From the ninth century onwards, Western Europe was an essentially rural society, in which an individual's condition was determined by access to the land. This was largely controlled by a minority of lay and ecclesiastical proprietors. It was a hierarchical society, in which the enserfed peasantry were subject to the domination of secular and ecclesiastical lords. The church possessed both economic and moral ascendancy. As Pirenne (1936) has argued, the church's conception of the feudal world 'was admirably adapted to the economic conditions of an age in which land was the sole foundation of the social order'. Land had been given by God to men in order to enable them to live on earth with a view to their eternal salvation. The object of labour was not to grow wealthy, and the monk's renunciation was the ideal 'on which the whole of society should fix its gaze'. To seek riches was to fall into the sin of avarice, and poverty was of divine origin (Pirenne 1936: 423).

In traditional societies, therefore, relative economic stagnation was also associated with social rigidity in respect of stratification systems. These societies, however, did not endure, and throughout the seventeenth, eighteenth and nineteenth centuries Western Europe, and much of the rest of the world, was transformed by the development of capitalist industrialism – the most significant element of the process which has been described as the coming of 'modernity'. The profound economic and social changes which took place throughout these centuries were accompanied by a developing critique of the traditional systems of belief which for over two millennia had served to explain material inequalities and render them legitimate.

In direct opposition to the idea that human beings are naturally or divinely unequal at birth, therefore, there developed from the seventeenth century onwards the argument that, by virtue of their humanity, all human beings were born *equal*, rather than unequal.[2] From this assumption derives the beginnings of a sociological approach to the explanation of inequality. If equality, rather than inequality, is assumed to be the 'natural' condition of human beings, then how are persisting inequalities to be explained and justified? If each individual is endowed with natural rights, why do some individuals dominate others? These questions remain as the central problems of social and political theory. In the sphere of political thought, some of the first answers to these questions were supplied by the social contract theorists. Hobbes (1588–1679) argued that in a state of nature life was 'nasty, brutish and short', characterized by the war of 'every man against every man'. The solution to this 'problem of order' was submission to the state, in the absence of which there would be chaos. Locke (1632–1704) also argued that the 'natural rights' to life, liberty and property are best protected by the authority of the state. In a famous statement which has resounded through history, Rousseau (1712–78) asserted that 'man was born free, and he is everywhere in chains'. He did not consider that complete equality could ever be achieved but argued that direct democracy, expressed through the 'general will', would afford the greatest protection for the individual. Thus the foundations of the argument that all 'citizens' were entitled to political rights, as expressed in universal suffrage and democratic institutions, were laid in the eighteenth century.

The passing of traditional society and the growth of capitalist industrialism was accompanied by an emphasis on the rationality of the modern social order. Not customary rules, but rational calculation, were held to be the principles which should govern economic conduct in the developing capitalist societies. The expansion of markets and transformation of the processes of production which accompanied the Industrial Revolution would have been difficult to achieve without the erosion of customary rights in trade and manufacture – which affected all its aspects and included cartels, wage and price fixing, restrictions on the mobility of labour and so on. Thus the political changes which created the formally free individual also created the landless labourer. This individual was, however, entitled to sell what only she or he possessed – labour, or the capacity to work. People themselves had become commodities.

The English and French revolutions were first amongst the political changes which accompanied the transition to capitalist industrialism. However, the 'bourgeois freedoms' which they achieved came under critical scrutiny from that foremost social theorist of the nineteenth century, Karl Marx. As described in the *Communist Manifesto*, Marx saw the unfolding of human history as an outcome of economic, rather than merely political, conflicts: 'The history of all hitherto existing society is the history of class struggles' (Marx and Engels 1962: 34). Inequality was, and always had been, a reflection of differential access to the means of production and what was produced. For Marx, state power was inseparable from economic power, and the 'sovereign individual' of capitalism was but a necessary condition of the development of the capitalist mode of production. Political equality could coexist with material inequalities and indeed, by defining the inequalities associated with the dominant system of production, distribution and exchange as 'non-political', bourgeois ideology served to make them legitimate. The landless labourers created as a consequence of political and economic change constituted a new class which was emerging as a consequence of the development of industrial capitalism – a class which would eventually transform capitalist society – the proletariat.

The development of capitalist industrialism has been identified as a major element in the transition to 'modernity'. The idea of modernity describes the development not just of industrialism *per se*, but also of the corresponding modes of surveillance and regulation of the population of nation states – nation states have been identified as one of the characteristic social forms accompanying the transition to modernity. This transition ushered in a world which is peculiarly dynamic, a world which is in the process of constant change and transformation.

In this book, 'class' will be discussed as a peculiarly modern phenomenon. To describe class as 'modern' is to suggest that it is primarily a characteristic of modern stratification systems, of 'industrial' societies, in contrast to the 'traditional' structures of inequality associated with ascribed or supposedly natural characteristics such as those of feudal estates or religiously defined hierarchies, as well as gender and race. This does not mean that 'classes' did not exist prior to modernity, but rather that the idea of 'class' has become one of the key concepts through which we can begin to understand it.[3] In the modern world, class-based organizations – that is, organizations claiming to represent classes and class interests, such as political parties, trade unions and organizations of employers and other interest groups – have been the dynamic source of many of the changes and transformations which have characterized the modern era.

'Class', therefore, is a major organizing concept in the exploration of contemporary stratification systems. However, although inequalities associated with the structures of production, distribution and exchange assume greater significance with the transition to industrialism, this does not mean that established forms of social distinction and differentiation simply disappear overnight. Customary inequalities, particularly those associated with ascribed statuses associated with age, gender and race, have persisted into the modern era.

Not only customary inequalities, but many of the ideas which underpinned them, persisted into the modern age. Hirsch (1977) has argued that the 'moral legacy' of pre-capitalist institutions supplied the social foundations for the developing capitalist order. The ideologies associated with religion and custom in traditional societies, besides identifying the levels of material reward which were properly associated with the different ranks in society, and giving hope for the future beyond this life, supplied a powerful moral justification for the unequal distribution of resources. They also included rules relating to individual behaviour such as truth, trust, customary social obligations and the restraint of appetites. Hirsch argued (1977: 117) that by the late twentieth century capitalism was facing a 'depleting moral legacy': 'The social morality that has served as an understructure for economic individualism has been a legacy of the procapitalist and preindustrial past. This legacy has diminished with time and the corrosive contact of the active capitalist values.' In a related argument, Goldthorpe (1978) extended the logic of Hirsch's analysis to argue that the period of rapid inflation in Britain during the 1970s was in part a consequence of the decay of the *status order*, that is, it reflected an erosion of customary assumptions which had provided a normative underpinning for the differential distribution of rewards in a market society. If customary assumptions relating to inequality have been and are being eroded, then how do unequal societies cohere, particularly given the presumption of a fundamental equality amongst human beings?

Theories of social differentiation

Inequality is a feature of all complex societies. One response, therefore, to the question posed above might be to argue that material inequalities are not, in themselves, necessarily a bad thing. Indeed, this has been a consistent theme in neo-liberal arguments concerning inequality. Such arguments distinguish between legal or formal equalities – for example, equality before the law, equality of opportunity – and equality of outcome. However, the pursuit of equality of outcome – for example, through programmes of affirmative action – contradicts, the neo-liberals argue, the principle of legal or formal equality. This is because positive or affirmative treatment for supposedly disadvantaged groups would treat the supposedly advantaged as less than equal. Thus in recent years we have witnessed, for example, the phenomenon of white male applicants to college courses in the United States utilizing equal-opportunity legislation in order to challenge the allocation of a quota of places on prestige courses to ethnic-minority applicants. Another important strand in neo-liberal arguments has been that, in any case, material inequalities are positively beneficial in modern societies. Economists such as Hayek (*The Road to Serfdom*, 2001) have argued that in a capitalist society, the pursuit of self-interest encourages innovation and technological advance. Inventors and entrepreneurs may succeed or fail, but society as a whole will nevertheless benefit from the advances which these dynamic individuals have achieved – mass transport and communication, consumer goods such as cars, washing machines and so on.[4] Capitalism is dynamic *because* it is unequal, and attempts at equalization will ultimately result in the stifling of initiative. Thus neo-liberals such as Berger have argued that: 'If one wants to intervene politically to bring about greater material equality, one may eventually disrupt the economic engine of plenty and endanger the material living standards of the society' (1987: 48).

These neo-liberal arguments have their parallel in the functionalist theory of stratification in sociology (Davis and Moore 1945; reprinted 1964). 'Social inequality', they argued, 'is thus an unconsciously evolved device by which societies insure that the most important positions are conscientiously filled by the most qualified persons' (1964: 415). In the particular case of advanced industrial societies, individuals must be induced to train for positions requiring a high level of skills, and compensated for having to take risks. In brief, this theory suggested that in industrial societies, characterized by a complex division of labour, a new consensus concerning inequality was emerging as a replacement for the old. Whereas the old consensus was grounded in customary, religious (and therefore non-rational) perceptions of worth, the new consensus reflected the rationality of modern industrial societies. Differentiated groupings are not perceived as necessarily antagonistic; they are, therefore, often described from within the functionalist perspective as socio-economic 'strata', rather than 'classes'.

The immediate origins of functionalist theories of stratification may be found in the Parsonian structural-functionalism which dominated sociological theory in the United States after the Second World War. (These ideas will be discussed at greater length in chapters 2 and 3.) Functionalist theories of stratification also reflected elements of Durkheim's analysis of the ultimate social consequences of the division of labour in industrial society. Durkheim (1968) was acutely aware of the negative consequences of the division of labour (poverty, social unrest, etc.) consequent upon the development of industrial capitalism, but he argued that, nevertheless, 'normal' forms of the division of labour would lead to the development of 'organic solidarity' – that is, solidarity through interdependence – in complex industrial societies.

Functional theories of stratification, therefore, suggested that inequality in complex societies was rendered legitimate via an emerging consensus of values relating to the societal importance of particular functions. It is important to recognize that such theories incorporate a moral justification of economic inequality which has been commonplace since the advent of economic liberalism: that is, in a competitive market society, it is the most talented and ambitious – in short, the *best* – that get to the top, and therefore take the greater part of societies' rewards. However, for many commentators, such arguments rest upon the presumption of equality of opportunity (as Durkheim expressed it, the 'equality of the partners to the contract' in the division of labour). Thus the conditions and possibility of equality of opportunities have loomed large in debates on stratification.

Equality of opportunity is a powerful justification for inequality. If all have an equal opportunity to be unequal, then the unequal outcome must be regarded as justified and fair, as a reflection of 'natural' inequalities of personal endowments, rather than of structured social processes. Although a true equality of opportunity has never, in fact, been achieved, the assumption that it was nevertheless a Good Thing dominated the (social) liberal consensus which prevailed in most Western societies after the Second World War, and which saw the extension of state expenditure on education, health and welfare. However, neo-liberals have always argued against such assumptions, and as we have seen in chapter 1, in recent decades the political and policy influence of such views has been increasing. Within the sociological field, Saunders (1990a, 1996) has argued for a return to the functionalist perspective in stratification theory and research.

Two closely associated arguments, therefore, have been used by functionalists to explain and justify material inequalities in a society of political and legal equals. These are, first, that unequal rewards provide a structure of incentives which ensure that talented individuals will work hard and innovate, thus contributing to the improvement of material standards for the society as a whole; and, second, that a broad consensus exists as to the legitimacy of their superior rewards, as such innovators are functionally more important to society.

Others, however, have stressed the continuing tensions, instability and tendencies to crisis which are associated with persisting structures of inequality. Marx predicted that the underlying structure of class inequality, associated with differential access to the ownership and control of productive resources, would lead, via the class struggle between labour and capital, to the revolutionary overthrow and eventual transformation of capitalist industrialism. Many theorists of stratification who are not Marxists, however, have also stressed the inherent instability of capitalist market societies, rather than any tendency towards an emergent consensus and stability. In contrast to the functionalists, 'conflict theorists' of stratification such as Dahrendorf (1959), Rex (1961) and Collins (1971) have emphasized the significance of power and coercion in any explanation of inequality. However, although such writers stress the persistence of conflict and are sceptical of the emergence of any genuine agreement concerning the existing structure of inequalities, they do not, unlike Marx, envisage the imminent break-up of the social and stratification order.

This is in part because persisting conflict exists in an uneasy tension with tendencies to regulation in capitalist market societies. This has been described by Polanyi (1957) as a 'double movement'. On the one hand, supporters of the 'self-regulating market' seek to eliminate all restrictions on its free operation (and the resurgence of neo-liberal social and economic policies, particularly in the USA and Britain, since the 1970s might be seen as an example of this), whilst on the other hand, movements for reform seek to limit the effects of 'market forces' (or its 'self-regulation'). As a consequence of this 'double movement', the consequences of the 'depleting moral legacy' which Hirsch identified may be argued to have been ameliorated by institutions developed within the framework of capitalism. Dahrendorf (1988), Lockwood (1974) and Rex (1986), for example, have all drawn upon T. H. Marshall's account of 'citizenship' (1963), arguing that the development of social citizenship (for example, universal provisions such as education and welfare state benefits) has contributed to the mitigation of class inequalities (chapter 6 below). During the twentieth century, there have been long historical periods (extending over many decades in countries such as Sweden) in which such a corporatist bargain has been struck between capital and labour (Therborn 1983). Crouch has described this as the 'mid [twentieth-]century social compromise' (1999: 53). This was in a broad sense a class 'compromise'. Governments of left and right supported social protections and increasing welfare, and left parties and their representatives did not seek to destabilize existing social arrangements radically. These arrangements may be described as characteristic of 'Fordism', a term that has been widely employed to describe the industrial and social order that emerged in many advanced capitalist societies after the Second World War. 'Fordism' was characterized by mass production, full employment (at least as far as men were concerned), the development of state welfare and rising standards of consumption.

One feature common to authors who may be characterized as working within the 'conflict' approach to social stratification is that they all identified social *classes* as the primary 'actors' within stratification systems in industrial societies. However, as we have noted, there is a marked lack of precision or agreement as to the definition and meaning of 'class'.

'Class', a multifaceted concept

Sociologists would argue that the use of the term 'class' in academic discourse is in fact quite different from its use in ordinary speech, the everyday use of the word being much closer to the notion of social distinction or prestige. This would seem to be confirmed by the journalistic view: 'observation of class difference has, over the years, been reduced to a question of style' (*Observer*, 6 October 1991). The use of 'class' to indicate lifestyle, prestige or rank is probably the most commonly used sense of the term. Here 'class' is bound up with hierarchy, of being 'higher than' or 'lower than' some other person or group. Rank is often indicated by lifestyles, and particular patterns of consumption. For example, in an often-repeated television comedy sketch of the 1960s, the 'upper class' was represented by a bowler hat, the 'middle class' by a trilby and the 'lower class' by a flat cap (*Frost over England*). Thirty years later, a conscious parody of the sketch (*Parsons on Class*, BBC2) had the 'upper class' wearing a deerstalker, the 'middle class' a peaked golfing cap, and the 'lower class' a football supporters' woolly hat. In the later programme, demonstrating that 'class' is a redundant term meant contrasting aristocrats who sent their children to state schools with low-paid workers who paid for private education, keen golf-club members who lived in local authority housing, and self-made men who had bought their own private shooting rights. In these kinds of debates, the 'end of class' rests on the argument that particular kinds of consumption practices are no longer tied to particular status groups.

'Class' is a word with a number of meanings. Although these will be extensively rehearsed throughout this book, it is nevertheless useful to attempt a summary at this early stage. With some oversimplification, three different meanings of the class concept may be identified:

- 'class' as prestige, status, culture or 'lifestyles';
- 'class' as structured social and economic inequality (related to the possession of economic and power resources);
- 'classes' as actual or potential social and political actors.

Sociologists, as well as journalists, have also paid considerable attention to class-differentiated lifestyles, as in Goldthorpe et al.'s (1969) discussion of the 'privatized' lifestyle of the 'affluent worker'. As we shall see in chapter 6, there has been a recent, and sustained, revival of sociological interest in the 'cultural' dimensions of 'class'. Occupational classifications have been devised by market research companies in order to give an indication of lifestyles and consumption patterns. When occupations are ranked according to their perceived levels of prestige or social standing, these are described as status scales.

A second common use of the 'class' concept is as a general description of structures of material inequality, reflected in differential access to economic and power resources (these could be the ownership of capital or productive resources, skills and qualifications, networks of contacts, etc.). Unequally rewarded groups are often described as 'classes'. These groupings are not characterized by any formal, legal distinctions; rather, they summarize the outcome, in material terms, of the competition for resources in capitalist market societies. A very common basis for classification in modern societies is occupation – for example, the *Office of National Statistics Socio-Economic Classification* (ONS-SEC). These occupational groupings are amongst the most useful indicators of patterns of material advantage and disadvantage in modern societies, and are widely used in social-policy, market and advertising research. Sociologists have also devised their own 'class' schemes.

'Classes' have also been identified as actual or potential social forces, or social actors, which have the capacity to transform society. As we have seen, Marx considered the struggle between classes to be the major motive force in human history. His views were certainly not shared by conservative commentators; nevertheless, from the French Revolution and before, 'classes' – particularly the lower classes – have been regarded as a possible threat to the established order. Thus 'class' is also a term with significant *political* overtones.

This threefold distinction can be used to illustrate a further set of class-related arguments that will be discussed extensively in this book. Class-related cultures and lifestyles, together with class-related economic locations, have been argued to give rise to specific class *identities* that form the basis of class-related political organizations and actions. That is, class *structures* give rise to particular forms of class *consciousness* that in turn result in class *actions* – what Pahl (1989) has described as the S→C→A chain. This causal argument, as we shall see, is highly problematic.

The use of the single word 'class', therefore, may describe rankings of lifestyles or social prestige, patterns of material inequalities, as well as revolutionary or conservative social forces. It is a concept which is not the particular preserve of any individual branch of social science – unlike, for example, the concept of marginal utility in economics. Neither is it possible to identify a 'correct' sociological perspective, or an agreed use of the term.

The variety of meanings which has been attached to the concept of class, it will be argued in this book, has contributed to the lack of clarity which characterizes many contemporary debates in stratification. However, two further sets of factors have also added to the general muddying of waters which were never particularly clear: debates in social theory, and the very rapidity of the social and economic changes that these theories sought to explain.

Social theory and social change

A preoccupation with inequality has long been a central issue for philosophy, politics and the social sciences more generally. However, as with all such issues, debates relating to inequality have been shaped by wider debates in social theory, and have also been affected by substantial changes in the historic social and economic contexts within which these debates have taken place. It has already been argued that the modern concept of 'class' emerged as a central issue with the development of capitalist industrialism, which has, over the last two and a half centuries, come to dominate the world. However, this period of recent history has itself been one of very rapid social change.

In relation to social theory, the emergence of the social sciences at the end of the nineteenth century was accompanied by a sustained debate as to the nature of the disciplines themselves (the so-called *Methodenstreit*, or disputes about methodology). Some argued that similar general principles applied in the social and in the natural sciences, and that law-like generalizations could be established in the social realm. This approach came to be known as 'positivism'. 'Humanist' critics of this position argued that, because of their subject matter, the social and natural sciences were radically different. As human beings are capable of independent thought and action, the nature of the social means that hermeneutic (interpretive) understanding, rather than establishing law-like generalizations, was the appropriate objective for sociological endeavour. This methodological debate was associated with a series of associated binary divisions (fact/value; agency/structure; culture/economy; social/economic) that continued into the twentieth century, culminating in the 'paradigm wars' of the 1970s and 1980s. Two contrasting, and conflicting, models of sociological research and theorizing were offered: positivist/quantitative versus interpretive/qualitative. Although McLennan (2000) has argued that these 'paradigm wars' are over, they nevertheless continue to have an impact on debates in class and stratification.

What Giddens (1982) and others have described as the 'orthodox consensus' that emerged in the social sciences during the 1950s and 1960s decisively shaped class analysis in sociology in the immediate postwar period. This 'orthodox consensus' had three elements. First, it was influenced by the logical framework of positivism; thus social science investigations were closely modelled on those of the natural sciences, and social facts treated as 'things'. Sociologists sought to establish general statements about social behaviour through factual observations. The second element of the consensus, the predominance of a broadly functionalist approach, has already been briefly described. The third element of this consensus, according to Giddens, was the influence of a conception of 'industrial society', whereby the technology of industrialism and its attendant social characteristics (rationality of technique, extensive division of labour and so on) were seen to be the main motor or force transforming the contemporary world.

Class and stratification theorists were at the forefront of critics of the 'orthodox consensus'. The 'conflict theorists' identified above led the anti-functionalist battalions in sociology, and much of the debate between 'functional' or 'consensus' approaches, on the one hand, and 'conflict' theories, on the other, took place on the terrain of stratification theory. Developments in systems of occupational stratification were a key feature of the industrial society thesis. It was argued that the stratification systems of advanced industrial societies would have a tendency to converge, and moreover that this would be in the direction of more open structures in which 'middle-class' occupations predominated (Mayer 1963). As the 'middle mass' expanded, so, it was argued, the conflict between classes would be reduced.

The industrial society thesis, therefore, encompassed important dialogues relating to class and stratification. It was developed at a time of apparent social stability as well as considerable optimism in some quarters. This 'mid-twentieth-century social compromise', as we shall see, rested on fractured foundations, but at the time it seemed to offer the prospect of permanent prosperity. In Harold Macmillan's often-repeated words of 1957: 'You have never had it so good': 'Go around the country, go to the industrial towns, go to the farms and you will see a state of prosperity such as we have never had in my lifetime – nor indeed in the history of this country' (news.bbc.co.uk/onthisday). This optimism proved to be unfounded. However, even in the 1960s and 1970s, class and stratification theorists and researchers were systematically challenging the rather comfortable assumptions of the 'industrial society' thesis (Goldthorpe 1967) – and indeed, this enterprise might be seen as a logical extension of 'conflict theory'. The critique of 'positivism', however, developed largely outside class and stratification analysis (but see Goldthorpe 1973), and has spawned a social theory 'industry' that has at times appeared to be in danger of taking over sociology in its entirety.

In the 1950s and 1960s, class and stratification theorists – as represented, for example, by writers such as Bendix and Lipset (1967b) – were emphasizing the importance of conflict, as well as stability. They appropriated the Marxist distinction between a class 'in itself' and a class 'for itself' – that is, between a class which existed as a historical reality, on the one hand, and a class which had acquired a consciousness of its identity and a capacity to act, on the other. Bendix and Lipset, however, viewed the question of class action as contingent – a class might, or might not, manifest a particular consciousness. This approach fits unproblematically with broadly 'positivist' modes of social investigation: 'classes' may be identified, factual observation will reveal whether they are 'class conscious' or not. From the 1950s there was a renewed sociological interest in European class-theoretical writings, particularly the work of Marx and Weber (these will be discussed in the next chapter). The US tradition of social stratification came in for particular criticism. It was argued that it focused upon social status or prestige, rather than class.

The developing interest in 'classical' class theory was paralleled by developments in sociological methods. As we have seen, 'classes' were conceived as objective entities that could be empirically investigated, and to this end, the occupational structure was conventionally regarded as providing a framework within which the 'class structure' could be located. The increasing methodological sophistication of the social survey was complemented by a huge increase in scope and capacity for data processing facilitated by the development of computer technology. As a consequence of this development, ambitious programmes of 'class analysis' were devised during the 1970s in which developments in class theory and survey analysis were combined (Wright 1997; Erikson and Goldthorpe 1993). This will be described as the 'employment-aggregate' approach to class analysis. One important feature of these empirical programmes is that they appeared to link two of the major aspects of class identified above: that is (a) class as a source of structured social inequality, and (b) class as a source of social and political identity, consciousness and action. As we shall see, the employment-aggregate approach developed into a major specialism within the field of 'class analysis'. In these research programmes, the S in the S→C→A chain was seen as deriving largely, if not entirely, from the economic dimension of class.

However, occupational measures of class have also been widely used to describe the broad contours of inequality in contemporary societies, and have not always been primarily concerned – or even concerned at all – with the issues of class consciousness and action. In nineteenth-century investigations of the poor, for example, the unfortunates had to be identified – indeed the empirical definition of 'poverty' absorbed much of the energies of early investigators. As, increasingly, extensive national statistics were gathered, so classification schemes were devised to bring order to the data. In a society where increasing numbers were dependent on paid employment, one obvious indicator of social advantage or disadvantage was occupation. Thus from the beginning of the twentieth century it became commonplace for statisticians to divide the population into occupational aggregates or classes, depending (more or less) on the material rewards accruing to particular

occupational groupings. The term 'class' is universally employed to describe these occupational aggregates, although they are clearly not of the same order as the 'classes' discussed
in the theoretical work of Marx and Weber. However, occupational indices developed in
the context of applied or policy research have constantly overlapped with theoretical discussions and empirical research relating to social class and to class consciousness and
action, and therein lies the source of much confusion.

Chapter 4, therefore, has a major focus on different strategies which have been developed
to investigate the employment or class *structure*. All of these accounts focus mainly upon
employment and the associated structure of occupations. However, although the structure
of employment in industrial societies is the major empirical source of the generation of
these 'classes', there is no agreed index of classification. It will be suggested that class
schemes can be usefully divided into three broad categories.

These are, first, the 'commonsense' schemes which lack theoretical pretensions, and
which arrange occupations into an approximate hierarchical order to which a number of
(hopefully not too arbitrary) cut-off points are applied. In an industrial society, occupation
is an excellent indicator of both levels of material reward and social standing, and over the
years such indices have been found to correlate with a range of factors, such as rates of
infant mortality, access to education, voting behaviour and so on. Second, there are indices
of occupational prestige or status, which attempt to measure the societal ranking or worth
of particular types of occupations within the population at large. Occupational prestige
scales were initially constructed with a view to the investigation of social mobility. The similarity of occupational prestige scales between different nation states, and the relative 'openness' (or otherwise) of occupational structures, have been essential data in the development
and investigation of the 'industrial society' thesis, which, as we have seen, Giddens has
described as a key element of the 'orthodox consensus' developed within postwar sociology. Both commonsense occupational indices and occupational prestige scales are descriptive indices. They are also hierarchical, and thus 'gradational' measures of a more or less
particular quantity (income, prestige, social standing and so on). However, the third
category of class index identified in chapter 4 – that is, 'relational' or theoretical class
schemes – has been constructed with explicit reference to class theories, particularly those
of Marx and Weber. Thus these indices claim to be a measure of the dynamics and actualities of class *relations*, rather than simply to describe structures of inequality or prestige.
The two major examples of theoretically grounded, relational class schemes which will be
investigated are the Marxist class scheme of Erik Wright and the neo-Weberian class
scheme of John Goldthorpe. Both of these authors claim that their class schemes are not
hierarchical or 'gradational', but 'relational'.

However, although these three different types of class scheme have been constructed for
very different purposes, there are in practice considerable similarities between the location
of occupations and employment statuses in the different schemes. Thus the three types of
scheme are often treated as equivalent. Nevertheless, the fundamental differences in the
bases and assumptions on which they have been constructed suggest that considerable care
should attend upon their application, particularly in respect of theoretical arguments relating to social class. The very different nature and claims of the different 'class' indices available have not always been widely acknowledged within the sociological community, and
this has been a further source of confusion in the area of 'class analysis'. This confusion,
as we shall see, has been somewhat clarified in recent discussions, and in many respects the
work of the major protagonists has tended to converge.

By the 1980s, empirical work in the area of 'class analysis' was dominated by the employment-aggregate approach. However, the very rapidity of social, economic and political change was increasingly serving to undermine what appeared to be some of its underlying assumptions and concerns. This was in large part a consequence of changes in the occupational ('class') structure itself. Towards the end of the twentieth century, there was a numerical and proportional decline, in the 'old' industrial countries, of the traditional working class. In countries such as Britain, America, Canada, Australia and much of Western Europe, there has been a massive decline in the numbers employed in heavy manufacturing and traditional extractive industries such as mining, steelmaking, shipbuilding and heavy engineering. The reasons for this decline are complex. Technological innovation has played a major part, as has technical obsolescence – newly automated processes simply require fewer people, new forms of energy replace old – but there have also been shifts in the global division of manufacturing labour to South East Asia and rapidly developing economies such as China and India. The collapse of heavy industry in the West was enormously accelerated by the impact of the world recession which followed upon the oil crisis of the 1970s. The economic restructuring which followed decline and massive unemployment did increase the number of jobs available, but mainly in the service economy of finance, retail and personal services. These changes have all led, as we have seen in chapter 1, to a decline in the numbers of what had long been considered to be the traditional 'working class', that is, geographically concentrated, manual employees in heavy industry. There has been a corresponding growth in non-manual, 'white-collar' employees, who had conventionally been regarded as located in the 'middle' classes or strata.

Together with these changes in the occupational structure, it has also been argued that 'work' as employment has become of considerably less significance in the shaping of social attitudes. People in employment spend less of their time in paid work, and increasing numbers of people are less dependent on paid work for their livelihood than in a previous era. In the older industrial countries, young people join the labour force at an increasingly later age, and the expansion of state provisions (in education, health and welfare) has made people less dependent on the sale of their labour in order to obtain the services they need. The continuing 'roll-back' of welfare states might imply that there is some need to modify these arguments, but nevertheless it is still argued that work as employment has been of declining importance, particularly as a source of social identity, since the second half of the twentieth century.

The real implications of these changes in work and employment were, however, hotly contested. In particular, in 1974 Braverman's influential book *Labor and Monopoly Capital* argued that the capitalist mode of production embodied an inherent tendency towards the routinization and 'deskilling' of labour. These tendencies affected all workers, and thus the apparent 'upgrading' of the labour force consequent upon the growth of non-manual employment was more apparent than real. White-collar workers, and even management, would in their turn become deskilled employees. Braverman's intervention stimulated considerable controversy as to the real nature of the changes, in class terms, which were occurring in respect of the occupational structure; but a (perhaps unintended) consequence of the revitalized debate on the class structure was that the question of class action was increasingly treated as a separate issue – or even not considered at all.

The question of class action, however, still remained problematic. The definition and relative size of the 'working class' might be contested, and the evidence of occupational class schemes might continue to demonstrate that occupational class and voting behaviour were still closely related; nevertheless, it would be difficult to make a strong case to the effect that the working class (or any other class) in the West has been engaged in sustained revolutionary activity since the end of the Second World War. The collapse of 'state socialism' in the Eastern bloc seems to have been accompanied by a turning away from socialist ideals, rather than their revitalization.

The growth of 'second-wave' feminism, which accompanied the increasing participation of women in paid employment, has also been of considerable importance in debates relating to the declining significance of 'class'. Class politics, it might be argued (as well as the institution of citizenship), was decisively shaped by the interests of male employees, as well as male owners and controllers of the means of material production. Men might have subordinated other men, and struggled for power and control, within the 'public' sphere of employment, politics and warfare, but, as the feminist critique demonstrated, women were subordinate not only in the public sphere but also within the 'private' sphere of domestic and family life. The orthodox terrain of class theory and analysis seemed to have little to contribute to an analysis of the position of women. The increase in women's employment also served to highlight major weaknesses as far as occupational class schemes were concerned. Such schemes had been devised in relation to a model of predominantly male employment. The persistence of occupational segregation by sex, despite the increase in the employment of women, meant that such schemes could no longer be implicitly treated as gender-neutral. The persistence of the gendered division of labour, however, continues to create apparently insuperable obstacles to the development of a single 'class' classification that would encompass both men and women.

Increasingly it appeared, therefore, that the leading empirical tradition in sociological 'class analysis' (that is, large-scale survey investigation) had little to offer as far as many of the apparently most pressing contemporary sociological topics were concerned. From the end of the 1970s, the resurgence of political and economic neo-liberalism was associated with a rapid increase in material inequalities (particularly in Britain and the USA), but this was not associated with an increase in anything resembling 'class' activism and/or identity. Indeed, some have argued that the failure of systematic, class-based action (particularly on the part of the (disappearing) 'working class') represents the major challenge to class analysis, not only in its employment-aggregate guise, but also in a broader sense (Pahl 1989; Savage 2000). Increasingly, although certainly not for the first time, 'class' and class analysis were rejected as outdated concepts and research strategies, irrelevant to the analysis of contemporary societies. Social theory went (some might say lurched) in new, and very different, directions.

The wider critique of 'class analysis'

Arguments as to the 'end of class', however, were not confined to the issues and topics (such as changes in the occupational structure, and the increase in women's employment) in relation to which the dominant 'employment-aggregate' approach appeared to be somewhat lacking. Increasingly, it began to be argued that significant 'societal shifts' were under way, and that the nature of these transformations meant that the 'class' concept was becoming redundant. It is sometimes suggested that these changes are in fact epochal and signify a significant shift in the development of capitalist industrialism. Many different labels have been used to describe this transition – from Fordism to post-Fordism, from modernity to postmodernity, from 'organized' to 'disorganized' capitalism. They describe the continuing break-up of older, mass-production industries and the growth of new, computer-based production and 'flexible specialization'. Individuals are being forced to adapt rapidly to these 'new times', and it is argued that long-term employment in mass industries and mass bureaucracies, which provided a solid foundation for the articulation of industrial-class action, is rapidly becoming a thing of the past. 'Postmodern' theorizing also involved a decisive rejection of the 'grand narratives', such as Marxism, as well as the 'industrial society' thesis, that had sought to give a coherent account of the evolution of 'modernity'. The 'global transformation of modernity' that is supposedly under way calls for 'a re-thinking of the humanities and the social sciences' (Beck and Sznaider 2006: 2), in which national organizations no longer serve as 'structuring principle(s) of societal and political action' (2006: 4). This, it is argued, will require a fundamental rethinking of the basic concepts of modernity, such as class.

As we have seen in chapter 1, one major theme which runs through these commentaries is that of individualization. As employment fragments, so individuals are forced to negoti-ate their own trajectories through an increasingly unstable labour market (Beck 1992, 2000b). In politics as much as in employment, it is argued, individualistic values are on the increase, and the old solidarities which fostered class identity and struggle have disappeared. As Beck has put it, social class is a 'zombie category', which is 'dead but still alive'. The past bases of collective identities, he argues, are no longer relevant, and society has been 'indi-vidualised'. Beck (Beck and Beck-Gernsheim 2002: 202) states that: 'Individualisation is a concept which describes a structural, sociological transformation of social institutions and the relationship of the individual to society . . . freeing people from historically inscribed roles . . . Individualisation liberates people from traditional roles and constraints . . . indi-viduals are removed from status-based classes . . . Social classes have been detradition-alised.' This detraditionalization, it is argued, affects not only classes, but also interpersonal relationships such as those within the family.

'Old politics' stands accused of 'productivism'; the 'new politics', it is argued, must rec-ognize that there are no objective class interests as such, but that there are many different points of antagonism, and thus potential for conflict and needs for representation. These kinds of argument, therefore, not only attempt to take on board the apparent decline in political significance of the old-style working class, but also to identify new foci of politi-cal concern. In contrast to the distributional issues which were the focus of the 'old poli-tics', it is argued that the growth of 'new social movements' has transformed the political scene. Such movements are concerned with the environment, and the rights of various groups which have been historically excluded from full economic and political participa-tion – women and subordinate ethnic groups in particular (Offe 1985b). The notion of rights is being extended, beyond those of adults, to include those of animals and children. It is a feature of new social movements that their support cuts across class boundaries, thus further weakening the basis of the old class politics, and class-based political action.

Globalization and the growth of postmodern culture, it is suggested, have swept away the last vestiges of traditionalism, and are in the process of eroding the powers of the state itself – which is in any case becoming increasingly irrelevant in circumstances of the 'new cos-mopolitanism'. In the West the corporatist bargains between capital and labour, associated with the 'mid[twentieth-]century social compromise' (Crouch 1999: 53) and 'Keynesian' economic policies (see p. 2) have largely crumbled; and state socialism has collapsed in the East. The whittling away of state and employment-related institutions and structures is leading, some have argued, to the emergence of systems of stratification that are primarily *cultural* in their origins, as individuals select and are drawn to, on the basis of their personal qualities and accomplishments, the symbols and lifestyles expressing their needs and preferences. Thus Waters (1996; see also Pakulski and Waters 1996) argues that stratification in contemporary societies, in which tastes and interests are constantly shifting, is 'status-conventional'. Indeed he argues that the 'class' basis of stratification has more or less disappeared. It is as consumers that many individuals express their environmental concerns; another example of this reasoning would be the supposed increase in significance of the 'gay' pound and dollar. In short, people's identities are being increasingly expressed and manifest through consumption, rather than production.

This emphasis on the significance of consumption is closely bound up with what has been described as the 'cultural turn' in the social sciences. Although 'postmodernism' is a term that seems, increasingly, to be slipping out of use amongst social theorists, nevertheless, the cultural turn may be legitimately regarded as one of its heirs. Putting a precise chronology on the cultural turn is problematic, not least because, it may be suggested, its ultimate origins are reflected in the *Methodenstreit* (see p. 17) of the late nineteenth and early twentieth centuries, briefly described above. Nevertheless, the cultural turn of the last two decades does represent (for some) a paradigm shift, a decisive turning away from positivism and 'factual' investigation towards an emphasis on interpretive understanding. Thus in relation to consumption, for example, the question would not be raised whether economic position *or* consumption patterns are *causal* in the creation of identities (see, for example, Phillips and Western 2005), but rather, consumption would be seen as one element in the ongoing practices that *constitute* identity. 'Culture' itself is seen as an autonomous, driving force in contemporary societies. For example:

> In societies with high information density, production does not involve economic resources alone; it also concerns social relationships, symbols, identities and individual needs . . . the operation and efficiency of economic mechanisms and technological apparatuses depend on the management and control of relational systems where cultural dimensions predominate over 'technical' variables. Nor does the market function simply to circulate material goods; it becomes increasingly a system in which symbols are exchanged.   (Melucci cited in Friedland and Mohr 2004: 5)

A theme running through many of the criticisms reviewed above focuses upon the question of whether 'classes' should still be regarded as actual or potential significant social forces in the late twentieth and early twenty-first centuries. Here the question of identity (consciousness) is crucial. These criticisms do not suggest, however, that capitalist societies are not still highly unequal. Following from this point, it may be suggested that, although 'work' as employment *may* possibly have declined as a significant source of social identity, work is still the most significant determinant of the material well-being of the majority of the population. Thus descriptive class indices continue to demonstrate the persisting structure of inequality in contemporary societies. It still makes sense to describe late capitalist society as being dominated by a 'ruling class' which is economically dominant, and has the capacity to influence crucially political and social life (Scott 1991). Nevertheless, far-reaching changes in societal organization, as well as the theoretical commentaries that have accompanied these changes, raise substantial challenges for class and stratification analysis.

In the next section, therefore, we will examine some of the implications of these theoretical paradigm shifts for the analysis of class, stratification and inequality.

Action and structure, economy and culture

One element of the sociological critique of positivism developed during the 1960s and 1970s – as expressed, for example, in Giddens's theory of 'structuration' – was the assertion that neither subject nor object, 'structure' nor 'action', should be regarded as having explanatory primacy. These arguments meshed with those already developed by some Marxist theoreticians – particularly historians such as E. P. Thompson (see chapter 3) – regarding the indivisibility of 'class' from the notion of consciousness. As already noted, questions of agency and structure were at the core of late nineteenth- and early twentieth-century debates (i.e. the *Methodenstreit*) concerning the nature of sociology as a discipline.

Agency/structure debates, it may be suggested, have the problems of causal explanation at their core. Put (very) simply, is human behaviour to be seen as being largely 'reactive', that is, a consequence of the pressures exerted by the social and economic institutions (markets, families, organizations and so on) within which all human beings are invariably located? Or is human behaviour better understood as an outcome of the actions of thinking, purposive agents? In practice, most sociologists have never placed themselves firmly on either side of this dichotomy. As Bottero (2005: 54) has noted:

> all the classical sociologists acknowledge the duality of social life, as an external constraint on the individual, but also constituted from the mass of individual actions. Each of them agrees that, on the one hand, individuals are constrained in their actions by wider social forces, but that on the other hand, the source of these external constraints lies precisely in the actions of ourselves and others. That is, we all of us actively create the social world, as purposive agents, interpreting and shaping our lives.

Nevertheless, as Bottero argues, despite this premise of duality of social life, many sociological explanations eventually collapse back on one side of the division or the other. This tendency need not, however, be seen as a problem, as we shall see in chapters 6 and 7 (although Bottero has argued otherwise).

The concept of class might be seen as encompassing this duality, as the bringing together of 'structure' and 'action' within a single concept. The S→C→A chain might be seen as combining structure and action in a single explanatory exercise, although the direction of the arrows renders structure the ultimate determinant. In fact, Lockwood (1981), whose work was crucial in the development of S→C→A explanatory arguments in modern analyses of class, has subsequently distanced himself from this reasoning (Savage 2000).[5]

The duality of action and structure is paralleled by a similar separation between the 'economic' and the 'social'. Classical sociologists, such as Weber and Durkheim, recognized this in their work and explored both the 'economic' and the 'social' as elements in sociological explanation (see discussion in Holmwood and Stewart 1983). This was especially recognized in the (re)formulation of the traditions of economic sociology, which insisted that economic life is 'embedded' in larger and all-encompassing social and cultural relations

(Granovetter and Swedberg 1992; Smelser and Swedberg 2005). Putting the matter some-what crudely, the framework of economic sociology argues that it is impossible to conceive of an 'economy' independently of some sort of functioning 'society' or encompassing set of social relations. Indeed, social relations necessarily precede exchange relations, and changes in the 'social' reflect changes in the 'economic' and vice versa. Again, the concept of class, as developed by Weber, Tonnies, Marx and the German tradition of sociology more generally, encompasses this 'embeddedness'. Pre-modern societies are seen as com-bining 'status' and 'class' in their forms of stratification, with modern societies showing an increasing differentiation and autonomization of economic class relations from the cultural and normative framework of traditional status.[6]

However, theoretical discussions associated with the 'cultural turn' incorporate an emphatic rejection of the separation of 'action' and 'structure', as well as the possibility of separating the economic from the social (Du Gay and Pryke 2002). As we have seen, this stance is often associated with arguments as to the declining significance – in fact, irrelevance – of the class concept as far as the analysis of contemporary societies is con-cerned. Even some of those working within a broadly defined 'class analysis' framework have argued that to (re-)recognize the significance of 'culture' means that: 'Insofar as values and norms are recognised as powerful in their own terms, this involves breaking from a tradition that links them to structural foundations. You cannot have your cake and eat it' (Devine and Savage 2005: 11). Thus, 'taking culture seriously involves breaking from stratification research, at least as conventionally conceived' (ibid.). Here Devine and Savage are pointing to the reorientation of stratification research from studies of class consciousness (following the effective failure of the S→C→A chain of reasoning) to studies of identity, where identi-ties are viewed not simply as 'reflections of position', but, rather, as 'claims for recognition'.

These are complex issues, which will be explored in greater depth in our discussion of the contribution of Bourdieu to class analysis in chapter 6. For the moment, the purposes of this book will best be served by making explicit some basic methodological assumptions underpinning our discussion in the chapters that follow. First, although it will be recognized that the *de facto* duality of social life means that according explanatory primacy to *either* agency *or* structure is problematic, it will be argued that as far as the analysis of inequality is concerned, an analytical separation (Archer 1982, 1996) has to be assumed. That is, agency and structure are indeed intertwined, but they may be analytically separated for the purposes of empirical research. A similar position will be taken with regard to 'the eco-nomic' and 'the cultural'. Whilst it will be recognized that 'the cultural' is indeed embed-ded in 'the economic' and vice versa, an 'analytical dualism' (Fraser 1998) that facilitates the separate social science exploration of the economic and the cultural will be assumed.

The reasons for taking this stance are very simple. Theorists of the 'cultural turn', in common with the humanist protagonists of the *Methodenstreit*, emphasize above all the self-constituting agent. In consequence, they hold back from causal explanation:

> While they assume that the social is constituted in and through orders of language, code, symbol and sign, humanists rarely, if ever, specify the contingent social conditions of its production or social productivity. For humanists, *interpretation is explanation.* (Friedland and Mohr 2004: 3, my emphasis)

If causes simply cannot be identified, and if the social world is indeed only a fluid, con-stantly changing world of representations, then this leads to a position in which it is highly problematic to identify policies or strategies that might bring about either emancipatory social change or a reduction in material inequalities.

In a similar vein, if culture and economy are (analytically) argued to be 'unitary' rather than 'dual' system(s) (Bottero 2005; Crompton and Scott 2005), then both empirical research and political debate will be similarly hampered. Indeed, an emphasis on the 'cultural' to the exclusion of the 'economic' has had the consequence, it has been argued, of deflecting discussion away from the significance of material inequalities. As an increasing number of authors have noted (Frank 2000; O'Neill 1999), an emphasis on the reflexive individual and a focus on individual identities rather than collective actions and outcomes has many resonances with neo-liberalism. The promotion of individual rights and recognition meshes well with the arguments of those who have criticized the way in which collective provision has disempowered individuals. Thus, as O'Neill (1999: 85) argues, there has been something of a 'convergence of a postmodern leftism with neoliberal defences of the market'.

Thus it may be argued that the 'identity politics' associated with the cultural turn have serious consequences for the politics of equality. If individual recognition is to be the primary political objective, then issues of redistribution become less important. It is paradoxical (to put it mildly) that this theoretical shift took place at precisely the same time that the intensification of capitalist economic activity was actually generating increasing levels of inequality. As O'Neill (2001: 81) puts it: 'the fragmentation of social citizenship is now accelerated by the New Right's curious adoption of left cultural relativism'. There is a very real danger of 'winning cultural battles but losing the class war' (ibid.: 82).

In short, empirical research and theoretical debates in relation to class and stratification, like other topic areas within sociology (family, race, gender and so on), have been influenced and shaped by wider developments and debates in sociological theory and methodology. These developments have not always been positive. In taking a position of analytical dualism in relation to both agency/structure as well as economy/culture, all that is being asserted is that in order to move forward our understandings in this area, parts need to be distinguished from wholes. Nevertheless, it is recognized that in practice, neither of the elements in these dichotomies can exist without the other. In relation to the study of class and inequality, it has been argued that some recent theoretical developments (in particular, the 'cultural turn') have served to blunt the cutting edge of sociological enquiry. It is true that the 'older' tradition of class analysis can be criticized as overly economistic, and somewhat determinist. Nevertheless, a concern with the *consequences* of inequality, it will be argued, should remain at the centre of our endeavours as far as class and stratification are concerned.

CLASS ANALYSIS: THE CLASSIC INHERITANCE AND ITS DEVELOPMENT IN THE TWENTIETH CENTURY

3

Introduction

As described in chapter 2, the term 'class' is widely used as a general label to describe structures of inequality in modern societies. Such descriptive accounts of inequality, however, will often incorporate explicit (or implicit) assumptions as to why a particular individual, occupation or social category should be located in a particular class. 'Class' has also been used in more abstract terms to describe a social force – most particularly by Marx, who described all history as 'the history of class struggles'. The notion that 'classes' can have transformative capacities is not limited to Marxism. The social forces (or 'actors') identified by class theorists such as Marx and Weber, however, do not correspond neatly to the class categories identified in descriptive accounts of the 'class structure'. Nevertheless, as we shall see in this chapter, both Marx's and Weber's theoretical accounts of social class have generated insights which have guided the particular allocation of individuals, occupations or social categories within specific class schemes. As a consequence of this practice, the 'classes' produced by the application of class schemes to the structure of employment have often been treated, implicitly, as if they also constituted actual or potential class actors. It will be argued that there are many difficulties with this assumption.

Social class and inequality have been amongst the central topic areas within sociology. It is not surprising, therefore, that the investigation of these topics over the last half century should have been significantly shaped by debates taking place within sociology itself. Thus, as we have already seen in the first chapter, debates in social theory, as well as the specific theoretical contributions of Marx and Weber, have also had an important impact on class analysis. Our primary objective in this chapter, besides giving an account of Marx's and Weber's classic contributions, will also be to explore the impact of these varying theoretical inputs on the developing project of class and stratification analysis.

The ideas of both Marx (1818–83) and Weber (1864–1920) continue to shape debates in class theory in the early twenty-first century. However, their contributions have been extensively reinterpreted and reformulated by successive generations. Of these two 'founding fathers', Marx was primarily a political activist, rather than an academic social theorist. From the 1960s, however, there was a revival of academic interest in Marx's work which ran in parallel with the theoretical debates in sociology which were then current – in particular, the developing critique of normative functionalism or the 'consensus' perspective (Lockwood 1964). As noted in chapter 2, the dominant paradigm in Anglo-American sociology in the 1950s and early 1960s was essentially positivist – that is, it held to the view that sociology was the study of observable and objective *facts* about the social world (rather than being concerned with *a priori* 'theories' concerning the nature of the world, as in theological or metaphysical speculation). It had a primary emphasis on the study of social structures or systems, rather than individuals. As the conflict theorists claimed, it was also concerned mainly with the functional coherence and normative integration of these systems, rather than with any conflicts or underlying tensions (Smelser 1988: 10). These kinds of sociological assumptions had also shaped the 'industrial society' thesis – that is, the idea that all industrial societies have a tendency to converge in a similar, non-conflictual direction (Kerr et al. 1973).

However, critics of positivism argued that social facts cannot be objectively located but are theory-dependent – that is, they are not simply 'out there' but are socially *constructed*. Thus even apparently objective facts such as Census data are gathered with regard to theoretical assumptions which may not always be explicit (Hindess 1973). The emphasis on social structures or systems was criticized (Wrong 1966) for its 'oversocialized' conception of human nature. The recasting of social theory was associated with an increasing emphasis on the significance of human *action*; it was emphasized that human beings are neither (to paraphrase Garfinkel 1967) structural nor cultural 'dopes' but act reflexively with the social world. The emphasis on stability and integration characteristic of normative functionalism was increasingly rejected in favour of perspectives that emphasized conflict rather than consensus, domination rather than integration (Rex 1961).

Sociology has continued to fragment into a number of separate paradigms, and it would be difficult, if not impossible, to describe a 'dominant paradigm' in contemporary sociology. These divisions have also been reflected in its sub-fields. Despite a common origin in Marx's and Weber's work, therefore, class theory in sociology has developed in a number of different directions, some of which are reviewed in this chapter. The concept of class has also been extensively drawn upon within history and geography, and some indications of its use within these disciplines will also be discussed.

Marx

Marx's aim was to provide a comprehensive analysis of capitalist society with a view to effecting its transformation; he was a committed revolutionary as well as a social theorist. In the *Communist Manifesto*, Marx and Engels (1962: 34) describe the course of human history in terms of the struggle between classes:

Free man and slave, patrician and plebeian, lord and serf, guild-master and journeyman, in a word, oppressor and oppressed, stood in constant opposition to each other, carried on an uninterrupted, now hidden, now open fight, a fight that each time ended, either in a revolutionary reconstitution of society at large, or in the common ruin of the contending classes.

There can be little doubt, therefore, as to the centrality of class in Marx's work, but, although the theme is constant, he nowhere gives a precise definition of the class concept. Indeed, it is somewhat poignant that his last manuscript breaks off just at the moment at which he appeared to be on the point of giving such a definition, in a passage beginning: 'The first question to be answered is this: What constitutes a class? – and the reply to this follows naturally from the reply to another question, namely: What makes wage-labourers, capitalists and landlords constitute the three great social classes?' (Marx 1974: 886).

For Marx, class relationships are embedded in production relationships; more specifically, in the patterns of ownership and control which characterize these relationships. Thus the 'two great classes' of capitalist society are bourgeoisie and proletariat, the former being the owners and controllers of the material means of production, the latter owning only their labour-power, which they are forced to sell to the bourgeoisie in order to survive. However, Marx did not have, as has sometimes been suggested, a 'two-class' model of society. It is true that he saw the bourgeoisie and proletariat as the major historic role-players in the capitalist epoch, but his analyses of contemporary events made it clear that he saw actual societies as composed of a multiplicity of classes. That is, Marx used the term 'class' both as an analytical concept in the development of his theory of society, and as a descriptive, historical concept. For example, in his account of the (1852) Bonapartist coup d'état in France, 'The Eighteenth Brumaire of Louis Bonaparte' (1962a), a variety of social groupings are identified including the landed aristocracy, financiers, the industrial bourgeoisie, the middle class, the petty bourgeoisie, the industrial proletariat, the lumpenproletariat and the peasantry.

Marx's account of antagonistic class relationships did not rest simply upon ownership and non-ownership by themselves. Rather, ownership of the material forces of production is the means to the exploitation of the proletariat by the bourgeoisie within the very process of production itself. The key to Marx's understanding of this process lies in the labour theory of value, a concept which Engels described as one of Marx's major theoretical achievements. In a capitalist society, argues Marx, labour has become a commodity like any other, but it is unique in that human labour alone has the capacity to create *new* values. Raw materials (commodities) such as wood, iron or cotton cannot by themselves create value; rather, value is added when they are worked on by human labour to create new commodities which are then realized in the market. The labour which is purchased (and therefore owned) by the capitalist will spend only a part of the working day in the creation of values equivalent to its price (that is, wages); the rest of the working day is spent in the creation of surplus value, which is retained by the capitalist. (Surplus value does not simply describe profit, but is distributed to a number of sources including taxes, payments to 'unproductive' labourers and new capital investment, as well as profits or dividends.) Thus even though the labourer may be paid a wage that is entirely 'fair', that is, it represents the value of this labour in the market, and the worker has not been cheated or swindled in any legal sense (cheating and swindling *may* occur, of course) – he or she has nevertheless been exploited.

It has been emphasized that Marx was concerned not just to provide a description of the nature of exploitation in class societies, but also to give an account of the role of social classes in the transformation of societies themselves. Thus, for Marx, classes are social forces, historical actors. For Marx, men (and, it should be said, women) *make* their own history, although not necessarily in the *circumstances* of their own choosing. Some commentators have suggested that for Marx a class only existed when it was conscious of itself as such. However, in *The Poverty of Philosophy* he appears to make an unambiguous distinction between a 'class in itself' and a (conscious) 'class for itself', when he writes of the proletariat that 'this mass is already a class in opposition to capital, but not yet a class for itself' (1955: 195). This ambiguity in Marx's work has been of considerable significance in the development of sociological analyses of class.

Marx's account of the generation of human consciousness is central to his theory of historical materialism, the social-scientific core of Marxist theory. This is summarized in the preface to *A Contribution to the Critique of Political Economy*:

> In the social production of their life, men enter into definite relations that are indispensable and independent of their will, relations of production which correspond to a definite stage of development of their material productive forces. The sum total of these relations of production constitutes the economic structure of society, the real foundation, on which rises a legal and political superstructure and to which correspond definite forms of social consciousness. The mode of production of material life conditions the social, political, and intellectual life process in general. It is not the consciousness of men that determines their being, but, on the contrary, their social being that determines their consciousness.   (Marx 1962b: 362–3)

Two related – and contentious – insights may be drawn from this account. First, that it is the economic 'base' that determines the political and ideological 'superstructure' of human societies; and second, that it is material being that determines human consciousness, rather than vice versa. These arguments may be illustrated via a summary of the account of the transition from feudalism to capitalist industrialism, as outlined by Marx and Engels in the *Communist Manifesto*. The relations of production in feudal society – the system of manorial estates held by right rather than purchase, with an unfree peasantry bound to labour on the land through feudal obligations – were the material basis of an ideological superstructure in which the existing social order was given divine justification through the Catholic church. Feudal society was static and technologically underdeveloped, and the network of customary rights and obligations which underpinned it acted as a hindrance to the development of the dynamic capitalist order. The feudal aristocracy was, however, ultimately unable to resist the power of the rising bourgeoisie, the 'revolutionary class' in the feudal context. Thus after centuries of feudal stagnation the transition to capitalism was nevertheless achieved – often accompanied by more or less violent events (such as, for example, the French Revolution). The triumphant bourgeoisie may have broken with feudal restrictions and consolidated their rights in the ownership of the means of production (that is, capital), but in creating the class that had only its labour to sell as its means of subsistence – that is, the proletariat – the bourgeoisie had created their own 'grave diggers': 'Society as a whole is more and more splitting up into two great hostile camps, into two great classes directly facing each other: Bourgeoisie and Proletariat' (Marx and Engels 1962: 35). The proletariat would constitute the revolutionary class within capitalist society, and through its struggles would usher in first socialism and eventually true communism.

Marx's distinction between base and superstructure has been the subject of extensive debate. He has been widely accused of economic reductionism – the assertion that the economic base *determines* social, political and intellectual development. Such a mechanistic model would, indeed, constitute a gross oversimplification of the complexities of human behaviour, and in a letter written after Marx's death his collaborator Engels emphasized that the theory of historical materialism should not be interpreted as claiming that the economic situation was the *sole* cause of human behaviour. Rather, he argued that although it might be 'ultimately' determinant, at any particular moment, other social relations – political, ideological – would also be affecting human actions. The base/superstructure debate, however, was not closed as a consequence of Engels's intervention.

Marxist theory has developed in a number of different directions. By the 1970s two broad strands within Marxism relating to the base/superstructure debate had emerged: 'humanist' and 'scientific'. As Urry (1981: 8) has noted, these perspectives incorporated 'the reproduction of certain of the problems which have already been encountered within orthodox sociology'. This was the structure/action debate; the contrast between, on the one hand, sociological perspectives which emphasize above all the significance of human action in explanations of social institutions and behaviour, and, on the other, the functionalist or structurally deterministic accounts of society which such 'action' approaches criticized. Thus, humanist Marxism – as in, for example, the work of Gramsci – tends to treat the base/superstructure distinction as a metaphor which can all too easily be interpreted in a deterministic fashion. Gramsci emphasizes the value of Marx's analysis as a means of developing a critique of the dehumanizing aspects of modern capitalism, a critique which will ultimately enable the actor to transcend his or her 'alienation'. As with the action approach within sociology, therefore, a central role is given to the human actor.

'Scientific' Marxism was the self-assigned label of French structural Marxists such as Althusser (1969) and Poulantzas (1975). Althusser argued that ideology and politics were not determined by the economy in a mechanistic fashion, as some simplistic interpretations of Marx had assumed. Rather, they should be seen as conditions of its existence and are therefore 'relatively autonomous' – although, echoing Engels, Althusser held that the economic was determinant in 'the last instance'. The work of Althusser and Poulantzas was also characterized by a distinctive (rationalist) epistemology, or view of how knowledge about the world is acquired. Knowledge about the social world, they argued, does not proceed by observation but through theoretical practice or 'science' – of which Marxism was an example. Thus we do not 'know' classes by observing them but rather through the theoretical identification and exploration of the class structure, and individuals are the 'bearers' or 'agents' of these structures of social relations. This approach, therefore, emphasizes above all the primacy of the identification and description of class *structures*. The manner in which individuals are distributed within these structures is, from their perspective, of comparatively minor importance; the important task for the 'scientist' is to identify the structure itself, and thus the 'real interests' of the individuals located within it. It is not difficult to see the parallels here with functionalism and structural overdeterminism in sociology (Connell 1982). Different classes are being identified according to their 'functional' relationship to the capitalist mode of production as a whole, which is described in Marx's account of the exploitation of workers within the labour process and the way in which different groups in society are related to this process.

As we have seen, Marx had drawn a distinction between a 'class in itself' and a 'class for itself'; this has been described as a distinction between a set of 'objective' conditions which define the class, and the 'subjective' consciousness which this class possesses (Braverman 1974). However, what is the nature of this subjective consciousness? It has been argued (Abercrombie and Turner 1978) that Marx's work provides two, conflicting, accounts of the generation of class consciousness. On the one hand, the passage cited above from the *Critique of Political Economy* could be used to argue that each class develops its 'own' consciousness: that factory workers, for example, will develop a common understanding of their exploited position. On the other hand, the same passage could be used to argue that the dominant class has the capacity to generate a dominant ideology – that the employers, for example, will have the capacity to generate amongst factory workers a belief that the prevailing arrangements are beneficial for all concerned. Thus in *The German Ideology*, Marx and Engels state: 'The ruling class are in every epoch the ruling ideas, i.e. the class which is the ruling *material* force of society, is at the same time its ruling *intellectual* force' (1970: 64). Thus a subordinate class may, as a consequence, hold to views which are at variance with its own 'objective' interests – a phenomenon which has been described by later Marxists as a 'false consciousness' of their true class situation.

Throughout the 1980s, the debate on class continued amongst Marxist theorists. Structural Marxism no longer has much influence – at least in part, it may be suggested, because of the electoral failure of the left during this period (see preface in Benton 1984). The collapse of 'state socialism' has also been widely interpreted as an empirical refutation of the Marxist theory of history. The revival of Marxist scholarship in the 1960s was accompanied by an optimism of the left which persisted throughout much of the 1970s. The 1980s, however, witnessed the electoral rise of the 'New Right' – Thatcherism in Britain, Reaganomics in the United States. Political theorists including Przeworski (1985), Laclau and Mouffe (1985) and Wood (1986) have examined the possibilities of the development of socialism in these changing circumstances. Much of this discussion has involved a fundamental revision of some basic Marxist political ideas. In particular, the central place which the proletariat or working class occupied within Marx's original writings has increasingly been called into question. Wood (1986: 3–4) has summarized these revisions (which she describes, somewhat scathingly, as the 'New True Socialism') as follows: first, the absence of revolutionary politics amongst the working class reflects the fact that there is no necessary correspondence between economics and politics (that is, the link between base and superstructure is regarded as tenuous, even non-existent). Second, there is no necessary or privileged relation between the working class and socialism, and so a socialist movement can be constituted independently of class (thus dissolving the link between 'class' and 'consciousness'). Third, socialism is in any case concerned with universal human goals which transcend the narrowness of material class interests and may therefore address a broader public, irrespective of class. Thus the struggle for socialism can be conceived as a plurality of democratic struggles, bringing together a variety of resistances to many forms of inequality and oppression (for example, those associated with gender and race).

These arguments amongst Marxist theoreticians have not been directly concerned with class and stratification research in sociology, but they have nevertheless had a considerable impact. The American sociologist Erik Wright (1989) has systematically developed both his 'class map' and his strategy of analysis in response to inputs from these sources. More widely, however, it may be suggested that contemporary debates within theoretical Marxism have contributed to more general arguments to the effect that 'class' is no longer a relevant analytical concept as far as early twenty-first-century societies are concerned.

Marx, therefore, saw classes as real social forces with the capacity to transform society. His class analysis did not simply describe the patterning of structured social inequality – although an explanation of this structuring can be found in the relationships to the means of production through which classes are to be identified. His theories have been enormously influential and are open to a number of different interpretations. Two major problems have been identified which are still the focus of considerable debate within sociology: first, the relative significance of the 'economy' (or class forces) as compared to other sources of social differentiation in the shaping of human activities; and second, whether or not consciousness is integral to the identification of a class. As we shall see, the position of Max Weber, the other major theorist whose ideas have been central to the development of sociological perspectives on class, was rather different on both of these issues.

Weber

The contrast between Marx's and Weber's analysis of class may at times have been overdrawn, but it cannot be doubted that their approaches to social science were very different. Marx was a committed revolutionary, Weber a promoter of 'value-free' social science; and although Weber could not be described as an idealist, he was highly critical of Marx's historical materialism. Marx claimed to have identified abstract social forces (classes) which shaped human history – although, as we have seen, the extent to which Marx considered such structures *can* be identified independently of human action is itself a topic of much debate. Weber, in contrast, was an explicit methodological individualist. That is, he argued that all social collectivities and human phenomena have to be reducible to their individual constituents, and explained in these terms. As far as class is concerned, for Weber:

> We may speak of a 'class' when (1) a number of people have in common a specific causal component of their life chances, in so far as (2) this component is represented exclusively by economic interests in the possession of goods and opportunities for income, and (3) is represented under the conditions of the commodity or labour markets.   (Gerth and Mills 1948: 181)

Thus 'class situation' reflects market-determined 'life chances'. The causal components contributing to such life chances include property, giving rise to both positively and negatively privileged property classes (that is, owners and non-owners), and skills and education, giving rise to positively and negatively privileged 'acquisition' or 'commercial' classes. Weber was aware of the (almost) infinite variability of 'market situations' and thus of the difficulty of identifying a 'class', and his discussion in *Economy and Society* (1978) incorporates the listing of over twenty positively and negatively privileged, property and acquisition, classes. This empirical plurality is resolved by Weber's description of a '*social* class', which 'makes up the totality of those class situations within which individual and generational mobility is easy and typical' (Giddens and Held 1982: 69). He identified as 'social classes' (a) the working class as a whole; (b) the petty bourgeoisie; (c) technicians, specialists and lower-level management; and (d) 'the classes privileged through property and education' – that is, those at the top of the hierarchy of occupation and ownership. In short, at the descriptive level, Weber's account of the 'class structure' of capitalist society is not too different from that of Marx, despite the fact that their identification of the *sources* of class structuring (production relationships on the one hand, market relationships on the other) *is* very different.

Marx and Weber, however, differed profoundly as far as the question of class action was concerned. For Weber: ' "classes" are not communities; they merely represent possible, and frequent, bases for communal action' (Gerth and Mills 1948: 181). 'Associations of class members – class organizations – may arise on the basis of all . . . classes. However, this does not necessarily happen . . . The mere differentiation of property classes is not "dynamic", that is, it need not result in class struggles and revolutions' (Giddens and Held 1982: 69–70). Indeed, in a passage which clearly refers to the Marxist notion of 'false consciousness' Weber writes that:

> every class may be the carrier of any one of the innumerable possible forms of class action, but this is not necessarily so . . . That men in the same class situation regularly react in mass actions to such tangible situations as economic ones in the direction of those interests that are most adequate to their average number is an important . . . fact for the understanding of historical events. However, this fact must not lead to that kind of pseudo-scientific operation which has found its most classic expression in the statement of a talented author, that the individual may be in error concerning his interests but that the class is infallible about its interests.   (Gerth and Mills 1948: 184–5)

Weber's historical sociology, therefore, was developed in conscious opposition to Marxist theories of historical development – at least in its more economistic versions – as in Weber's analysis of the genesis of modern capitalism in *The Protestant Ethic and the Spirit of Capitalism*. In this book, he explored the unintended consequences of Calvinist ideology, and its impact on historical development, through an examination of the 'elective affinity' between Protestantism and the 'spirit of capitalism', which affected the development of capitalism itself. Weber argued that rational, ascetic Protestantism, as developed within a number of Calvinist churches and Pietistic sects in Europe and America during the seventeenth century, provided, through its rules for daily living (diligence in work, asceticism, and systematic time use), a particularly fruitful seedbed for the development of capitalism. It would be misleading to argue that Weber had developed his argument in order to advance an alternative, 'idealist' interpretation of history; he did not seek 'to substitute for a one-sided materialistic an equally one-sided spiritualistic causal interpretation of culture and of history' (Weber 1976: 183). However, as Marshall (1982: 150) has argued, the question as to whether Marx's materialist or Weber's pluralistic account of the rise and development of capitalism is to be preferred is not, ultimately, an empirical one but, rather, a question of the 'validity of competing frameworks for the interpretation of social reality'. Although Weber's account of the rise of capitalism cannot be described as 'idealist', therefore, it does lead, inevitably, to an account of the relationship between the 'ideological' and 'material' realms of human activity which would be in conflict with Marx's analysis.

Weber's analysis is also to be distinguished from Marx's in that he denies not only the inevitability of class action and conflict, but also the identification of class as a primary source of differentiation in complex societies. For Weber, ' "classes" and "status groups" are phenomena of the distribution of power within a community' (Gerth and Mills 1948: 181), and in certain circumstances status may be the predominant source which regulates entitlements to material rewards. Status is associated with honour and prestige and, indeed, may often come into conflict with the demands of the market, where, to use an old phrase suitably adapted: 'every man (and woman) has his (or her) price'. In contrast: 'in most instances', wrote Weber, 'the notion of honour peculiar to status absolutely abhors that which is essential to the market: higgling' (Gerth and Mills 1948: 193). Thus in Weber's analysis the feudal lord or abbot, for example, would belong not to a dominant class but to a status group.

'Status', in Weber's writings, is a complex concept. First, there is the meaning which has already been described: that which reflects the etymological link with 'estate' or '*Stände*' and describes positions which represent particular life chances or fates for the status group in question. Second, status groups have been identified as 'consciousness communities', as when, for example, Collins (1971: 1009) describes status groups as 'associational groups sharing common cultures . . . Participation in such groups gives individuals their fundamental sense of identity.' Third, as we have seen in the previous chapter, status has been used to describe consumption categories or 'lifestyle', as 'the totality of cultural practices such as dress, speech, outlook and bodily dispositions' (Turner 1988: 66).

The crucial differences between Marx's and Weber's accounts of class may be summarized as follows: first, for Marx, class relationships are grounded in exploitation and domination within *production* relations, whereas, for Weber, class situations reflect differing 'life chances' in the *market*; second, Marx's historical materialism gives a primacy to 'class' in historical evolution which is at odds with Weber's perspective on historical explanation; and finally (and following from this point), whereas for Marx class action is seen as inevitable, for Weber classes 'merely represent possible, and frequent, bases for communal action' (Gerth and Mills 1948: 181).

Class and sociology after the Second World War

Sociology had been well established in the United States before the Second World War, and 'At the beginning of the 1950s . . . one could find large numbers of studies dealing with almost every aspect of behaviour in the United States. No other society had ever been subjected to such detailed examination' (Bendix and Lipset 1967a: 6). A strong tradition of empirical investigation, therefore, was well established. This included research into social stratification, which, as in studies such as Warner's (1963) anthropologically inspired *Yankee City* series, first published in the 1940s, had a focus on occupational inequality and social mobility, often in small communities. As has frequently been noted, in such studies 'class' was in practice operationalized as a particular dimension of the Weberian concept of *status* in that it was mainly concerned with social prestige rankings within the community. The pre-eminent sociological theorist in the United States was Talcott Parsons; as we have seen, the structural functionalism which characterized his approach had a tendency to emphasize order rather than conflict, and thus to direct attention away from the conflict and tensions in society which are the focus of *class* (rather than status) analyses.

Sociology in Britain was relatively underdeveloped in the 1950s, and had been much influenced by the Fabian tradition of social improvement and reform. Thus a preoccupation with structured social inequality had always been present. An example of this tradition of British 'political arithmetic' would be Glass's *Social Mobility in Britain* (1954), which had used an occupational (class) scale in its statistical analyses of social mobility. In continental Europe, sociology was more deeply rooted in established traditions of philosophy and social theory. The intellectual diaspora which was a consequence of the rise of fascism brought many European scholars to the United States and Britain, and with them an increasing emphasis on the significance of 'theory' in sociology.

The first major reader in the field of class and stratification to be published in English after the Second World War – *Class, Status and Power* (1953; 2nd edn 1967), edited by Reinhard Bendix and S. M. Lipset – reflected this mingling of influences. The title was itself a deliberate play on a section of Weber's *Economy and Society*, 'Class, Status, and Party', which had been of considerable significance in shaping sociological thinking about 'social class'. The importance of the distinction between economic 'classes' and 'status rankings' (the latter describes the conceptualization of class in Warner's research) was increasingly emphasized. However, the use of the 'class' concept by the different contributors to the volume reflected the variety of definitions of the term which has been noted in chapter 2. Thus there were a number of papers on class theory, in which class was discussed as an abstract force, whereas other contributions used the same word – class – to describe the occupational aggregates used in, for example, empirical analyses of residential segregation. Bendix and Lipset's article – 'Karl Marx's theory of social classes' (1967b) – provided a guide to 'Marx on Class' for a whole generation of sociology students in Britain and America.

Bendix and Lipset identified a 'basic ambiguity', which has already been noted, in Marx's theory concerning class action:

> on the one hand, he felt quite certain that the contradictions engendered by capitalism would inevitably lead to a class-conscious proletariat and hence to a proletarian revolution. But on the other hand, he assigned to class-consciousness, to political action, and to his scientific theory of history a major role in bringing about this result.   (1967b: 11)

In other words, is class consciousness, and therefore conflict, inevitable, or not? As Bendix and Lipset demonstrated, Marx's own work provided an extensive discussion of the circumstances in which class consciousness *might* develop (conflicts over the distribution of material resources, alienation and deskilling within the labour process, concentration of workers within factories, combinations to raise wages, increasing polarization within society and so on), but, they argued, ambiguity still remained as to whether it *would* develop. However, if the question of class consciousness is viewed as contingent rather than inevitable (and this, it will be remembered, was Weber's position), then the question becomes an empirical one – in what circumstances does class consciousness develop? As Lockwood has noted: 'once shorn of its deterministic assumptions, the Marxian problem of the relationship between class position and class consciousness could become a subject of far-reaching and systematic sociological inquiry' (1958; 1989: 217).

The development of theoretically informed accounts of the 'class structure'

The way was laid open, therefore, for the analytical and empirical separation of the specification of the class structure from the question of consciousness, between the 'objective' and 'subjective' dimensions of class, even if linked within the S→C→A chain. Within this emerging sociological perspective, a central problem is that of the identification of the class structure itself – that is, a structure of positions which may or may not give rise to consciousness. The structure of employment became the major focus of such attempts.

Dahrendorf's work was extremely influential in this regard. In *Class and Class Conflict in an Industrial Society* (1959: 151), he drew upon the work of both Marx and Weber in deriving the class structure from 'positions in associations (i.e. occupations) co-ordinated by authority and defin[ing] them by the "characteristic" of participation in or exclusion from the exercise of authority'. In a similar vein to Bendix and Lipset, he argued that: 'The general theory of class consists of two analytically separable elements: the theory of class formation and the theory of class action, or class conflict' (1959: 153). This analytical separation of 'structure' and 'action', as we have seen, assumed considerable significance in sociology and has had an important effect on the development of 'class analysis'.

Like Dahrendorf, Lockwood in *The Blackcoated Worker* drew upon the theoretical analyses of both Marx and Weber in his now-classic 1958 account of a 'socioeconomic group that had long been a discomfort to Marxist theory: the growing mass of lower non-manual or white-collar employees' (1958; 1989: 218). (In fact, Lockwood's research focused entirely on clerical occupations.) He described 'class position' as including three factors: 'market situation', that is, 'the economic position narrowly conceived, consisting of source and size of income, degree of job-security, and opportunity for upward occupational mobility'; secondly, 'work situation', or 'the set of social relationships in which the individual is involved at work by virtue of his position in the division of labour'; and finally, 'status situation', or the position of the individual in the hierarchy of prestige in the society at large. Experiences originating in these three spheres were seen as the principal determinants of class consciousness (1989: 15–16). It must be emphasized that Lockwood was not merely concerned descriptively to locate clerks in the class structure. A central issue in his work is the question of class consciousness and action, and he explored the differentiation of 'class situation' within the clerical category which gave rise to variations in the level and type of trade union activity amongst clerical workers – trade unionism is here being viewed as an expression of class consciousness. Nevertheless, in maintaining, like Dahrendorf, an analytical separation between structure (formation) and action, Lockwood's work left open the possibility that 'class analysis' might come to have a primary focus on one or the other. Although, therefore, his original work was concerned as much with the question of class consciousness and action as it was with class structure, it might be suggested that one of its enduring legacies has been that it provided, within a neo-Weberian framework, the means to locate empirically particular groups of occupations within the 'class structure'. In particular, Lockwood's concepts of 'work' and 'market' situation were key elements in Goldthorpe's (Goldthorpe with Llewellyn and Payne 1980, 1987) development of a theoretical class scheme, based on the occupational structure, which has been widely employed in empirical research (as we shall see in the next chapter, Goldthorpe now uses the term 'employment relations', rather than Lockwood's concepts).

Another sociologist who has devoted considerable effort to the theoretical identification of a 'class structure' within the structure of employment relationships is the American Marxist Erik Wright. Wright's initial development of his Marxist 'class map', which was to become the basis of his own theoretical class scheme, was carried out in a conscious dialogue with structural Marxism (Wright 1976). Thus, although Wright's theoretical perspectives are clearly very different from those of Lockwood, Dahrendorf, Goldthorpe and other 'left Weberians', his work is, like theirs, an attempt to identify sets of 'class positions' within the structure of employment. Wright's earlier work was much influenced by Braverman, whose *Labor and Monopoly Capital* (1974) was modelled on Marx's analysis of the labour process in *Capital*, vol. 1. Braverman argued that with the development of mass production, work had become increasingly routinized and, as a consequence, there had been a continuing 'proletarianization' of the labour force – despite the apparent increase in 'white-collar' or 'middle-class' employment. Braverman's account of the 'deskilling' of craft work and the rationalization of the labour process had a considerable impact on industrial sociology. In respect of class analysis, however, his work had the effect of driving a further wedge between structure and action: 'No attempt will be made to deal with the modern working class on the level of its consciousness, organization, or activities. This is a book about the working class as a class *in itself*, not as a class *for itself*' (1974: 26–7; emphasis in original).[1] His account, therefore, focused entirely on developments within the labour process and did not discuss the possibility of class resistance or action. Thus, although it is highly unlikely that Braverman would have had any sympathy with structural Marxism, his work had a similar impact. The 'analytical separation between class formation and class action' (Dahrendorf) was increasingly coming to represent distinct areas of theoretical and empirical activity (Crompton and Gubbay 1977).

Since the Second World War, therefore, we can trace the emergence of a distinctive sociological strand of 'class analysis'. Marxist and Weberian theories of social class are employed, as in the work of authors such as Lockwood, Dahrendorf and Braverman, to generate theoretical accounts of how particular jobs and occupations might be located within a structure of class positions. Increasingly, these accounts are used to elaborate and refine a predominant empirical approach within social stratification as a whole, in which employment aggregates are described as 'classes'. That is, 'classes' are identified theoretically within the structure of employment. Following from Bendix and Lipset's appropriation of Marx's distinction between a class 'in itself' and 'for itself', class structure and class action are regarded as analytically separable. Thus these theoretically identified employment aggregates may be regarded as 'classes' – although the question of class action is contingent, rather than inevitable. This strategy, therefore, brings together within a single framework theoretical analyses of social class and empirical analyses of inequality. It is an approach with tremendous explanatory and analytical promise but, as we shall see, it also embodies a number of serious, and probably irresolvable, difficulties.

Class and history

We have summarized above a number of sustained attempts, deriving from different theoretical perspectives, to identify *a priori* a 'class structure' located within the structure of work and employment. A number of different factors served to push class analysis in this direction, including the established convention in American and British sociology of identifying 'classes' as occupational aggregates, the influence of both structural functionalism and structural Marxism, and the revival of sociological interest in the labour process. However, these developments ran in parallel with other approaches to the study of social class, which tended to be associated with a humanistic, rather than a structuralist, Marxist perspective, and a methodological approach which drew primarily upon history and anthropology.

A broadly historical approach to the topic of social class, similar to that found in the work of Weber and Marx, has been a constant theme in the work of sociologists. In Britain, the work of Bottomore (1991) and Bauman (1982) might be cited as examples. From the 1960s there was a continuing dialogue between sociology and history, much of which has been concerned with the concept of 'class' (Stedman Jones 1976; Neale 1983; Abrams 1980). A major example is E. P. Thompson's *Making of the English Working Class*, first published in 1963. In this book, and in his other work, Thompson argues explicitly against the more determinist versions of the model of economic 'base' and ideological 'superstructure' which had been developed from Marx's work. As Kaye (1984: 172) has argued: 'In his historical studies . . . Thompson has persistently pursued an intellectual struggle against those varieties of Marxism and social science which are characterized by economic determinism and the denial of human agency.' A rejection of determinism and emphasis on human agency might suggest the possibility of close parallels with Weber, but Thompson has from the first been associated with a tradition of Marxist history which, in Britain, has a lengthy pedigree. This tradition includes authors such as Maurice Dobb, Christopher Hill and Eric Hobsbawm, who have written extensively on the development of capitalism and the transition from feudalism, the English Revolution, rural protest and the development of empire. The concept of 'class', and class struggle, has a central place in all of their writings, but Thompson's account of the 'making' of the English working class in the eighteenth and nineteenth centuries develops a distinctive perspective on 'class' which has had a major impact. Although his work is focused on the British case, it has been extremely influential in other countries.[2]

Thompson defines 'class' in the manner of an abstract force which nevertheless has real consequences: 'By class I understand a historical phenomenon, unifying a number of disparate and seemingly unconnected events . . . I emphasize that it is a *historical* phenomenon. I do not see class as a "structure", nor even as a "category", but as something which in fact happens' (Thompson 1968: 9). Like Marx, Thompson sees class as embedded in relations of production, but he is emphatic that classes cannot be discussed or identified independently of class *consciousness*: 'class experience is largely determined by the productive relations into which men are born – or enter involuntarily. Class-consciousness is the way in which these experiences are handled in cultural terms: embodied in traditions, value-systems, ideas, and institutional forms' (1968: 10). Thompson's emphasis on the significance of experience and consciousness has led to criticisms from other historians that his work is excessively culturalist – that is, it represents a shift away from the investigation of *economic* structures and relations which, it may be argued, should occupy a central place in any Marxist historical investigation (Johnson 1979). This specific point relating to Thompson's work will not be pursued here – although the interrelationship between the 'economic' and the 'cultural' will be explored in some depth in further chapters of this book (see in particular chapter 5). For the moment, however, we will explore a topic of some relevance to class analysis in sociology, and which assumes a central place in Thompson's work – that is, the possibility (or otherwise) of identifying a class 'structure' independent of class consciousness.

Kaye has argued, following Wood, that Thompson has 'reformulat[ed] class analysis as class-struggle analysis' (1984: 201), but nevertheless Thompson does not claim that there are no 'objective' class relations. As we have seen, Thompson is explicit that the productive relations which determine class experience have an existence apart from the individual, but he *does* insist that 'class is a relationship, and not a thing . . . "It" does not exist, either to have an ideal interest or consciousness, or to lie as a patient on the Adjustor's table' (1968: 11). In taking up this position, Thompson was arguing against what he perceived to be the dominant sociological approach to 'class analysis', which was briefly described in the previous section of this chapter. He was equally critical of the structural-functional approach of Parsons and Smelser as well as the 'conflict' approach of Dahrendorf (1959). Smelser (1959) had carried out a detailed historical study of the Lancashire cotton industry which had used Parsons's 'general theory of action' in order to construct a set of empty theoretical 'boxes' to be filled by empirical research. This was informed by the principle that structural differentiation created new roles which then functioned more effectively in the new circumstances. On an extreme reading of this approach, human actors are thereby reduced to puppets. Dahrendorf had developed a model of the 'class structure' in which 'classes are . . . based on a structural arrangement of social roles' (1959: 148). Thus Dahrendorf's analysis focuses on the structuring of these roles, rather than on their incumbents: 'Classes are based on the differences in legitimate power associated with certain *positions*, i.e. on the structure of social roles with respect to their authority expectations. It follows from this that an individual becomes a member of a class by playing a social role' (Dahrendorf 1959: 149; my emphasis). It is not difficult to see how this approach would be at variance with that of Thompson, who describes Dahrendorf's work as 'obsessively concerned with methodology', and as excluding 'the examination of a single real class situation in a real historical context' (Thompson 1968: 11).

Although Thompson was a fierce critic of overly 'structural' approaches to class, he nevertheless held to a broadly 'Marxist' account of the role of classes, and class struggle, in the shaping of British history. However, contemporary social history has been much affected by the 'cultural turn', and has moved 'beyond' Thompson and towards a rejection of materialist explanations (Joyce 1995). Thus although Cannadine (2000) makes a strong case for the reinsertion of class into both historical and contemporary accounts of the British situation, his argument focuses, above all, on how people *think* about class. For Cannadine (2000: 19), throughout history, 'class' has been 'thought' within one or other of three basic frameworks that could all be applied to the analysis of the same society. These are first, finely graded hierarchies of rank; second, oppositional 'two-class' models ('us' and 'them'); and third, three-class models that identify collectivities based on wealth and occupation. Politicians, Cannadine argues, have been instrumental in determining which model of class (and therefore perspective on an unequal world) is accepted as legitimate by the populace: 'the task of politicians is the creation and manipulation of social identities' (Cannadine 2000: 171). As Britain has experienced no major revolutions, or social disruptions, all three versions of 'class' have been continuously available, and 'the history of class in Britain . . . can only be written as the history of multiple identities . . . This history of class is as much about the history of *ideas* about society as it is about society itself' (ibid.).

Although Cannadine's account is interesting and thought-provoking, his rendering of the class concept as being largely focused on the question of identity has the consequence (as in other, similar, 'ideational' accounts of class) of removing the cutting edge of the class concept in relation to inequality. Thus he defines a 'classless' society as 'one in which the majority of people do not think about the social order in terms of a formal or informal hierarchy, in terms of an upper, middle and lower class, or in terms of a great divide between "us" and "them"' (Cannadine 2000: 185). As inequalities of wealth and power have been persistent throughout recorded history, it is unrealistic, he argues, to define a 'classless' society as one in which inequalities have been abolished. It may indeed be 'unrealistic' to envision a complex society as having a complete absence of social and economic differentiation, but nevertheless, to abandon efforts to understand the nature of inequalities, and how they might be addressed, might effectively contribute to their legitimation – described in chapter 2 above as 'winning cultural battles but losing the class war' (p. 26). We will be returning to this theme in our discussion of Fraser's work later in this chapter, but for the moment, we will continue with our account of the history of sociological analyses of 'class'.

The intertwining of structure and action, economy and culture

Methodologically speaking, the development of 'theoretical' or 'relational' employment-based class schemes, on the one hand, and historico-cultural ethnographies, on the other, represent opposite poles in the development of 'class analysis'. However, these are by no means the only direction that class analysis has taken in sociology. The development of theoretical class schemes, focused on the structure of employment, depends on the analytical separation of the study of class structure from that of class action, of 'subjective' and 'objective' dimensions, but the validity of this separation has always been contested – and not only by those committed to an ethnographic approach. For example, Stark (1980) has been highly critical of Braverman's separation of the investigation of a class 'in itself' from a class 'for itself'. He argues against the type of class analysis which 'proceeds by identifying the members who "make up" the class; this aggregate is then given the properties of a purposive actor' (1980: 96–7). As a consequence of this separation, he argues, Braverman's history was empirically inadequate in that it did not examine either worker resistance or the purposive strategies of the emergent managerial class. Rather than simply identifying classes as aggregates of 'places', Stark argues, in a manner reminiscent of Thompson, for a 'relational' approach:

> a class is not 'composed of' individuals; it is not a collection or aggregation of individuals. *Classes*, like the social relations from which they arise, exist in an antagonistic and dependent relation to each other. Classes are constituted by these mutually antagonistic relations. In this sense . . . the object of study is not the elements themselves but the relations between them. (1980: 97)

Thus the transformation of method, he argues, must also be accompanied by a shift in the level of abstraction of class analysis, away from an obsessive overconcern with the 'mode of production' to the study of the interaction of organizations and groups.

Stark's arguments, therefore, may be seen as an example of the ongoing parallel between debates in Marxist theory and those in mainstream sociology during the 1960s and 1970s. Giddens, whose work was influential in developing the critique of positivism, first developed his ideas on 'structuration', which has become the core of his social theory, in his book *The Class Structure of the Advanced Societies* (1973, 1981). He introduced the concept of 'structuration' as a means of focusing upon '*the modes in which* "economic" relationships become translated into "non-economic" social structures' (1981: 105), that is, *social* classes.[3] Two types of structuration were identified. First, mediate structuration describes the links between particular market capacities – the ownership of productive property; the possession of educational and technical qualifications; and manual labour-power and identifiable groups in society. Mediate structuration is governed by the extent of social mobility. Second, proximate structuration points to the factors which shape local class formation, including relationships of allocation and authority within the enterprise (here Giddens's discussion has close parallels with Dahrendorf's), and the impact of 'distributive groupings' in the community and neighbourhood. Thus Giddens's initial identification of a 'social class' incorporates both structure and agency. On the question of class consciousness, Giddens extends the original Marxist concept to a number of levels. He argues that 'structuration' will result in a common class *awareness*, but not necessarily class *consciousness* – that is, any sense of opposition to other social classes. He argues that, in contrast to Marx's analysis, a *revolutionary* consciousness which might lead to the transformation of society is most likely to develop at the historical moment of the emergence of the capitalist order, when material disparities are at their greatest and the imposition of authoritative control most rigorous. In mature capitalism, in contrast, the working class is characterized merely by *conflict* consciousness, and social democracy is the characteristic form of developed capitalist society.

Giddens's account of the 'class structure', therefore, reflected the developing critique of positivism and structural overdetermination within sociology itself, in that class relationships were presented as being *actively* structured, rather than simply being taken as given. The introduction of the notion of 'structuration' has led his subsequent work in a more methodological direction, and he has not returned to a further substantial treatment of class analysis.[4] The question of action arises at two points in his analysis; first, that which relates to the 'structuration' of the different classes, and second, the nature and possibilities of class action once 'structuration' has occurred. Given this emphasis on the active structuring of class relationships, it is not surprising that Giddens's approach to class analysis struck a resonant chord with historians influenced by Thompson's work.[5]

The possibilities of the development of class consciousness and action consequent upon class formation have also been a continuing focus of empirical research in British sociology. Much of this work was stimulated by Lockwood's influential article 'Sources of variation in working class images of society' (1966). For the most part, Lockwood argued that individuals 'visualise the . . . structure of their society from the vantage points of their own particular *milieus* and their perceptions of the larger society will vary according to their experiences . . . in the smaller societies in which they live out their daily lives' (1966: 249). He thus developed a typology of working-class images of society ('traditional proletarian', 'traditional deferential' and 'privatised'), which corresponded to variations in the characteristic 'work' and 'community' situations experienced within the working class. Thus particular cultural and structural locations are seen as corresponding to particular 'class' images.

Lockwood's account of working-class 'images of society' drew upon an existing corpus of contemporary, anthropological, community-based research (see Frankenberg 1966), such as Dennis et al.'s 'Coal is our life' (1969, first published 1956), a study of a mining village in Yorkshire. The harsh working conditions of the miners generated a strong sense of (masculine) occupational solidarity, and this 'us and them' workplace consciousness is complemented and reinforced by close kin and community ties, resulting in 'traditional proletarian' consciousness (see also Gouldner 1954). A simultaneous exploration of structure and action, economy and culture, was a feature of such case studies. This approach was carried over into the enormously influential 'affluent worker' research (Goldthorpe et al. 1968, 1969, 1970), which investigated the phenomenon of working-class 'embourgeoisement'. Reflecting the sociological preoccupations of the period, one of the major issues investigated in the 'affluent worker' study was the 'problem' of working-class consciousness – or rather, the lack of it.

Savage (2000) has argued that the question of class consciousness – specifically, 'working-class' consciousness – became something of an obsession in British sociology during the 1970s, even as Lockwood's model was 'collapsing under the weight of counter empirical evidence' (Devine and Savage 2005: 7). It stimulated a number of empirical studies which explored the link between particular occupational groups, structural locations and social imagery – for example, Newby's (1977) study of agricultural workers, Brown and Brannen's study of shipbuilders (1970) – as well as wide-ranging review and debate (Bulmer 1975). This empirical research demonstrated that 'class' consciousness was incoherent and often contradictory, rather than being capable of being 'read off' from work and community locations (see also Mann 1973). Nevertheless, this kind of work makes no empirical separation between the investigation of structure and action, economy and culture, and usually took the form of the case study, rather than relying primarily on the large-scale sample survey (Marshall 1988).

Empirical studies of social class influenced by this perspective have often taken the form of micro-level studies of particular groups and occupations, within their specific social context. Much of this work has overlapped with the sociology of work and occupations, in particular that stimulated by the 'labour process' debate (Crompton and Jones 1984; Smith 1987). Devine and Savage (2005: 8) have argued that the problems, revealed by these studies, in giving a coherent account of class consciousness led to an 'impasse' in class analysis in Britain that precipitated a 'retreat from the "cultural" pole of enquiry' and a focus of energies on a 'better appreciation of the "structural"' (as in the work of Goldthorpe and Wright). It is possible to suggest, however, that rather than a 'retreat from the cultural' on the part of class and stratification researchers, what had in fact taken place was a major split within sociology itself. For, by the 1980s, and much influenced by then-fashionable currents in social theory, the 'cultural turn' was well under way.

Class, inequality and the 'cultural turn'

Besides its impact on the development of social history, Thompson's work has also been influential in the area of cultural studies, within which there has developed an approach to 'class analysis' very different from that of those who have concentrated upon the identification and investigation of the macro-level class structure. Much of the earlier work in this tradition was influenced by Gramsci's humanist Marxism.[6] As we have indicated above, Gramsci rejected the base/superstructure dichotomy of economistic Marxism, and emphasized the pervasive importance of culture and ideology to the persistence of structures of class domination. Culture, he argued, is neither apolitical, nor a mere reflection of the ideology of the dominant class. Central to Gramsci's thought is the concept of *hegemony*, that is, the manner in which the active *consent* of the subordinate classes to their domination is achieved. Thus 'every struggle between classes is always also a struggle between cultural modalities' (Hall 1981); winning the struggle of ideas is as important to the 'class struggle' as are economic and political struggles.

Thus within cultural studies there have been developed ethnographic accounts of the manner in which individuals in different classes both resist and reproduce their class situations. An influential example of this genre is Willis's *Learning to Labour* (1977), a study of working-class male adolescents. Willis illustrated how, in his terms, the explicitly oppositional working-class culture (that is, opposed to 'middle-class' values, including conformity, an emphasis on the importance of formal education and so on) which was developed within the school context nevertheless reflected that within the working-class world of work which these youths were about to enter, and thus, paradoxically, reinforced their subordination.

It is a feature of this cultural approach to class analysis, therefore, that no distinction is made between 'structure' and 'action', and that 'culture' is defined as encompassing both the meanings and the values which arise amongst distinctive social groups and classes, as well as the lived traditions and practices through which these meanings are expressed and in which they are embodied (Hall 1981: 26).

The cultural turn, however, has involved not simply a (re-)emphasis on the significance of culture, but also a turning away from economic or structural explanations and analysis. Resistance has become a matter of 'subcultural style', as in Hebdige's (1979) analysis of the fashions and music of working-class youth. In part, these arguments reflect the widespread assumption that there has occurred some kind of 'societal shift', as discussed in chapter 2. The supposed shift from 'modern' to 'postmodern' societies has been associated, it has been argued, with a collapse of the boundaries between economy and culture (Lash and Urry 1994; Crook et al. 1992). The rejection of 'grand narratives' of the kind associated with the Marxist theory of history was associated with an emphasis on the discursive and narrative foundations of knowledge – and indeed, even of institutions themselves (Foucault 1972). Pushing the argument even further, it has been argued that more and more areas of the economy are, effectively, devoted to cultural production and reproduction. The 'aestheti-cization of production', it is suggested, has meant that sign value has become more important than exchange value in the structuring of commodities (Baudrillard 1972).

Not surprisingly, an emphasis on the overwhelming significance of symbols, discourse and difference is often associated with arguments to the effect that class is 'no longer a relevant concept'. Indeed, as already noted in chapter 2, the turn to culture incorporated a shift, in discussions of inequality, from economic questions of redistribution to cultural questions of recognition. Thus inequality becomes rendered as largely 'cultural'. For example, Fraser (1995, 2000) suggests that the 'culturalist' theories of contemporary society that fuse economic inequality seamlessly into the cultural hierarchy result in an all-too-present danger of 'displacement'. That is, economic inequalities are effectively subsumed within, or displaced onto, cultural concerns. In such a model, 'to revalue unjustly devalued identities is simultaneously to attack the deep sources of economic inequality; [and] no explicit politics of redistribution is needed' (2000: 111). Such 'vulgar culturalism', Fraser argues, is nothing more than the mirror image of the 'vulgar economism' that character-ized cultural or status differences as deriving directly from economic inequalities.

The cultural turn, therefore, was a major theoretical shift that resulted in the increasing questioning, even rejection, of 'class analysis' in the closing decade of the twentieth century. With hindsight, however, it may nevertheless be seen as having had some positive effects. Few would now subscribe to 'vulgar economism', and culture, discourse and subjectivity are now taken more seriously. In particular, Bourdieu's approach to class analysis is widely regarded as combining both 'economy' and 'culture', and there has been a considerable revival of interest in his work.

Social class, social geography and the turn to 'realism'

Another perspective which developed during the 1970s, and which has been particularly influential within human geography and urban sociology, was a return to *political economy*.

As the label implies, this strand of analysis tends to be interdisciplinary, and has often been informed by Marx's work. In these discussions, the concept of class has often been employed in a somewhat eclectic manner, and has incorporated both objective and subjective, aggregational and relational, dimensions of class analysis.

This urban sociology and radical geography have been highly responsive to current developments in social thought, and have been much influenced, in succession, by structuralist Marxism (Castells 1977), political economy, the rediscovery of the labour process and the 'deskilling' debate (Massey 1984), philosophical realism (Sayer 1984), debates about 'postmodernism' (Harvey 1990) and, most recently, the 'cultural turn'. There has also been a continuing focus on the interpretation of contemporary social developments; in particular the debates relating to the restructuring of Western economies following the recession of the late 1970s and early 1980s have loomed large in empirical and theoretical discussions in Britain. This flexibility and openness of approach have been a source of both strength and weakness. On the one hand, they have encouraged a theoretical pluralism which appropriately reflects the complexity of the issues under investigation. On the other, the somewhat eclectic approach to be found within the new human geography has resulted in a tendency to borrow and mix concepts developed within rather different theoretical traditions, and a failure to appreciate that the confusions thus imported have resulted in a number of pseudo-debates which have not proved particularly fruitful.[7]

The influence of Marxism within urban sociology has meant that there has been a continuing emphasis within it on the significance of class *structure*. This has often been taken, in an unproblematic fashion, to be represented by the occupational structure. As a consequence, radical urban sociology has made extensive use of occupational class schemes – in all their variety (Sarre 1989). Thrift and Williams (1987: 5) distinguish five major concepts which are 'fairly consistently used in a class analysis, namely class structure, the formation of classes, class conflict, class capacity and class consciousness'. These concepts are more or less appropriate at different levels of analysis, which they describe as spatial – cross-national, regional, individual communities – as well as temporal. Class structure, which is defined as 'a system of places generated by the prevailing social relations of production' (1987: 6), is 'the most abstract' of the five concepts, and Thrift and Williams emphasize that class structure 'is only one element of class and it is unfortunate that in the literature it has all too often become an end in itself' (1987: 7) – a comment which may be taken as a criticism of structural Marxism. Thus they do not claim that the class structure alone determines action, and stress that other social forces such as 'race, religion, ethnicity and gender, family and various state apparatuses' will 'not only blur the basic class divides but also generate their own divisions' (1987: 7).

The formation of classes, class conflict, class capacity and consciousness, they argue, demands a relational approach, as these processes can only be studied in the context of action, that is, actions (struggles) which shape the very emergence of 'classes' themselves. Here we have in their discussion of 'class' aspects which have close parallels with E. P. Thompson's Marxist humanism, but these are used in combination with a 'class structural' approach.

Urban sociology has also been much influenced by the 'realist' theoretical approach. Philosophical realism became influential as a possible solution to the theoretical problems raised by the critique of positivism (Keat and Urry 1975, 1981). Thus realism does not reject the natural science model out of hand, but argues that empirical regularities do not, in themselves, establish the full extent of our knowledge. Rather than mere constant conjunction, a 'realist' causal explanation must answer the question of why these realities exist in terms of the causal mechanisms that generate them (Layder 1990). Thus 'realism' directs attention not just at events, but at the underlying processes or mechanisms which produce them. These relatively enduring social entities are held to have causal properties which give rise to events – but the mere existence of a causal property does not mean that an event *will* occur. The realization of particular causal properties often depends on the blocking, or realization, of others, and empirical investigations guided by 'realist' principles have reflected this complexity (Bagguley et al. 1989). 'Realist' accounts have tended to focus on class *formation*, which has many parallels with Giddens's account of 'structuration'. In the 'realist' approach, therefore, class structure and class action would not be separated.

Thus, for example, Keat and Urry claim that:

> The term 'class' is used by Marx in a realist manner. It refers to social entities which are not directly observable, yet which are historically present, and the members of which are potentially aware of their common interests and consciousness. The existence of classes is not to be identified with the existence of inequalities of income, wealth, status or educational opportunity. For Marx, and generally for realists, class structures are taken to cause such social inequalities. The meaning of the term, 'class', is not given by these inequalities. Rather it is the structure of class relationships which determines the patterns of inequality. (1975: 94–5)[8]

Keat and Urry are particularly critical of what they describe as the 'positivisation' of class in American stratification studies, that is, the identification of 'classes' as aggregates of individuals without reference to 'causal properties' but 'in terms of various kinds of demographic, social, and psychological criteria' (1975: 95). Thus in his subsequent work (Abercrombie and Urry 1983; Lash and Urry 1987), Urry has taken a socio-historical approach in his empirical investigations of the class structure. In particular, he has devoted considerable attention to exploring the emergence of the 'service class', and its 'causal powers' in contemporary capitalism.

Theoretical 'realism' within urban sociology, therefore, sees classes as having 'causal powers' which are 'realized' in the struggle with other classes. Thus empirical analyses informed by this approach are often socio-historical in their approach. Savage et al.'s (1992) work on the middle classes in Britain provides a clear statement of this approach to 'class analysis'. As indicated above, the major focus of the 'realist' approach is upon class *formation*, and this is reflected in their work. They argue that the 'middle classes' have access, to varying degrees, to three assets – or potential 'causal powers'. These are, first, property; second, organizational assets (that is, access to positions in organizational hierarchies, and the power that goes with them); and third, cultural assets, that is, the 'styles of life', or 'habitus' (see the discussion of Bourdieu, chapter 6), which serve to buttress and perpetuate structures of power and advantage (there are obvious parallels between cultural assets and the Weberian concept of status). Savage et al. draw upon a wide range of empirical material to suggest how relatively stable social collectivities have emerged on the basis of these 'causal powers'.

The 'realist' approach, therefore, may be characterized as having its major empirical focus upon processes of class formation, rather than upon descriptions of the class structure. The emphasis upon the contingency of the realization of particular 'causal powers' means that, in practice, empirical accounts of the processes of class structuring carried out within this framework are multidimensional. The stress upon contingency and multidimensionality within the realist approach is a source of both strength and weakness. In particular, it is difficult to provide empirical tests of association and causal relationships – as, for example, those who have developed theoretical class schemes (such as Goldthorpe and Wright) have attempted to do.

Nevertheless, the spatial mapping of 'class' continues as a significant research resource within social geography, in particular, the development of 'geodemographics', that is, typifying residential areas in social terms. A brief discussion of this approach may be found in the next chapter (see p. 54).

Conclusions

Marx and Weber, despite their very real theoretical differences, both conceptualized social classes as groups structured out of *economic* relationships, and both saw classes as significant social 'actors' in the context of capitalist industrialism. For Marx, class struggle would have a central role in the ultimate transformation of capitalism. Weber did not hold to this view, but there can be little doubt that he saw class conflict as a major phenomenon in capitalist society. In the early twenty-first century, a criticism that is increasingly made of both authors (particularly Marx), and indeed, of 'class analysis' in general, is that such arguments place too much emphasis on the significance of economically determined classes at the expense of other, competing sources of social identity such as nationality, gender, locality or ethnic group. In short, it is argued, nineteenth-century sociology cannot adequately grasp the complexities of early twenty-first-century society.

This chapter has not discussed these arguments in any detail (they will be examined in chapters 5 and 6), but as we have seen there have developed within Marxism theoretical approaches to class which have modified considerably – indeed, abandoned – the economism of earlier theoretical conceptualizations. The discussion above has been mainly concerned with the fate of the class concept itself, particularly in relation to the ongoing debates relating to structure and action in sociology. Weber's rejection of the inevitability of the development of class consciousness and thus action was an element in his overall rejection of Marxist economism and determinism. In sociology (and history), however, the question of class consciousness has been incorporated into a more general debate concerning the nature of social reality, which has crucially shaped the perspectives of a number of different authors who would all claim to be doing 'class analysis' – although the diversity of their work belies the common label.

In the course of this chapter, there have emerged a series of dichotomies relating to both sociology and class analysis, some of which may be summarized as follows:

Sociology
structure   action

Class analysis
class in itself   class for itself (Marx)
objective   subjective (Braverman)
class formation   class action (Dahrendorf)
aggregational   relational (Stark)

The persistence of such dichotomies in the social sciences has often been criticized, as when, for example, Bourdieu writes that:

> One can and must transcend the opposition between the vision which we can indifferently label realist, objectivist or structuralist on the one hand and the constructivist, subjectivist, spontaneist vision on the other. Any theory of the social universe must include the representation that agents have of the social world and, more precisely, the contribution they make to the construction of the vision of that world, and consequently, to the very construction of that world. (1987: 10)[9]

It might be argued, however, that although Bourdieu has described the essence of sociological 'good practice', the overarching theory that would successfully achieve this integration has not yet been developed, or rather, there is certainly no consensus that it has been. Giddens's theory of 'structuration', as well as the development of philosophical 'realism', have both been offered as theoretical solutions,[10] but neither has gained universal acceptance; there is no dominant theoretical paradigm in sociology. In the light of these constraints two, rather different, emphases on the question of 'action' have been identified within discussions relating to class. These are, first, an insistence upon the active construction of classes themselves (class formation or 'structuration'), as when, for example, Therborn writes that: 'Classes must be seen, not as veritable geological formations once they have acquired their original shape, but as phenomena in a constant process of formation, reproduction, re-formation and de-formation' (1983: 39) – that is, an insistence upon the role of action in the constitution of 'classes' *in* themselves. Theories of class formation can be distinguished from theories of class action – the question of whether a 'class' acts *for* itself. Weber, as we have seen, would regard such a possibility as contingent, and this would also be Bendix and Lipset's position. To adopt the first position, some may suggest, renders the second redundant – a class 'in itself' is simultaneously a class 'for itself'. In contrast, the second position assumes that the examination of class structure may be undertaken independently of the examination of class action.

These past debates are not mere abstractions. They have crucially affected not only perceptions of class, but also the way in which research into social class has been carried out. In the next chapter, therefore, we will focus on the work of class analysts whose starting point is the class *structure* – that is, attempts to measure 'social class'. As we shall see in our conclusions to chapter 4, an increasing focus, throughout the 1980s and 1990s, on the measurement of 'class' led to criticisms of such approaches as 'economistic' and structurally 'overdetermined'. These criticisms contributed to a growing emphasis on the cultural *construction* of social classes (one of our major topics in chapter 6). Class 'culturalism' has many parallels with the 'action' approach discussed in this chapter. However, as has been argued in chapter 2 (and as will be argued more extensively in our conclusions to chapters 6 and 7), these (apparently) mutually exclusive 'binaries' should be perceived, rather, as *interdependencies*, and as argued in chapter 1 (p. 6): 'in order to grasp the totality of social inequality and its persistence, we have to be prepared to work *across* and with [apparently] conflicting approaches and methods'.

MEASURING THE 'CLASS STRUCTURE'

4

Introduction

In this chapter, our discussion will focus primarily on empirical accounts of class *structures*, and the research programmes associated with this approach. In relation to the methodological contrasts examined in chapter 2, it should be noted that all of the approaches to class analysis discussed in this chapter may be described as broadly 'positivist', and assume an analytic separation between 'structure' and 'action'. With the exception of geodemographic classifications (see below), they have a focus, above all, on the *economic* dimension of 'class', as manifest in the structure of positions (occupations) associated with systems of capitalist production.

The division of the population into unequally rewarded categories is commonly described as a 'class structure'. In contemporary societies this usually means a focus on the structure of employment. The division of the occupational order into economic 'classes' is probably the most frequent 'taken-for-granted' use of the class concept in sociology (Westergaard and Resler 1975). However, it is important to distinguish between, on the one hand, class schemes which simply *describe* the broad contours of occupational inequality and, on the other, 'theoretically' derived class schemes which purport to incorporate, at the empirical level, the actualities of class *relations* – that is, the processes whereby these inequalities emerge. There is a wide variety of employment-based class schemes, constructed for a variety of different purposes. A simple but important point – which is all too often overlooked – is that all class schemes are social constructs, or rather, the constructs of social scientists. Therefore different class schemes, when applied to the same occupational structure, can produce rather different 'class maps'. For example, it is a feature of Wright's neo-Marxist scheme, which will be discussed later in this chapter, that it produces more 'proletarians' than other classifications.

In this chapter, different class schemes will initially be discussed in relation to two broad analytical categories. These are, first, occupational class schemes which have been devised primarily for use as commonsense descriptive measures, which often overlap with subjective scales of occupational prestige or social ranking. In this section, we will also briefly discuss other descriptive classifications (geodemographics) based on residence. Second, we will examine 'theoretical' occupational class schemes, often constructed with explicit reference to the theoretical approaches of Marx and Weber. It may be objected that no system of classification can be said to be independent of 'theoretical' assumptions, even if they are not overt (Hindess 1973). Nevertheless, the differentiation between class schemes on the basis of their theoretical claims is commonplace (Nichols 1979; Marshall et al. 1988), and, as we shall see, the development of particular theoretical schemes has been associated with the development of distinctive research programmes of 'class analysis' using the scheme in question.

In previous chapters, the diversity both of definitions of the 'class' concept, as well as of approaches to 'class analysis', has been described. Thus, although the 'employment-aggregate' approach to class analysis, which is the main focus of this chapter, is certainly a very important development in the field of class analysis, it is not the only way in which class has been investigated empirically. We have drawn attention to socio-historical and case-study research which has explored the *processes* through which classes are structured, not only through patterns of ownership and control, but also as a consequence of technical change and development, political struggles, etc. Explorations of class formation have often focused upon changes in the labour market and structures of employment – as in, for example, Braverman's (1974) account of the 'deskilling' of the labour process.

More generally, over the last decade or so, the *de facto* plurality of empirical approaches to the study of social class has been increasingly recognized as a sociological reality. The 'employment-aggregate' approach generated two major comparative research programmes, each with its own 'theoretical' class scheme, that dominated much research and discussion in the field of 'class analysis' through the 1980s and into the 1990s. These were the CASMIN (Comparative Analysis of Social Mobility in Industrial Societies: Goldthorpe), which developed a neo-Weberian occupational scheme, and the Comparative Project on Class Structure and Class Consciousness (Wright: more usually known as the Comparative Class Project), which developed an explicitly Marxist scheme. Both of these research programmes have now come to an end, and as we shall see, have actually converged in some important respects. However, an important development of the Goldthorpe (or 'Nuffield') class scheme has been its incorporation into the revised 'official' class scheme in Britain, the National Statistics Socio-Economic Classification (NS-SEC, now ONS-SEC). This class scheme has an explicit (and sociological) theoretical rationale, and it is anticipated that this will form the basis of a European-wide social classification.

In this chapter, therefore, we will describe 'commonsense', descriptive class schemes, Wright's Marxist class scheme, the Goldthorpe/Nuffield class scheme and finally, the ONS-SEC. First, however, we will consider some basic, and problematic, issues raised by the strategy of using occupation as a proxy for 'class'.

Occupations

The economic, technical and social changes brought about by the continuing development of capitalist production, distribution and exchange have been accompanied by a continuing division of labour and differentiation of occupations. The point need not be laboured that 'occupation' has become, for the majority of the population, probably the most powerful single indicator of levels of material reward, social standing, and 'life chances' in general in modern societies (Blau and Duncan 1967: 6–7). Thus throughout the twentieth century and into the twenty-first, it has become commonplace for social researchers of all kinds (in academia, government and commercial agencies, and so on) to divide up the occupational structure into aggregates corresponding to different levels of social and material inequalities, which are commonly known as 'social classes'. Reid (1981: 6), for example, defines a 'social class [as] a grouping of people into categories on the basis of occupation', and Parkin has asserted that: 'The backbone of the class structure, and indeed of the entire reward system of modern Western society, is the occupational order' (1972: 18).

However, despite its acknowledged usefulness as a social indicator, there are a number of difficulties in using occupation as a measure of 'class' (Reid 1998: 11–13). Four major areas of difficulty may be identified. First, there is the fact that only a minority of members of contemporary societies will be 'economically active', and therefore have or be seeking an occupation, at any time. A variety of strategies are available for allocating the 'economically inactive' (children, old people), or those without an occupation, to an occupational class. These include giving all household members the same 'class' as that of the 'head of household' or 'main breadwinner', and locating the retired in the 'class' indicated by their last occupation. It has been argued that this strategy has been a reasonably successful one (Marshall et al. 1996). However, the minority of the long-term unemployed, including people who have never had a job at all, present a continuing problem for employment-based class schemes.

Second, although 'class processes' – that is, the structures of production and market relationships – will obviously have an important impact on the occupational structure, there are also other factors, in particular the ascriptive (or status) differences associated with gender, race and age, which are of considerable significance in structuring the division of labour. It is important also to recognize that many of the claims made by occupational groups in the constant jockeying for material advantage which is a feature of the activities of trade unions and professional groupings are in fact *status* claims, for example, those related to established relativities which have historically been fiercely protected by skilled-craft groupings and professional occupations. The occupational structure, therefore, will also bear the imprint of these other factors which are not, strictly speaking, the outcome of capitalist *class* processes. Sayer and Walker (1992) have taken these kinds of argument even further, arguing that the division of labour should be seen as an independent axis of occupational structuring, whose effects are often confused with 'class' processes.

Third, occupational title does not give any indication of capital or wealth holdings, that is, property relations (this point has been extensively argued by Westergaard 1995). As Nichols has argued, 'in the . . . "social classes" of the census the owners of capital are lost to sight' (1979: 159).[1]

The fourth area of difficulty relates to the capacity of occupational class schemes to describe class relations in a theoretical sense. The Marxist distinction between the 'technical' and the 'social' division of labour has been used to argue that 'occupation' does not grasp the essential components of the Marxist class concept: 'Occupation typically refers primarily to sets of job tasks, that is, it refers to positions within the technical division of labour . . . the concept of class refers primarily to the social relations at work, or positions within the social division of labour' (Abercrombie and Urry 1983: 109). An entire strategy of class analysis – Wright's Marxist model – has been based on this conceptual division.

Although Weber's approach to social class was very different from that of Marx, he too regarded social classes as something more than occupational aggregates. For Weber, a social class is made up of the 'totality of those class situations within which individual and generational mobility is easy and typical'. Thus Goldthorpe, a leading neo-Weberian class analyst, initially identified mobility boundaries as crucial to the identification of 'social classes' (however, in recent years his position on this issue has been substantially modified).

'Commonsense' occupational class schemes invariably reflect some kind of hierarchical ordering of occupations, although the assumptions underlying the hierarchy are not always made explicit. These can include income or other material benefits, social status, 'cultural level' and so on. Subjective scales of occupational rankings are similarly hierarchical, 'gradational' classifications. In contrast, what are here described as theoretical schemes or approaches attempt to encompass in their construction the actualities of class *relationships*.

The investigation and analysis of occupational *hierarchies* – particularly subjective rankings – has been closely associated with models of society which have stressed the importance of the social solidarity and functional interdependence associated with the division of labour in complex societies, whereas the development of theoretical class analysis and 'relational' class schemes has had more of an emphasis on cleavage and conflict. Thus the dominant paradigm in sociology (normative functionalism) established in the United States after the Second World War was associated with a view of the occupational structure as a hierarchy of rewards and prestige into which the population was sorted according to its capabilities. In Davis and Moore's (1945) functional theory of stratification, the structure of social inequality was seen as a mechanism through which the most appropriate and best-qualified persons were allocated to the functionally most important positions in society, and, as a consequence, the question of individual 'status attainment' has been a key topic in stratification research in the United States (Blau and Duncan 1967).

In contrast, 'conflict' theories of stratification considered the division of labour and the development of 'classes' to be likely to be a non-resolvable source of conflict and tension in society. This difference is reflected in the class schemes of those authors, such as Goldthorpe and Wright, whose analysis has been grounded in Marx's and Weber's theoretical arguments. Davis and Moore's theory has also been criticized from within a modified functionalist perspective which incorporates aspects of a 'conflict' view. How can some occupations, it was argued, be regarded as functionally 'more important' when, in a highly complex society, *all* occupations are necessary in respect of the whole? (Consider the chaos when public service workers go on strike.) The 'sacrifices' made by those undergoing training (in terms of earnings forgone) are usually made by others (parents) and, in any case, are massively overcompensated by the subsequent level of reward. Systems of stratification can also bring with them rigidities, and levels of social conflict, which are positively *dysfunctional* as far as the social order is concerned (Tumin 1964).

Descriptive occupational and status hierarchies and the analysis of 'social classes'

In Britain, in the past the most frequently used class scheme has been that of the registrar-general – for example, much of the empirical material in Reid's (1998) comprehensive summary of occupational class differences in employment, mortality, family arrangements, education, politics and so on is organized using the registrar-general's classification. It was first developed in 1913 by a medical statistician (Stevenson), who was engaged in a wider debate concerning levels of infant mortality. As Szreter (1984) has demonstrated, Stevenson, although no eugenist himself, initially developed the scale in the context of a debate with eugenists such as Francis Galton, who believed that the social and occupational structure more or less reflected a natural hierarchy of ability and morality in society. From the first, therefore, the registrar-general's scheme has been hierarchical.

The registrar-general's social-class classification was devised with the aim of including within each category unit groups:

> so as to secure that, as far as is possible, each category is homogeneous in relation to the general standing within the community of the occupations concerned. This criterion is naturally correlated with . . . other factors such as education and economic environment, but it has no direct relationship to the average level of remuneration of particular occupations.   (HMSO 1966: xiii)

It has been through a number of revisions since its inception (Hakim 1980), and has been superseded by the ONS-SEC, but the most commonly used version, devised for the 1971 Census, was:

I		Professional etc. occupations
II		Intermediate occupations
III	(N)	Skilled non-manual occupations
III	(M)	Skilled manual occupations
IV		Partly skilled occupations
V		Unskilled occupations

As Reid's (1998) compendium *Class in Britain* demonstrates, these occupational groupings correlate with a wide range of inequalities in income, health and education. Nevertheless, the registrar-general's scale contained a number of anomalies and difficulties in the classification of particular occupations (Nichols 1979). In older versions of the scale, the category of 'manager' presented particular problems, and drawing the boundary between manual and non-manual employment has been a constant source of contention. These and other classification difficulties resulted, from the 1951 Census onwards, in the creation of a more detailed classification of socio-economic groups (SEGs, also used by Reid 1998). The seventeen-point SEG scale included details such as size of establishment in relation to 'managerial' occupations, and collapsed versions have been widely used in government surveys such as the General Household Survey.[2]

Despite the fact that they have been subject to a process of almost constant revision, occupational class schemes used by government departments have nevertheless remained remarkably similar in their broad outlines – managerial and professional occupations at the top, unskilled workers at the bottom – and this is also true of the ONS-SEC. Other industrial countries have developed very similar scales – for example, the Nordic Occupational scale developed in the Scandinavian countries, and a scale of socio-economic status devised by the United States Bureau of the Census which closely resembles the registrar-general's SEG scale and was utilized by Blau and Duncan (1967), who also devised their own socio-economic scale. Another scale in wide commercial use is Social Grade, developed first for the National Readership Survey and commonly used by market research agencies. This divides the population into A, B, C1, C2, D and E – corresponding to upper middle, middle, lower middle, skilled, semi-skilled and unskilled working classes (there are separate categories for the self-employed and unemployed). Again, the occupations comprising the different 'classes' closely resemble those of the other hierarchical scales in general use.

Another descriptive strategy, identifying a multiplicity of 'classes', that has become of increasing importance in market- and policy-oriented research is geodemographics, or residential area classifications (Burrows and Gane 2006; Butler et al. 2007). As Burrows and Gane (2006: 795) argue, 'from the point of view of marketing professionals knowledge of where someone lives is a particularly powerful predictor of all manner of consumption practices, values, tastes, preferences and so on'. The two most commonly used classifications are ACORN and MOSAIC, both developed and owned by commercial companies. The basis of these classifications is postcodes, rather than occupations. A wide variety of data items taken from the Census, as well as from commercial sources (purchasing behaviour such as in-store loyalty cards, for example) is statistically manipulated to generate detailed descriptive groupings, by postcode, which are then characterized by numerous categories and subcategories ranging from 'Symbols of success' (example of a subcategory: 'Golden empty nesters') to 'Welfare borderline' (example of a subcategory: 'Bedsit beneficiaries').

It has been argued that geodemographic classifications combine both 'class' and 'status' in a single measure. That is, these classifications encompass both economic situation ('class') and cultural ('status') signifiers:

> 'White van culture', for example, involves an economic positioning ('Blue collar enterprise') [of which 'White van culture' is a subcategory] along with the identification of key cultural signifiers that are played out through acts of consumption: the white van, tabloid newspapers, certain forms of music, and so on. (Burrows and Gane 2006: 806)

These classifications have parallels with Bourdieu's (1986) national mapping of tastes and cultural practices in *Distinction* (discussed in chapter 6), in which he attempts to synthesize diverse forms of differentiation. However, as will be argued later in this chapter, multidimensional classifications (such as geodemographics) are difficult to maintain given the changing nature of tastes (and indeed, residential desirability) – it is perhaps no accident that they have been developed and maintained by commercial organizations. This is not to argue that these classifications are not extremely useful in the contemporary mapping of patterns of inequality and its outcomes – for example, Butler et al. (2007) have used the MOSAIC classification in examining the association between secondary school choice and educational performance (the topic will be explored in some depth in chapter 7). These classifications are increasingly important to social geographers. 'Where someone lives' is, in many important respects, a crucial identifier of 'who they are'. Nevertheless, 'what someone does' – that is, their occupation – is an equally crucial 'identifier', and, pragmatically, a much simpler and more straightforward way of identifying 'classes'.

Marsh (1986) has described the registrar-general's and other, similar scales as describing 'groups differentiated by lifestyle'; this label would be particularly appropriate to market research, where occupational coding is often carried out on the doorstep (an excellent source of information concerning 'lifestyle') by the interviewer concerned. The registrar-general's and market researcher's 'class' categories have also often been described as status or prestige scales (Weber 1948 described status groups as being differentiated 'above all, by different styles of life'). However, the 'prestige' label is probably more appropriate for occupational scales which have been deliberately constructed according to the reputed prestige or desirability of occupations.

Occupational prestige scales have often been described as 'subjectivist'; that is, as reflecting the subjective assessment of the relative prestige of occupations within a population. One of the earliest and best-known of such scales is that of North and Hatt, constructed in 1947 in the United States for the National Opinion Research Center (NORC) in Chicago, where a cross-section of ninety occupations were ranked by a national sample of the population on a scale ranging from 'excellent' to 'poor' standing (see Reiss 1961). The resulting scale of occupational prestige closely resembles that of the socio-economic classifications reviewed earlier: higher professional and powerful occupations such as physician or Supreme Court justice being ranked at the top, and low-skilled occupations such as street sweeper and garbage collector at the bottom. There proved to be a very high statistical correlation between the results of the earlier and later scaling exercises, and a comparison of similar 'subjectivist' rankings carried out in a number of other countries suggested that there was also a high level of cross-national consensus on occupational prestige rankings (Hodge et al. 1967).

These empirical findings supplied a justification for two, closely related, functionalist arguments concerning social stratification. First, the wide measure of recorded agreement concerning the relative prestige of different occupations corresponded to the distribution of material rewards and power attached to the occupations in question. It was therefore argued that the results of this 'moral referendum' (Parkin 1972) concerning occupational prestige suggested that the distribution of occupational inequality was, indeed, regarded as legitimate by the population at large, and that, as Davis and Moore had argued, the actual pattern of material rewards and status rankings reflected the functional importance of different occupations for the society, as well as being a measure of the training and talent required to fill these positions (Davis and Moore 1945). Second, the cross-national similarity of the prestige rankings of particular occupations was argued by Hodge et al. to reflect an underlying 'logic of industrialism', a theoretical argument which Giddens (1982) has identified as a central component of the 1960s' 'orthodox consensus'. All industrial societies, it was argued, required a similar division of labour and associated structure of occupational prestige (or 'classes'). These two conclusions are brought together in the following extract:

> Development hinges in part upon the recruitment and training of persons for the skilled, clerical, managerial, and professional positions necessary to support an industrial economy. Thus, acquisition of a 'modern' system of occupational evaluation would seem to be a necessary precondition to rapid industrialisation, insofar as such an evaluation of occupations insures that resources and personnel in sufficient numbers and of sufficient quality are allocated to those occupational positions most crucial to the industrial development of a nation.   (Hodge et al. 1967: 320)

Similar scales of occupational ranking have also been constructed in Britain – for example, the Hall–Jones scale which was developed as part of a major investigation of social mobility in Britain immediately after the Second World War (Glass 1954). Goldthorpe and Hope (1974) constructed a new scale for the Oxford Mobility Study where respondents were asked to rank a set of twenty occupations in terms of their 'perceived social desirability' (rather than scoring individual occupations, as in the construction of the NORC scale). Respondents then nominated twenty of their 'own' occupations for inclusion in the ranking.

However, Goldthorpe has been highly critical of both functionalist theories of stratification and inequality, as well as the associated 'logic of industrialism' arguments, which have developed out of work relating to the NORC scale. His approach shares much with that of those authors, such as Lockwood, Dahrendorf, Rex and Collins, who emphasized not interdependence and integration, but the significance of persisting economic and political inequalities, and the social conflicts and competition associated with them, in the shaping of the stratification order. The conflict perspective was highly critical of the capacity of hierarchical scales of prestige or lifestyle to render any account of *class* conflicts. Such scales, it was asserted, measured social status, rather than class, and the apparent agreement on matters such as prestige rankings was an indication not of any moral consensus, but rather, simply represented a general awareness of the empirical distribution of material and symbolic rewards to particular occupations (Parkin 1972: 40–1). The relative distribution of rewards described in hierarchical schemes reflected, it was argued, the *outcome* of class processes, rather than giving any account of the underlying structure of class *relations* which had brought them about.

A parallel argument has been developed by Wright (1979), who built upon Ossowski's (1963) distinction between *gradational* and *relational* class theories in his critique of existing empirical approaches to 'class analysis'. Gradational class schemes – such as prestige or income hierarchies – describe but do not explain. Gradational differences, Ossowski emphasized, are the *outcome* of class relations. Wright divided relational conceptions of class into two categories: (a) those deriving primarily from Weber's work, where 'class' is seen as deriving from social relations of exchange; and (b) those deriving primarily from Marx's theories, where 'class' is seen as grounded in production relationships.

Thus these kinds of criticism of empirical 'class analyses' using commonsense and hierarchical scales have led to the development of 'theoretical' (or 'sociological') class schemes (Crompton 1991); that is, class schemes which attempt to divide the population into 'social classes' which correspond to the kinds of groupings described by Marx and Weber. As has been noted in chapter 2, this strategy attempts to bring within a single framework of analysis theoretical approaches to social class and the detailed empirical investigation of the 'classes' themselves. As we have seen, two such programmes of class analysis, associated with particular 'relational' class schemes, have achieved particular prominence since the 1970s: Erik Wright's explicitly Marxist class scheme, and that devised by John Goldthorpe, which has often been described as 'Weberian'.

Theoretical ('relational') class schemes: Wright

Wright has followed a self-consciously Marxist project, a central feature of which has been his efforts to develop a Marxist class scheme; as he has put it, one of the central objectives of his work has been 'to generate a concept capable of mapping in a nuanced way concrete variations in class structures across capitalist societies' (1989: 274). His project has been developed in constant dialogue with other Marxist theoreticians, and in the light of empirical research findings generated by the Comparative Project on Class Structure and Class Consciousness, the international research project co-ordinated by Wright. Wright is quite frank that his goal of generating an adequate Marxist 'class map' has not, as yet, been achieved. However, in his efforts to move towards an adequate measure, his class scheme has been through a series of transformations.

Like Goldthorpe, Wright is critical of orthodox sociological strategies for measuring the 'class structure'. He dismisses hierarchical or gradational schemes as 'static taxonomies': 'While it might be the case that most of the participants in the storming of the Bastille had status scores of under 40, and most of the French aristocracy had scores above 70, such labels do not capture the underlying dynamics at work in the revolutionary process' (1979: 8). Thus we have, yet again, the criticism that such schemes do not tap the dynamics of class *relationships*. Wright also draws a sharp distinction between 'class' and 'occupation' (1980). Occupations, he argues, are understood as positions defined within the *technical* relations of production; classes, on the other hand, are defined by the *social* relations of production.

> a carpenter transforms lumber into buildings; a doctor transforms sick people into healthy people; a typist transforms blank paper into paper with words on it, etc. Classes, on the other hand, can only be defined in terms of their social relationship to other classes, or in more precise terms, by their location within the social relations of production.   (1980: 177)

Thus, he argues, occupational aggregations cannot produce 'classes', and his own empirical work has used especially gathered survey data to locate individuals within his successive class schemes: 'The basic strategy I have used . . . has been to elaborate the ways in which class relations are embodied in specific *jobs*, since jobs are the essential "empty places" filled by individuals within the system of production' (Wright 1989: 277).

Individual jobs are then located within Wright's class scheme, which has been derived from explicitly Marxist principles. Notions of control and exploitation within the social relations of *production* are central to Wright's analysis (it should be noted that he has consistently maintained a distinction between his own approach and Weberian approaches to the measurement of social class, which he characterizes as being grounded in *market* relationships). In developing the first version of his scheme, he argued that the social relations of production can be broken down into three interdependent dimensions: (a) social relations of control over money capital, (b) social relations of control over physical capital, and (c) social relations of authority – that is, control over supervision and discipline within the labour process (1980: 24). One of Wright's major preoccupations has been to give an empirical account of the 'middle class', or 'nonproletarian employees', in contemporary capitalist societies. Braverman (1974) had argued that the growing stratum of employees such as supervisors, or lower managerial and administrative workers, had a 'foot in both camps' (that is, bourgeois and proletarian), in that it both 'receives its petty share in the prerogatives and rewards of capital, but . . . also bears the mark of the proletarian condition' (1974: 407). Wright's initial solution to this paradox was to develop the concept of 'contradictory class locations'. Such jobs were said to represent positions which are 'torn between the basic class relations of capitalist society'.

Wright's first starting point was from the three basic positions within class relations in capitalism; the bourgeoisie, who are characterized by their economic ownership, and exercise social control over both the physical means of production and the labour-power of others; the proletariat, who are characterized by neither ownership nor control – even of their own labour-power – which is in fact purchased by the bourgeoisie; and the petty bourgeoisie, who own and control their means of production even though they do not control the labour-power of others. To these basic class positions Wright added three contradictory locations: (a) managers and supervisors, who, even if they do not legally own the means of production, nevertheless exercise *de facto* control over both the material means of production and labour-power; (b) semi-autonomous employees, who, even if they do not own or control the material means of production, nevertheless retain control over their own labour-power; and (c) small employers. This generates six 'class positions', locating individuals within a 'class map' according to the extent to which they possess economic ownership, control and autonomy – or lack of it – within the process of production. Specific information on these topics has been gathered via large-scale sample surveys carried out by Wright and his collaborators (Wright 1985: appendix II).

Wright's first class scheme was subject to a number of theoretical criticisms which eventually resulted in a recasting of his original model. Most fundamentally, Wright came to the opinion that his original class map had not, as he had argued, provided an analysis of the Marxist account of *exploitation* within capitalist relations of production but, rather, had merely given a descriptive account of *domination* (Wright 1985: 56–7). Domination is, of course, a significant aspect of class relations but it may be viewed as essentially epiphenomenal – that is, as being a consequence of exploitative class relationships, rather than their cause.

Wright's solution to this theoretical problem was to develop the work of John Roemer, who had applied game-theoretic principles to Marx's analysis in order to give an account of exploitation. Wright summarizes Roemer's basic strategy as follows:

> The basic idea of this approach is to compare different systems of exploitation by treating the organization of production as a 'game'. The actors in this game have various kinds of productive assets (i.e. resources such as skills and capital) which they bring into production and which they use to generate incomes on the basis of a specific set of rules. The essential strategy adopted for the analysis of exploitation is to ask if particular coalitions of players would be better off if they withdrew from this game under certain specified procedures in order to play a different one. (Wright 1985: 68)

If a group would be better off by withdrawing from the first game, and entering into an alternative game (and their previous partner would be worse off as a consequence), then exploitation can be said to be taking place under the conditions of the original game.

In his development of the analysis of exploitation (rather than domination), Wright distinguishes four types of assets, the unequal ownership or control of each of which forms the basis of different types of exploitation. These are: labour-power assets (feudal exploitation), capital assets (capitalist exploitation), organization assets (statist exploitation) and skill or credential assets (socialist exploitation). No actually existing society ever consists of a single form of exploitation, and thus, empirically, classes with particular assets may be simultaneously exploited through one mechanism of exploitation and exploiters through another mechanism. Through this complex chain of abstract reasoning, therefore, Wright developed a further 'class map' reflecting relations of exploitation, rather than domination (see figure 4.1).

As can be seen from figure 4.1, the number of Wright's classes has increased from six to twelve. The major difference between Wright's earlier and later approaches, however, is that whereas the presence or absence of work autonomy was central to the identification of significant 'contradictory' class groupings in Wright's first scheme, this element is absent from the second version. Rather, such groupings are now identified through their possession of expertise and skills, as well as their position in organizational hierarchies. It has been pointed out that this development of Wright's analysis has a close parallel in Weberian approaches to the identification of the individual's 'class situation', as such assets clearly differentiate groups 'according to the kind of services that can be offered on

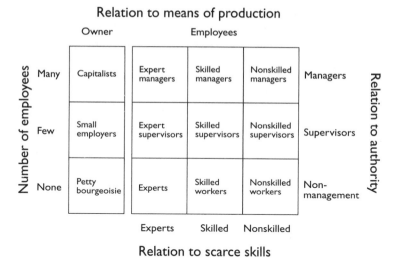

Figure 4.1 Wright's second class scheme: relations of exploitation

Source: Wright (1997: fig. 1.3)

the market . . . and will thus have an impact on individual "life-chances"' (Rose and Marshall 1986). Wright would not reject such suggestions, and indeed has suggested (Wright 2005: 27) that 'for certain kinds of questions there will be little practical difference between Marxist and Weberian analyses'. Nevertheless, he argues that 'The pivotal difference [i.e. between Marx and Weber] is captured by the contrast between the favourite buzz-words of each theoretical tradition: *life chances* for Weberians, and *exploitation* for Marxists' (Wright 1997: 31).

Wright's class scheme has to be evaluated in the context of his work as a whole – although the theoretical elaboration of his scheme has occupied a significant place within this corpus. Besides the empirical evaluation of his own approach to social class against other strategies of operationalizing the 'class structure',[3] Wright's aim has been to test empirically a number of basic Marxist assumptions. Thus, for example, he has, like Goldthorpe, been highly critical of liberal analyses concerning the class trajectory of 'industrial societies'. Wright and Singlemann (1982) have used empirical data classified by Wright's class categories (using the first version) in an analysis of the American occupational structure which appeared to demonstrate that, contrary to Blau and Duncan's optimistic assumptions relating to occupational 'upgrading', the American class structure was undergoing a process of 'proletarianization'. Wright and Singlemann's evidence suggested that Braverman's thesis of the 'deskilling' of the labour force could be sustained at the macro-level. Within given economic sectors there was 'a systematic tendency for those positions with relatively little control over their labor processes to expand during the 1960s and for those positions with high levels of autonomy to decline' (1982: 198). These tendencies had been to some extent masked by the growth of semi-autonomous employment, particularly in the state sector, but they predicted that this would be checked by a decline in state employment given the growing 'fiscal crisis' of the state.

However, in a later paper (Wright and Martin 1987) which draws upon further evidence (and uses the second version of Wright's scheme), Wright argues that, contrary to the predictions of his earlier argument: 'In terms of the working class . . . the 1970s were a period of relative de-proletarianization . . . In no case is there any evidence that the prolonged stagnation of the 1970s generated a tendency for the proportion of managers, supervisors and experts within sectors to decline . . . these results [run] consistently counter to our theoretical predictions' (1987: 16). Indeed, all of the evidence points in the *opposite* direction: 'The implication of these analyses, then, is unmistakable: the results are more consistent with what we construe to be the post-industrial society thesis than the traditional Marxist proletarianization thesis' (1987: 18). Wright does not as a consequence reject Marxist analysis. The globalization of capitalist relations, he argues, suggests that national units of capitalism are not necessarily representative of capitalism as a whole and, in any case, such internationalization means that there will be a tendency for managerial class locations to expand more rapidly in the core capitalist countries and proletarian positions to expand more rapidly in the Third World. In any case, he suggests that the extent of the incompatibility between Marxist and liberal theories of industrial development may have been overdrawn, as the effects of the material conditions posited in postindustrial theory can, using his revised class framework, be described in class terms.

Wright also uses comparative data drawn from Sweden and the United States to develop his arguments relating to class structure and politics. The long tradition of left-corporatist social democracy in Sweden has shaped not only the 'class' (that is, occupational) structure, as compared to the United States, but has also, perhaps paradoxically, resulted in a heightened salience of 'class thinking' and thus class attitudes which are more polarized. Thus he is careful always to stress that the effects of class structure are mediated by politics. Here his position is very similar to that of Goldthorpe (Goldthorpe with Llewellyn and Payne 1980; 1987: 350), who suggests that the interests of the 'mature' working class in Britain would be best served by some version of 'left democracy'. Similarly, Wright states that 'the heart of the positive struggle for socialism is radical democracy' (Wright 1985: 287). Thus, despite their very different theoretical orientations and strategies of analysis, it would seem that Wright and Goldthorpe are in broad political agreement on a number of contemporary issues.

The empirical questions that Wright addresses have, not surprisingly, been shaped by his broader theoretical interests – hence, for example, the extensive attention he has given to the question of class consciousness (see Wright 1997: part IV). However, he has also used his comparative material to explore topics similar to the major concerns of the CASMIN project – most notably, the question of the permeability of class boundaries and intergenerational mobility. Rather to his surprise, he found that an analysis of the permeability of class boundaries (as measured by class mobility, friendships and cross-class marriages) revealed that the authority boundary was always more permeable than the skill boundary (Wright 1997: 230). From a Marxist standpoint this was unexpected, as the control of the labour of others would be considered more significant than the possession of individual skills – indeed, this finding might be considered as confirming a 'Weberian' view of class.

However, notwithstanding such negative (or surprising) findings, Wright has always been explicit that his continuing commitment to a Marxist class scheme stems from his primary commitment to Marxist theory as an organizing theoretical framework, which he claims is still 'the most coherent general approach to radical, emancipatory social theory' (Wright 1989: 322). Ultimately, his choice 'remains crucially bound up with commitments to the socialist tradition and its aspirations for an emancipatory, egalitarian, alternative to capitalism' (1997: 37).

Theoretical ('relational') class schemes: Goldthorpe

Goldthorpe's class scheme was constructed via the aggregation of occupational categories within the Hope–Goldthorpe scale of 'general desirability' (described above) into a set of 'class' categories. The key concepts guiding the allocation of occupations to classes were initially 'market' and 'work' situation; two of Lockwood's three factors comprising 'class situation' (see chapter 2 above):

> we . . . bring together, within the classes we distinguish, occupations whose incumbents share in broadly similar *market* and *work* situations . . . That is to say, we combine occupational categories whose members would appear, in the light of the available evidence, to be typically comparable, on the one hand, in terms of their sources and levels of income and other conditions of employment, in their degree of economic security and in their chances of economic advancement; and, on the other hand, in their location within the systems of authority and control governing the processes of production in which they are engaged.   (Goldthorpe with Llewellyn and Payne 1980; 1987: 40)

The Hope–Goldthorpe categories which formed the basis of the scheme also incorporated employment status: 'Thus, for example, "self-employed plumber" is a different occupation from "foreman plumber" and from "rank-and-file employee" plumber' (1987: 40). The seven categories of the original Goldthorpe class scheme have often been aggregated into threefold service-intermediate-working-class categories in empirical discussions of the British material.

The use of Lockwood's concepts of 'work' and 'market' situation ('market' situation being taken directly from Weber's work) has meant that Goldthorpe's class scheme has often been described as 'neo-Weberian'.[4] Lockwood's concepts had originally been developed in his study of clerical workers (1958), and his description of 'work situation' identified elements such as proximity to authority, level of work autonomy, nature of workplace supervision, etc. in describing a clerk's 'class situation'. Thus Goldthorpe's initial descriptions of the derivation of his class scheme included references to monographs describing the 'work situation' of various occupations. Like Wright's, Goldthorpe's class scheme has been modified, and indeed Goldthorpe has now rejected any notion that work tasks and roles play any part in the construction of the scheme (Erikson and Goldthorpe 1993: 42). He now describes his scheme as being constituted in terms of *employment relations* (Goldthorpe 2000). This strategy has been incorporated into the recent ONS-SEC class scheme, described below.

The publication in Britain (in 1980) of Goldthorpe's work on social mobility was subject to considerable criticism, particularly from feminists (for example, Stacey 1981; Stanworth 1984). The Nuffield mobility survey had sampled only men; women were only included in the study as wives. Goldthorpe's class scheme itself was moulded to the contours of men's employment and did not differentiate very well between the kinds of jobs held by women. In particular, the original version of the scheme tended to crowd women into a single 'class' category – III (routine non-manual employment). Not only, however, did the scheme appear to be a rather crude instrument as far as women's employment was concerned, but the placing of lower-level clerical jobs in the 'Intermediate' (class III) category seemed to make little sense as far as women were concerned. Whereas for a man (until fairly recently) a clerical job was usually but a stepping-stone to a managerial position, for most women, these were dead-end jobs with few prospects of promotion (Crompton and Jones 1984). Goldthorpe's practice of allocating all members of the household to the class of the 'male breadwinner' was also extensively criticized, particularly given the increasing number of married women in employment.

Although Goldthorpe has at times appeared to be very resistant to feminist criticisms (e.g. Goldthorpe 1983), as it developed, his work incorporated important changes. The class position of the household is now inferred from that of the 'dominant' breadwinner, who might be male or female. More importantly, class III was divided into two categories (a and b), reflecting the concentration of women in low-level white-collar work. When the class scheme is applied to women, class IIIb is treated as class VII. The class scheme has been further elaborated by dividing class IV (a and b) into self-employed with, and without, employees. A further modification, following participation in the CASMIN project, has been to identify farmers and employees in agriculture separately (the agricultural sector is substantial in some of the countries – e.g. Ireland – taking part in the CASMIN project).

The arrangement of occupations into 'classes' in the Goldthorpe scheme closely resembles that of conventional hierarchical schemes reflecting prestige and/or lifestyle, such as the ABC scheme used by market researchers, or that of the registrar-general. However, Goldthorpe is adamant that his class scheme does not have a hierarchical form but, rather, reflects the structure of class (employment) *relations* (1980; 1987: 43). Goldthorpe's scheme has been subject to a wide range of criticisms. In particular, its 'relational' (and therefore non-hierarchical) nature has been questioned (Marsh 1986; Prandy 1991).

Although Goldthorpe's scheme has often been described as neo-Weberian, his recent work has stressed that the measure should not be regarded as deriving from any particular theory (although Goldthorpe 2000, discussed below, has subsequently developed a *post hoc* 'causal narrative'); rather, it should simply be seen as a 'research instrument'. In later clarifications of his original position, Goldthorpe has made it clear that the scheme is to be judged on the basis of the empirical findings it generates, rather than on any 'theoretical' basis:

> its [i.e. the scheme's] construction and adaptation have indeed been guided by theoretical ideas – but *also* by more practical considerations of the context in which, and the purposes for which, it is to be used and the nature of the data to which it is to be applied. In turn, the crucial test of the schema, as of any other conceptual device, must lie in its performance: it must be judged by the value that it proves to have in enquiry and analysis.   (Erikson and Goldthorpe 1993: 46)

Thus in Goldthorpe's early work, on social mobility in Britain, the construction of a class scheme is only the starting point for his overall strategy of 'class analysis'. It divides the occupied population according to their employment relations, but it must then be established to what extent actual 'classes' have been formed within this structure, or, to use Goldthorpe's phrase, the extent to which a class can be said to have a 'demographic identity'; that is, whether classes have emerged as 'specific social collectivities . . . collectivities that are identifiable through the degree of continuity with which, in consequence of patterns of class mobility and immobility, their members are associated with particular sets of positions over time' (1983: 467). Thus patterns of social mobility are crucial to the identification of a 'class'. Once the extent of demographic identity has been established, the further question may be pursued as to the extent to which 'sociopolitical class formation' has also taken place; that is, 'the degree of distinctiveness of members of identifiable classes in terms of their life-chances, their life-styles and patterns of association, and their sociopolitical orientations and modes of action' (1983: 467). For example, Goldthorpe suggests that, in Britain, the extent of mobility associated with classes III and V of his scheme implies that these 'classes' are inchoate and unformed and thus highly unlikely to generate class-based socio-political action (1980; 1987: 335). In contrast, he argues, Britain possesses a 'demographically mature' working class which might be expected to generate systematic socio-political action, as well as an emerging 'service class' which, although not as stable as the working class, is nevertheless in the process of development as a significant social force.

Goldthorpe's initial approach to class analysis, therefore, followed a systematic structure→ consciousness→action model which, as we have seen, has occasioned much criticism.[5] Goldthorpe does not ignore the question of class action but he draws an analytical separation between class formation and class action and treats them empirically as quite separate phenomena. The scheme itself is not seen as drawing upon any systematic theoretical position, and Goldthorpe has argued that (1983: 467): 'class analysis begins with a structure of positions, associated with a specific historical form of the social division of labour . . . . It is . . . in no way the aim of class analysis to account for either a structure of class positions or for [sic] the degree of class formation that exists within it in functional terms.' Here he was distancing himself from functionalist accounts of the social structure, and he has subsequently developed a similar argument in respect of Wright's Marxist account.

Goldthorpe's work on the CASMIN project (Erikson and Goldthorpe 1993) has moved away somewhat from some of the considerations which informed his original work on social mobility in Britain. In his comparative work there is less of an emphasis on the processes of demographic class formation, as described above. Rather, Erikson and Goldthorpe's major concern has been to explore cross-national continuities in the relative social mobility experiences of occupational groups (or 'classes'). This topic will be more comprehensively addressed in chapter 7. Erikson and Goldthorpe have used this work to criticize liberal theories of 'industrial society'. Liberal theorists of industrial society had suggested that, as industrialism developed, the technical 'logic of industrialism' would mean that opportunity structures would become more open and class differences would be eroded (Kerr et al. 1973; Blau and Duncan 1967). This equalization of opportunities would mean that rates of social mobility would increase. Instead, Erikson and Goldthorpe argue that, although there may have been an increase in *absolute* rates of social mobility, the class difference in *relative* mobility rates persists; that is, that there is 'constant social fluidity' across different societies. However, Goldthorpe's apparent move away from the problematics of class formation has been much criticized as being a leaving of his Weberian 'roots' (Scott 1996).

The ONS-SEC

The impetus towards the development of a new British social classification derived from a number of considerations, in which changes in the nature of employment itself have played a major part. The shift from manufacturing to service employment had been accompanied by an increase in the proportion of women in the labour force, particularly since the 1970s. As has been noted above, it was argued that existing employment-based classifications did not adequately reflect this changing industrial and sexual composition of the labour force.

Table 4.1 The ONS-SEC

Analytic classes	Operational categories	
1.1	L1	Employers in large organizations
	L2	Higher managerial occupations
1.2	L3	Higher professional occupations
2	L4	Lower professional and higher technical occupations
	L5	Lower managerial occupations
	L6	Higher supervisory occupations
3	L7	Intermediate occupations
4	L8	Employers in small organizations
	L9	Own account workers
5	L10	Lower supervisory occupations
	L11	Lower technical occupations
6	L12	Semi-routine occupations
7	L13	Routine occupations
8	L14	Never worked and long-term unemployed
	L15	Full-time students
	L16	Occupations not stated or inadequately described
	L17	Not classifiable for other reasons

Source: Derived from ONS/HMSO 2002: 8, table 2

Similarly, it was also the case that occupational classifications were problematic in that those without an occupation – the retired, and also the long-term unemployed – could not be classified. A review of social classifications was instituted in the 1990s, and during the course of the review, a further criticism that was increasingly articulated was that both the registrar-general's Social Class and SEG schemes rested on obscure, or absent, conceptual bases and operational rules (Rose and O'Reilly 1997). These kinds of criticisms led to the development of a new British 'social class' scheme, the National Statistics Socio-Economic Classification (NS-SEC, now ONS-SEC).

The ONS-SEC has eight (subdivided) 'analytic classes', which are based on fourteen functional and three residual operational categories (table 4.1). The information required to create the classification is an individual's occupation, together with details of employment status – whether an employer, self-employed or employee; whether a supervisor, and the number of employees at the workplace (the parallels with Wright's second class scheme may be observed here).

In comparison to the old registrar-general's Social Class scheme, two differences in the ONS-SEC are immediately apparent. First, the classification identifies small employers and the self-employed (class 4) as a separate category, and second, the never worked and long-term unemployed have been incorporated into the scheme as class 8. Category L14 (class 8) is described as an optional category, and L15, L16 and L17 are residual categories that are excluded when the classification is collapsed into actual classes. A feature of ONS-SEC is that it may be collapsed into eight-, five- and three-class versions (table 4.2).

Two series of questions are needed in any census or survey in order to derive the ONS-SEC: three questions on occupation and five questions on employment status/size of organization. Look-up tables incorporating the Standard Occupational Classification 2000 are included in the *National Statistics Socio-Economic Classification User Manual* (ONS/HMSO 2002).

Table 4.2 Collapsed versions of ONS-SEC

Eight classes	Five classes	Three classes
1 Higher managerial and professional occupations Large employers and higher managerial occupations Higher professional occupations	1 Managerial and professional occupations	1 Managerial and professional occupations
2 Lower managerial and professional occupations		
3 Intermediate occupations	2 Intermediate occupations	2 Intermediate occupations
4 Small employers and own account workers	3 Small employers and own account workers	
5 Lower supervisory and technical occupations	4 Lower supervisory and technical occupations	3 Routine and manual occupations
6 Semi-routine occupations	5 Semi-routine and routine occupations	
7 Routine occupations		
8 Never worked and long-term unemployed	Never worked and long-term unemployed	Never worked and long-term unemployed

Source: ONS/HMSO 2002: 10, table 3

Conceptual basis of the ONS-SEC

The ONS-SEC is grounded in the Weberian observation that 'class situations' reflect socio-economic differences as represented by *life chances* in the market (Weber 1948). It is made explicit that 'employment is not the only determinant of life chances' (ONS/HMSO 2002: 2); thus the scheme does not, indeed cannot, encompass all sources of social and economic inequality:

> The (O)NS-SEC aims to differentiate positions within labour markets and production units in terms of their typical 'employment relations' . . . Labour market situation equates to source of income, economic security and prospects of economic advancement. Work situation refers primarily to location in systems of authority and control at work . . . the (O)NS-SEC categories thus distinguish different positions . . . as defined by social relationships in the work place – i.e., how employees are regulated by employers through employment contracts . . . The category names used for the (O)NS-SEC do not refer to 'skill' . . . The categories describe different forms of employment relations, not skill levels . . . Changes in the nature and structure of both industry and occupations has rendered the (manual/non-manual) distinction both outmoded and misleading.   (ONS/HMSO 2002: 2, 4)

The ONS-SEC has been developed from the 'Goldthorpe' (or Nuffield) class scheme, as noted above. Goldthorpe (2000) has recently developed a theoretical rationale (or 'causal narrative') for his class scheme that seeks to account for the different forms of employment regulation. Employment contracts are contracts through which employees agree, in return for a wage, to place themselves under the authority of the employer. However, the labour that is bought from the employee cannot be physically separated from the individual person selling it (Edwards 2000). From the employer's point of view, therefore, the major objective is not just one of *enforcing* compliance, but also of inducing the employee to behave in a way that supports the employer's objectives. Employees always have some non-negligible amount of discretion – that is, they are possessed of individual 'agency'.

Thus as far as the employer is concerned, there are two main sources of 'contractual hazard'. The first is the difficulty in monitoring the work performed. How can the employer ensure that the employee is expending sufficient effort? The second is the level of specific skills, expertise and knowledge ('human capital') possessed by the employee. How can the employer ensure that these skills, etc. are used to the employer's best advantage?

The difficulties in measuring the quantity of work done will be least when measurement can be based on actual output (for example, pickers, loaders, fillers and packers). In these occupations, the payment of employees is calculated in return for discrete amounts of work done, and there is little to be gained by encouraging workers to invest in the acquisition of human assets (training, etc.). Such types of employment are, therefore, characterized by a *labour contract*.

At the opposite pole to the labour contract is the *service relationship*. Here the 'problem of agency' is at its most acute. There is an asymmetry of information between employer and employee – that is, the particular skills and knowledge of the employee are simply not accessible to the employer. For example, a large corporation may have a legal department, but those responsible for hiring and paying the lawyers will not necessarily themselves be experts in the law. The element of discretion in professional work such as law makes it particularly difficult to monitor with any precision. It is therefore especially important for the employer to gain the commitment of these kinds of employees. Thus the prospective elements attached to such jobs are crucial – share option schemes, promotion opportunities and so on – and it is worthwhile for the employer to invest further in the 'human capital' of employees.

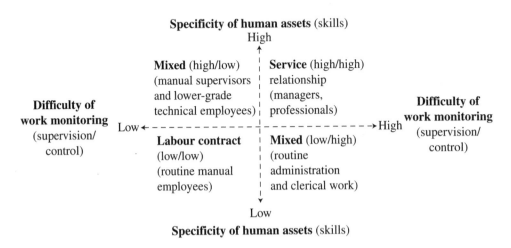

Figure 4.2 Goldthorpe's analytical scheme of employment relationships

Source: Adapted from Goldthorpe (2000: 223)

Goldthorpe combines two measures into a single scheme, as in figure 4.2. These are the specificity of human assets and the difficulty of monitoring work. It can be seen that the service relationship is located in the high/high quadrant, whereas the labour contract is low/low.

Logically, there are two other mixed forms of the employment contract. First, there are difficulties of work monitoring but not of asset specificity. Here Goldthorpe places occupations such as routine non-manual clerical work. Second, there are circumstances in which there are problems of asset specificity but not of output monitoring. Here Goldthorpe places manual supervisors and lower-grade technical employees.

ONS-SEC, therefore, combines employment status – whether a person is an employer (large or small), self-employed or employee – with the characteristic modes of employment regulation specific to particular categories of employee. Goldthorpe's specification of employment relationships maps on to the ONS-SEC categories as in table 4.3.

ONS-SEC is clearly constructed and operationalized, as well as being theoretically grounded. It has been extensively validated both as a measure and as a predictor (e.g. of health and educational outcomes). It is relatively simple to use, and indeed, has been used from the 2001 Census onwards. It has been extended so as to include those not in employment, and it is grounded in a more nuanced understanding of both employment status and employment relations. The scheme's flexible construction makes its use appropriate across a range of research topics and situations. The refinements of the scheme, together with the updating of the Standard Occupational Classification, means that a standard criticism of the registrar-general's Social Class scheme – that it failed to describe adequately the individual class situation of women – is no longer such a serious problem. ONS-SEC is to be welcomed as a substantial improvement on the registrar-general's Social Class scheme. Any system of social classification is relatively expensive to set up, test and maintain, and ONS-SEC is likely to remain standard for many years to come.

This does not mean that the scheme is beyond criticism. As table 4.3 suggests, two of the 'classes' (classes 4 and 8) fall outside its theoretical rationale. More generally, as noted above, critics of occupational classifications have emphasized the fact that, in practice, the 'life chances' associated with the occupational positions or slots generated within the scheme cannot be separated from the characteristics (such as sex, or level of education) of the individuals occupying the slots (Blackburn 1998). Blackburn and his colleagues (see Prandy 1998) have more fundamental criticisms to make of categorical schemes such as the

Table 4.3 ONS-SEC categories and employment relationships

ONS-SEC category	Employment relationship
1 Higher managerial and professional occupations Large employers and higher managerial occupations Higher professional occupations	Service
2 Lower managerial and professional occupations	Attenuated service
3 Intermediate occupations	Attenuated service/mixed
4 Small employers and own account workers	Not applicable
5 Lower supervisory and technical occupations	Mixed
6 Semi-routine occupations	Modified labour contract
7 Routine occupations	Labour contract
8 Never worked and long-term unemployed	Not applicable

Goldthorpe scheme and ONS-SEC. They argue that the dividing lines between the categories are in essence arbitrary. Why, for example, should a firm with twenty-four employees be 'small' whilst one with twenty-six employees is 'large', thus defining positions in different 'class' locations? Blackburn and Prandy, therefore, advocate the use of a simple hierarchical scale (the 'Cambridge scale') rather than a categorical classification, and indeed, have argued that such a scale is a better measure of social inequalities (Jones and Macmillan 2001).

A feature that ONS-SEC shares with all employment-based classifications – as those who developed the scheme are well aware – is that some may criticize it as 'incomplete' as it does not cover all aspects of social and economic inequality. It is concerned with class inequalities deriving from employment status and employment relationships, rather than with inequalities associated with gender, race, age and locality. It may be suggested that particular occupational (ONS-SEC) distributions associated with gender, race, age, etc. – for example, the concentration of women, and young people, in low-level service occupations – are in essence *outcomes* of inequalities of age and gender. Of course, inequalities of gender, race, etc. will in turn be exacerbated by inequalities of occupational distribution. It should always be remembered that employment-based classes are relatively blunt instruments, and they should be seen as proxies for 'real' class divisions and not as attempts to grasp them in all their complexity.

Any system of classification is limited in the number of dimensions that can be incorporated into it. ONS-SEC is focused solely on employment status and employment relationships. It does not, therefore, include substantial holders of wealth or capital, arguably one of the most important groups in any class system. More particularly, it does not incorporate cultural dimensions, which many sociologists regard as central to the discourse of 'class analysis'. It would be difficult, if not impossible, to incorporate a 'cultural' dimension systematically into such a scheme. There might well, for example, be cultural artefacts – such as tastes in music or holidays – that are systematically associated with occupational categories, but by their very nature are fluid and changing. To return to our discussion of geodemographics, the category of 'White van man' has only emerged over the last one and a half decades, and might well fade away during the next. The work required to update the 'cultural' dimension systematically would simply be too onerous and expensive to be worthwhile.

Conclusions

This chapter has reviewed a number of different strategies (or classification schemes) through which the structure of employment in industrial societies may be divided in order to produce statistical aggregates which are then labelled 'social classes'. Many such schemes are largely descriptive in their intentions – that is, they provide a convenient measure of the broad contours of structured social inequality in late twentieth- and early twenty-first-century capitalism. They also supply a (somewhat rough and ready) indication of 'lifestyle' and associated social attitudes. Different schemes have been used in a wide variety of social science and other contexts – for example, research on social policy, market research, research on voting behaviour and social mobility. The range of different theoretical and practical applications for which different class schemes are utilized suggests that it is not possible to identify particular schemes which are 'right' or 'wrong'; rather, different schemes are more or less appropriate for particular tasks. Nevertheless, sociologists have at times appeared to be reluctant to accept such theoretical and methodological plurality, and there have been extensive arguments about which particular scheme is 'superior' – arguments which extend across a range of different issue areas. For example, Marshall et al. (1988) have compared in some detail the registrar-general's, Goldthorpe's and Wright's class schemes. It is difficult, however, to see what is actually gained from this exercise, as the class schemes in question were devised for different purposes and on the basis of different (implicit and explicit) theoretical assumptions.

Employment-derived class schemes have also been used to provide evidence for theoretical debates – for example, concerning the nature and future trajectory of 'industrial societies' (Wright and Singlemann 1982; Wright and Martin 1987), or to test Marx's and Braverman's arguments concerning 'proletarianization' (Rose et al. 1987). This chapter has drawn particular attention to the class schemes associated with the development of the theoretical programmes of class analysis of Goldthorpe and Wright. These programmes were generated as part of a widespread critique within sociology of approaches to the study of society which emphasized order, rather than conflict, within the stratification system and employed subjective and/or intuitive occupational rankings in their 'class' analyses. Relational schemes, in contrast, attempted to capture the underlying divisions and conflicts associated with class in capitalist industrial societies.

Both Goldthorpe and Wright were engaged, in the 1970s and 1980s, in extensive programmes of empirical research to which their (rather different) definitions of 'class' are central. Their respective energies have produced a considerable quantity of published materials, and associated debates, which merit separate books in themselves (indeed, such volumes have appeared: Clark et al. 1990; Wright 1989). Nevertheless, however distinguished these sociologists (and the research teams associated with them) are, the point must be emphasized that neither Wright nor Goldthorpe, nor the 'employment-aggregate' approach in general, represents 'class analysis' in its entirety. In our outline of the work of the two authors in this chapter, we have drawn attention to the points of difference between them – differences which they, too, have emphasized (see in particular Goldthorpe and Marshall 1992). Nevertheless, Goldthorpe and Wright also share a broad similarity of approach to 'class analysis' in that both locate the 'class structure' in the employment structure, and both have adopted the technique of the large-scale sample survey. This approach has produced a number of important empirical findings. However, national-level sample surveys are not sufficient to explore many of the topics within the field of 'class analysis' as a whole.

Many of these difficulties stem from the theoretical and empirical problems of separating action from structure, economic from cultural, factors in social research. The 'failure' of the S→C→A model, arguably explicit in Marx's theories, as well as in Goldthorpe's earlier work, has been argued to reflect the essential weakness of the 'class analysis' project as a whole (Savage 2000: 40). In this book, it will be argued that although it is indeed the case that action and structure, economy and culture, are intertwined, this does not preclude their separation as far as empirical research is concerned. However, in these conclusions we will draw together some of the critical strands relating to the 'employment-aggregate' approach. As we have seen, many of these rest, in essence, on its perceived inadequacy in providing a sustained account of human (class) action. In addition, the approach has been criticized for failing to take sufficient account of cultural or normative factors as far as both the structuring of classes and the location of persons within this structure are concerned.

Indeed, the national-level survey approach is not particularly suitable for the exploration of the actual *processes* of class formation. Wright derives his account of class formation from Marx's analysis. Goldthorpe's 'causal narrative' focuses on abstract employment relations, but these take place in organizations within which particular values and normative assumptions prevail – for example, ideas about 'proper' jobs for men and women (to say nothing of age- or ethnicity-appropriate positions). Moreover, classes are also forged in localities, and in associations such as political parties. These processes are more usually investigated via a holistic, case-study approach.

In this chapter, we have explored the widespread assumption that 'class' is described by the occupational structure – indeed, 'class structure' and 'occupational structure' are often taken to be synonymous. This convention stems from the practice established by early twentieth-century statisticians such as Stevenson of dividing up the population into unequally rewarded occupational orders or 'classes'. Stevenson was engaged in a debate with eugenists, not with Marx or Weber. It is not surprising, therefore, that 'class' schemes such as the Registrar-General's should correspond only fortuitously to the theoretical concerns of these classical sociologists.

In Britain, the new official class scheme (ONS-SEC) is theoretically (sociologically) grounded, and therefore can no longer be dismissed as 'atheoretical'. Nevertheless, the more general problems associated with operationalizing classes via employment aggregates still apply. No account of wealth holdings is given in occupational classifications.[6] Moreover, the occupational structure *is* shaped by cultural and normative assumptions that are treated, even in relational class schemes, as external to both the organization of employment and the allocation of people within the employment structure. As we shall see in the next chapter, these kinds of criticisms resonated with the 'cultural turn' within sociology, which itself was part of a series of developments that effectively denied both the theoretical and practical significance of 'class'.

AN UNTIMELY PREDICTION OF DEATH AND A TIMELY RENEWAL

5

The report of my death was an exaggeration.
Mark Twain

Introduction

Chapter 4 has considered a range of different strategies developed for the measurement (operationalization) of the 'class structure' via the structure of employment. The question of the most appropriate measure of social 'class' became a central issue for an important debate within postwar Anglo-American sociology: 'consensus' versus 'conflict' approaches. It was argued that normative functionalism had laid an unwarranted emphasis on integration and consensus, thus obscuring the very real conflicts that characterized industrial capitalist society. The stability and (apparent) cross-national similarity of occupational rankings had been interpreted as a manifestation of this supposed consensus, as well as providing an empirical demonstration of the 'industrial society' thesis. In contrast, those sociologists who stressed the significance of social conflict emphasized the need to develop measures of social *class*, rather than descriptive occupational hierarchies. Thus in the 1970s and 1980s there were developed sociological measures of the structure of employment which, in contrast to 'gradational' or status schemes, purported to reflect, theoretically, the structure of actual class *relations* in capitalist societies. Two major empirical programmes of 'class analysis' – those of Goldthorpe and Wright – have been developed using such schemes.

The theoretical underpinnings of both schemes have been criticized. Scott (1996; see also Morris and Scott 1996) has argued that Goldthorpe has lost sight of the Weberian programme of 'class analysis' which was its original starting point. Following Weber, Scott draws a distinction between an individual's 'class situation' and 'social classes'. As we have seen in chapter 3, for Weber a 'class situation' is indicated by property and market relations; social classes are actual strata as indicated by mobility processes. Scott argues that: 'Despite Goldthorpe's continued use of the phrase "social class", his new categories are not social classes at all. They are nominally defined economic categories of class situations that have been designed to maximise the predictive powers of the schema in comparative research' (1996: 215–16). Gubbay (1997: 76) has developed a similar critique of Wright's Marxist version of employment-aggregate class analysis. He argues that although Wright began his class project with a *relational* class scheme – that is, a scheme 'deriving from a theory about society as a totality which identifies relations between "classes" as crucial to its dynamics' – the subsequent revisions of the scheme means that it has lost this capacity. Gubbay concludes that 'the drive to demonstrate the fruitfulness of his approach in empirical research on the statistical correlation of his class categories with income and consciousness, has moved him far away from Marxist class analysis' (1997: 80).

However, as both research programmes have now ended, debates about which class scheme is 'best' have become less important. As noted in chapter 4, there has been something of a convergence between Goldthorpe and Wright, and in any case, it would seem that, in practice, the different schemes and scales are in fact measuring very similar phenomena. For example, Hout et al.'s (1993) defence of 'class analysis' (by which they meant the employment-aggregate approach) found that the class ratio of earnings in the US was 4.2:1 for men and 2.5:1 for women using Wright's scheme, and 4.9:1 for men and 3.6:1 for women using Erikson and Goldthorpe's. There has been much heated debate about which scheme is the 'best', but all class schemes are in fact highly correlated with each other, and their categories overlap to a considerable extent, particularly in their collapsed versions, which are used with great frequency (Emmison 1991; see also Jones 1988; Prandy and Blackburn 1997).

Goldthorpe and Wright may be viewed as the leading practitioners of a distinctive sociological approach to class analysis which was developed during the 1960s and 1970s. The impetus for this approach, as has been described in previous chapters, came from the use of theoretical accounts of 'social class', drawn from the work of Marx and Weber in order to develop theoretical, relational employment classifications which described the 'class structure'. Both Goldthorpe and Wright considered it to be particularly important to distinguish between 'class' and 'status'. These accounts were then operationalized through the large-scale sample survey, a method of research whose capacities were enormously enhanced by the advent of computers and electronic data processing. This approach brings together, within a single framework, the theoretical analysis of social class with the empirical analysis of class inequalities and class structures. It is an approach with tremendous promise, but also severe limitations. There are insoluble difficulties in the identification of 'class' independently of the other factors which structure employment relations, and the nature of the links between class structure and class consciousness or action cannot be sufficiently explored through survey data. Both Goldthorpe and Wright are clear that the concept of 'class' refers to social *relationships*, but these relationships cannot be adequately grasped through approaches which rest, in the last instance, on the aggregation of *individual* attributes (Ingham 1970).[1] Both Goldthorpe and Wright have revised their class schemes, and attempted to clarify their positions. These clarifications have revealed the inherent limitations of both approaches, as well as their converging paths. However, to paraphrase Goldthorpe and Marshall, employment-aggregate class analysis now appears as a far more limited project, intellectually as well as politically, than it once did (1992: 15).

Nevertheless, during the 1970s, 1980s and 1990s, the dominance of Wright's and Goldthorpe's quantitative research programmes meant that debates about the continuing significance (or otherwise) of 'class' often took the form of arguments concerning the continuing strength of the association between occupation (or job) and a variety of attitudinal and behavioural factors (e.g. Clark and Lipset 1991). That is, the 'employment-aggregate' approach was implicitly taken to represent 'class analysis' as a whole.[2] Besides the apparent attenuation of 'traditional' occupational class-associated behaviours (such as voting behaviour[3]), changes in the occupational structure – the proportionate decline of 'working-class' occupations, the increase in the employment of women – have also served to undermine this approach. However, as we have already seen in chapter 2, questionings as to the relevance of 'class' extended beyond the criticisms developed in respect of this one particular approach to 'class analysis'. In the rest of this chapter, therefore, we will develop a brief account of recent changes in societal organization and functionings (both national and global) that have contributed to the argument that 'class' is no longer a useful or appropriate concept as far as the analysis of contemporary societies is concerned. First, there are changes in the structure of work and employment; second, the apparent failure of class analysis to address the 'gender question'; and third, what appears to be the increasing irrelevance of class politics. In these critiques, two major emergent themes will be identified: first, the thesis of increasing 'individualization', and thus the irrelevance of 'collectivist' concepts such as class, and second, arguments to the effect that cultural, rather than economic, theories and concepts have become more appropriate for the sociological analysis of 'postmodern' societies.

Changes in the structure of work and employment

In this book, frequent reference has already been made to one of the single most significant structural changes that has contributed to the claim that 'class' is no longer of major significance in 'Western' societies – the proportional and numerical decline of the 'old (male) working class'. The industrialization of China and South East Asia has been accompanied by the decline of heavy manufacturing in the West, the United States' 'steel belt' has become a 'rust belt' and in Britain, once dependent single-industry localities in South Wales and the North-East have ceased to manufacture this most basic commodity of 'industrial society'. Other major industries, such as shipbuilding, have suffered a precipitate decline in the level of worldwide demand, whilst what construction remains is predominantly in non-Western countries. Post-Second World War expansion in the West had seen the rapid growth of manufacturing to meet the demand for consumer goods – notably vehicles – but increasing competition and the saturation of home markets has also led to a marked decline, particularly in Britain, in these industries. The postwar boom was already coming to an end by the 1960s, but the worsening of the economic crisis, exacerbated by the world oil price rises of the early 1970s, led to a further collapse of manufacturing industry in the West.

Throughout the 1970s, governments in Britain had attempted to grapple with the worsening economic situation through a further extension of the broadly 'corporatist' bargain which had been consolidated during the period of postwar expansion – what Crouch (1999: 53) has described as the 'mid-[twentieth-]century social compromise'. This had involved the adoption of Keynesian policies of state economic management – a policy of full employment, which governments attempted to maintain by controlling demand through taxation and other fiscal policies – in combination with increased levels of state provision of education, health and welfare.[4] In 1974, the Labour government in Britain entered into a 'social contract' with the trade union movement, in which the unions agreed to regulate the wage demands of their members in exchange for an increased right to participate in the shaping of government policies. These policies were not successful in stabilizing the economy, and inflation continued to rise, as did rates of unemployment – a phenomenon which was given the suitably unpleasant title of 'stagflation'.[5] They culminated in the 1979 'winter of discontent', during which public-sector workers, whose wages had declined sharply as a consequence of the 'social contract', went on strike.[6]

The Conservative government which was then elected pursued policies in sharp contrast with those of the 'social contract'. Industries in decline were no longer protected, and government 'intervention' in the economy was restricted to attempts to control the money supply. Trade unions were excluded from access to state power – indeed a full-frontal attack was mounted on their position, and legal rights (such as those embodied in the Trade Unions and Labour Relations Act 1976) they had achieved during the 1970s were simply removed. Under the influence of neo-liberal economic theories the Conservative government spearheaded a return to 'market forces' in the regulation of economic affairs, which involved the selling of state monopolies such as gas, telecommunications, electricity and water, the increasing 'privatization' of welfare, the application of 'quasi-market' principles to those areas remaining within the state's orbit (such as schools, universities and hospitals), and the promotion of individual entrepreneurship.

These neo-liberal policies contributed further to the headlong collapse of manufacturing. There was a sharp rise in unemployment, and a decline in trade union membership, which dropped from 13.2 million in 1979 to 10 million in 1989, standing at 7.7 million in 2002. Employment in manufacturing declined by 3 million between 1971 and 1988, from 8 million to 5 million employees. New jobs were created during the economic restructuring of the 1980s, but these were largely in the service economy, and in the UK service employment increased from 53 per cent to 73 per cent between 1973 and 1993. This decline in employment in manufacturing, which has taken place in all late industrial economies, has resulted in a further decline in those occupations which have by convention been described as 'working-class'. The decline in working-class employment, as already noted in chapter 1, has also been associated with the erosion of working-class communities (for example, in coalmining and old industrial areas), and, it is argued, increasing individuation.

The labour market has been progressively fragmented, with a growth of flexible and non-standard employment such as part-time work, short-term contracts and self-employment (see Beatson 1995). Between 1993 and 1997, only 38 per cent of new jobs created in the UK were for full-time, 'standard' employees. Jobs were increasingly characterized by apparent insecurities, deriving from managerial practices such as organizational 'delayering' (for example, removing supervisory and managerial positions) and 'outsourcing' (subcontracting catering, cleaning and other tasks once carried out 'in-house'). It was suggested that self-employment would rise to meet the needs of outsourcing, as would non-permanent forms of employment such as fixed term contracts. Even by the year 2000, Beck was still describing 'the Brazilianization of the West' – that is, a massive shift towards casual, insecure employment – as virtually inevitable (Beck 2000b). These developments have been associated with increasing insecurity of employment and the supposed decline of the long-term career (see chapter 8).

However, recent research suggests that in Britain job tenure has not declined markedly in recent years, and a third of the UK workforce has been with the same employer for over ten years (Nolan 2003). Thus in aggregate, jobs are not becoming more insecure, rates of self-employment are not rising, and most employees have permanent contracts of employment (Taylor 2002). Nevertheless, it might be suggested that employment in Britain has historically been relatively lacking in regulations and protections and thus relatively flexible in any case.[7]

According to Beck (1992: 143), these kinds of change have resulted in the development of an 'individualized society of employees' in a 'risk-fraught system of flexible, pluralized, decentralized underemployment'. As we have seen, as a consequence, Beck (Beck and Beck-Gernsheim 2002) has argued that social class is a 'zombie category', which is 'dead but still alive'. 'Work' in the sense of an occupation once provided a focus for the development of class-based identities in industrial societies, but as a consequence of increasing insecurity and flexibility in the labour market, Beck argues, both 'class' and 'status' are losing their significance.

In the 1990s, these changes were described as a move from prevailing 'Fordist' to 'post-Fordist' techniques of production and labour organization (Murray 1989; Sabel 1982). 'Fordism', it is argued, was characterized by large-scale mass production of cheap, uniform commodities, the detailed division of labour, and extensive hierarchical organization of productive activity. Hence the label 'Fordist', which describes the system of mass, assembly-line production of cars developed by Henry Ford in the United States during the early decades of the twentieth century. It is the system of production in manufacturing which Braverman (1974) described as the 'degradation of work' in monopoly capitalism. 'Post-Fordism', in contrast, is supposedly characterized by flexible production techniques on smaller, dispersed sites. The emphasis is on product variety and rapid response to consumer demand – in contrast to Henry Ford's famous statement that customers could have any colour car they wanted, as long as it was black.

Two major strands may be identified in the arguments summarized above. There has been, first, a move towards increasing flexibility and insecurity in employment, and second, a precipitate decline of employment-based communities, both in a geographical sense and in the erosion of a sense of 'belongingness' once associated with large, well-established employers that had provided a 'job for life'. Empirically, the *actual* growth of job insecurity may be questioned. However, what cannot be questioned is the decline of geographically based employment communities, which has removed a significant locale within which traditional, collectivist, 'working-class' ideologies were generated. The reorganization (and removal) of production (and administration) have had important consequences, and in an influential text, Sennett (1998) has argued that flexible working and the end of long-term career predictability have undermined the contribution of employment to the formation of individual identities. In the circumstances of modern organizations, he argues, trust has broken down, and relationships have been fragmented, as human beings no longer have deep reasons to care about one another (Sennett 1998: 148).

This is in part because management practices have changed and developed. 'High-commitment' (or 'high-performance') human resource practices, which seek to obtain a greater discretionary effort from employees, have been widely introduced in many contemporary organizations. These include teamworking and quality circles, individual appraisals and training, and performance-related pay. Indeed, it has been argued that: 'we do not have "hands" in today's organisations. The popular view is that organisations are opting, by choice or necessity, to engage with hearts and minds instead' (Thompson and Warhurst 1998: 1). Individualized career development is also central to high-commitment management practices. Rather than (as in the past) being sponsored through a fixed and stable bureaucratic hierarchy, individuals are encouraged to self-develop through what is often a fluid and changing organizational structure. Thus increasingly employees are being 'worked on' in order that they may develop an 'entrepreneurial self' (Rose 1989).

The emphasis on employee 'performance' in 'high-commitment' management has led some authors to argue that the nature of work as employment is in the process of being transformed. 'Work', it is argued, is becoming increasingly 'cultural' rather than 'material'. The generalization of the service relationship within the organization (as, in innovations such as 'total quality management', every department becomes a 'customer' of another department) has rendered an increasing number of employees both 'producers' and 'consumers'. Service work in particular depends for its successful accomplishment on the 'performance' of service employees (Du Gay 1993, 1996). Thus Du Gay argues that the boundaries between production and consumption are increasingly blurred.

It is not difficult, therefore, to understand how, over the last forty years, changes in the nature of work as employment have led to both increasing individualism and a decline in 'class'-based identities. However, what can be questioned is the validity of the assertion, by theorists such as Beck, that 'class is dead' as a consequence of these changes. As we shall see, although as individuals people may not have a strong sense of class 'belonging' (indeed, the question may be raised as to whether this element of collective identity was ever particularly strong; see Savage 2000), nevertheless, class processes continue to have a major impact on people's lives. Another theme, to which we will return, that emerges from this discussion of the changing nature of employment is the increase in the significance of culture, and consumption, *within* the employment relationship.

The expansion of women's employment

The 'industrial society' which was consolidated from the second half of the nineteenth century onwards was developed on the 'male-breadwinner' model of the gender division of labour. Married women were excluded from paid work (i.e. became 'housewives') on the assumption that the male 'breadwinner' was paid a 'family wage' (see Glucksmann 1995).[8] As a consequence, the 'Fordist' occupational hierarchy became increasingly masculine. As we have seen, the growth of male-dominated industrial employment was also paralleled by the increasing development of social protections, notably those associated with the welfare state. Welfare state institutions, such as occupational pensions and other social benefits, were explicitly created on the assumption that the male-breadwinner model was the norm. Thus women received many social benefits via their 'breadwinner' (Esping-Andersen 1990; Pateman 1989).

However, the expansion of welfare-state-led service provision (as well as the expansion of other state-provided services such as education and health) was a major source of employment growth for women. Thus the basis of the male-breadwinner model was being eroded even as its principles were being consolidated in national institutions and policies. Other factors were also leading to the growth of women's employment, including 'push' factors such as rising levels of education, effective fertility controls and the growth of 'second-wave' feminism, as well as 'pull' factors including the buoyant labour markets of the 1950s and 1960s. Service expansion was fuelled not only by state expenditure and job creation, but also by the growth of financial, leisure and business services.

Thus for a significant category of people – women – paid employment is becoming considerably *more* important in their lives. In all of the OECD countries, women's employment has grown rapidly since the Second World War – particularly since the 1960s. This rise was almost entirely accounted for by an increase in the employment of *married* women. The recession of the 1970s and 1980s was not accompanied by any great decline in women's employment – indeed, many of the service-industry jobs which were created as a consequence of economic restructuring were low-level 'women's jobs'. Women's continuing participation in the formal economy was also accompanied by both the rise of 'second-wave' feminism and an improvement in their levels of academic and work-related qualifications, and women are increasingly achieving higher-level positions within employment. In Britain, women's employment rates continued to increase rapidly during the 1980s. Although the trend is still upwards, the rate slowed somewhat during the 1990s, a decade in which 'increasing female participation in the labour market was entirely concentrated among women with children' (Dench et al. 2002: 31).

The developing structure of employment in the West, therefore, is not only service-based but increasingly feminized. The increasing employment of women presented a number of problems for employment-aggregate class schemes. Our discussion (in chapter 3) of difficulties associated with employment-aggregate class analysis has identified two which are particularly germane to the 'woman question'. These are, first, the difficulties of separating and identifying the mechanisms of 'class' from the large number of other factors structuring the labour market. These include ascriptive properties associated with gender, race and age, as well as other status factors such as the traditional or customary prestige and advantages associated with particular occupations. As a consequence of these processes, women and men tend to be concentrated into different occupations – the phenomenon of occupational segregation. The same occupational class scheme, therefore, will describe a rather different 'class structure' for men and women. The second difficulty is how to categorize the 'economically inactive' – and in the case of women 'housewives' have presented a particular problem.

Within the employment-aggregate approach, an empirical convention had long been established where a woman was allocated the same class position as that of the male 'head of household'. This convention reflected the predominant division of market and domestic labour between the sexes characteristic of the mid-twentieth century, where the male 'breadwinner' went 'out to work' whilst women retained the primary responsibility for the domestic sphere. It might be argued, therefore, that the conventional 'male model' of the occupational class structure simply reflected the *de facto* predominance of men within the structure of employment. For example, Giddens wrote that: 'Given that women still have to await their liberation from the family, it remains the case in the capitalist societies that female workers are largely peripheral to the class system' (1973; 1981: 288). This convention, however, was difficult to sustain, given the continuing increase in women's employment which has taken place since the Second World War.

Both Goldthorpe and Wright have responded to feminist criticisms. When Goldthorpe's major national investigation of the British class structure was published (Goldthorpe with Llewellyn and Payne 1980; 1987), it was subjected to extensive criticism on the grounds that it focused entirely on men, women only being included as wives (Goldthorpe 1983, 1984b;

Heath and Britten 1984; Stanworth 1984; Crompton 1989b, 1996c). However, Goldthorpe argued that, as the family is the unit of 'class analysis', then the 'class position' of the family can be taken to be that of the head of the household – who will usually be a male. Arguments concerning the extent to which women are disadvantaged within the structure of employment merely serve to prove his point. Far from being a case of intellectual sexism, his approach actually recognizes the discrimination which women suffer. To incorporate women's employment on the same terms as men's, he argued, would lead to confusion. Many women work in lower-level white-collar jobs ('Intermediate' class locations in Goldthorpe's original class scheme), and to incorporate their occupations would result in the generation of 'excessive' amounts of spurious social mobility. He also argued that his empirical evidence had demonstrated that a woman's 'conjugal' class is in general more significant than her 'occupational' class in determining her socio-political attitudes. This finding gives further support to his overall strategy.

Wright's analysis generally takes the individual, rather than the household, to be the unit of class analysis. However, in respect of economically inactive housewives (and other members of the household, such as children), Wright (1997: 246–7) employs a strategy similar to that of Goldthorpe. Thus he introduces the notion of a 'derived' class location, which provides a 'mediated' linkage to the class structure via the class location of others. Wright is sensitive to the issue of gender, and the fact that gender is a major sorting mechanism within the occupational structure as well as reciprocally interacting with class (as in the 'male-breadwinner' model of the gender division of labour; see Wright 1997: ch. 9). Nevertheless, he argues that while gender is indeed highly relevant for understanding and explaining the concrete lived experiences of people, it does not follow that gender should be *incorporated* into the abstract concept of 'class' (Wright 1989: 291). Thus in his empirical work, 'class' and 'gender' are maintained as separate factors.

We can see, therefore, that in responding to feminist criticisms, both Goldthorpe and Wright insist that class and gender should be considered as *distinct* causal processes. This analytical separation of class and gender may be seen as part of a more general strategy within the employment-aggregate approach in which the continuing relevance of 'class' is demonstrated by the empirical evidence of 'class effects' (Goldthorpe and Marshall 1992). Although, therefore, Goldthorpe and Wright have apparently developed very different approaches to 'class analysis', their underlying approach to the articulation of gender with class is in fact the same. It may be suggested that this stems from the similarity of the empirical techniques used by the CASMIN and Comparative Class projects: that is, the large-scale, cross-nationally comparative, sample survey. This kind of research proceeds by isolating a particular variable – in this case, employment class – and measuring its effects.

Although today, these debates about 'where to put the women' might seem rather old-fashioned, they usefully clarified some important points in relation to the complex project of 'class analysis' as a whole. First, both Wright and Goldthorpe are broadly correct when they emphasize that 'gender' and 'class' should be seen as *separate* axes of inequality. The inequalities of class and gender (and age and race) are indeed intertwined, but they do not necessarily have similar roots. Indeed, it has been persuasively argued (Fraser 2000; Sayer 2005) that gender inequalities are more fruitfully to be seen as inequalities of status, reflecting the subordinate position of women in relation to men, rather than as economic class inequalities. Nevertheless, gender relations are constitutive of employment relations and conditions, and this means that (as we have seen in chapter 4) attempts to develop a 'theoretical' account of employment relations that exclude gender (as well as other attributes such as sex and race) will inevitably be partial. However, as has also been argued in chapter 4, it is difficult for a single measure (occupational or otherwise) to encompass multiple dimensions of inequality, and those that have been developed tend to be rather unstable and require frequent updating.

The second important point of clarification relates to whether the individual, or the household, should be considered as the 'unit' of 'class analysis'. Putting the question this way describes it as a measurement problem, but there is more at stake than this. As a measurement problem, there can be no correct answer to the question as put, as it will depend upon the topic under investigation. For example, an exploration of the class correlates of trade unionism would use an individual measure, whereas an investigation into social mobility would use a household measure. Indeed, it is extremely important to remember that the family has a major role in determining the location of individuals within the 'class structure'. Family relationships do not in and of themselves *create* classes and class relationships, but they play the major role in reproducing them, and the family is the major transmission belt of social advantage and disadvantage. As Erikson and Goldthorpe (1993: 233) put it: 'The family is . . . the unit of class "fate" . . . the economic decision-making in which family members engage . . . is typically of a joint or interdependent kind. The family is, at the "micro" level, a key unit of strategic action pursued within the class structure.'

Indeed, women's increasing equality with men is one of the factors that has contributed to rising levels of *inequality* in society as a whole. Rising levels of education amongst women have contributed to an increase in marital homogamy. As Ermisch and his colleagues (2006) have demonstrated, assortative mating, where 'like marry like', is a major factor in the intergenerational transmission of economic status. In all countries, better-educated women are more likely to be in employment, and they are also likely to be in partnerships with better-educated men. Less well-educated women are likely to be in partnerships with less well-educated men, and household inequalities are rising. Gregg and Wadsworth demonstrate for Britain an increasing polarization between working and workless households: 'individuals who are either single or who have non-working partners increasingly don't work whereas those with working partners do' (2001: 798) – and lone-parent households, of course, have a high rate of joblessness.

Class, politics and action

In the 1980s and 1990s, feminist thinking made a major contribution to the 'identity politics' which, it has been argued (and as already discussed in chapter 2), has largely replaced 'old' class politics. From the beginning of the 1980s, left-leaning parties suffered successive electoral defeats in both Britain and the United States, and there was a neo-liberal 'return to the market' in government policies ('Reaganomics' in the US, 'Thatcherism' in Britain). Towards the end of the 1980s, government regimes in the self-proclaimed state 'socialist' countries in the Eastern bloc progressively collapsed.[9] They have been replaced by governments which have, with varying degrees of enthusiasm, embraced the doctrine of neo-liberalism and 'market forces'.

A powerful subtext in these debates is that the 'failure of the left' is also a failure of socialist theory; that socialists have remained encumbered for too long by the trappings of outdated ideologies which required revision and updating. The major thesis associated with such arguments, which reflects the changes discussed above, is that the decline of mass production, and with it a mass labour force, has led to the declining significance of the (mass, male) 'working class' and thus of class *politics*. The political parallel of mass production was Keynesian economics in combination with varying degrees of centralized planning and organization; when such political accommodations finally collapsed at the end of the 1970s the vacuum was filled by the neo-liberal 'return to the market', which has further fragmented class politics. Thus 'class', at least in its now obsolete mass, manual, male, working-class dimensions, is of declining significance, and must be replaced by a new emphasis on ecological and feminist issues, a concern for internationalism together with a move away from authoritarian centralism, and a recognition of the centrality of consumption, rather than outdated 'productivism' (Hall and Jaques 1989: 11–12).

This apparent decline of 'class politics' seemed also to signify the unravelling of yet another element of the 'industrial society' thesis which, as has been described in previous chapters (pp. 17, 28), was a significant element of the 'orthodox consensus' which prevailed in postwar sociology in Britain and America. This was the Lipset–Rokkan thesis concerning the institutionalization of class politics (1967). It argued that as nation states mature, political divisions (parties) come to reflect relatively stable class cleavages in society. Thus political representation allows for the expression of class interests within the framework of democratic politics. This model was extensively criticized, but the British case, in broad outline, did correspond to the bipartisan 'class containment' model; with the middle and upper classes tending to vote Conservative, the lower and working classes for Labour. Nevertheless, as we have noted, both parties gave broad support to 'welfarist' policies such as increased educational provision, the development of public housing, and support for the National Health Service. However, from the 1960s onwards, the link between class and voting has apparently become increasingly tenuous – that is, a process of 'dealignment' (between employment class and voting behaviour) has occurred (Clark et al. 1993).

The significance of 'new social movements' which, according to Offe (1985a), have 'transformed the boundaries of institutional politics' has also been emphasized. Offe describes the 'old politics' – that is, the major political issues in Western Europe from the immediate postwar years until the early 1970s – as being centrally concerned with issues of economic growth, distribution and security. As described by the Lipset–Rokkan thesis, old politics was also marked by a considerable degree of consensus – on the desirability of economic growth, of welfare provision and so on – and distributive conflict organized politics along broadly 'class' lines; parties of the unionized working class competing with bourgeois parties which included both the old and elements of the 'new' (that is, lower-level, white-collar) middle class. However, the accommodative basis of the old politics has been challenged by both the New Right and the growth of new social movements, which include the peace movement, ecological movements and human rights and feminist movements.

The neo-liberal New Right was highly critical of the extent of state involvement characteristic of the 'old politics', which it saw both as acting as a brake upon economic recovery and as eroding the base of individual responsibilities and undermining civil society. New social movements are similarly critical of the state's capacity to resolve the major problems which they identify, but, Offe argues, they seek not to 'roll back' the state or 'reprivatize' civil society but to *transform* political action through the development of a non-institutional politics which will bring about permanent changes. The feminist slogan 'the personal is political' may be used to describe this approach to political action, which is also characterized by relatively non-hierarchical modes of organization, mass protests (for example, against the Iraq war) and, often, direct action.

New social movements, Offe argues, represent a significant break with class politics. The bases of their organization do not correspond to socio-economic classes, or their corresponding left/right ideologies, but '[are] rather coded in *categories* taken from the movements' issues, such as gender, age, locality etc., or, in the case of environmental and pacifist movements, the human race as a whole' (Offe 1985b: 831; my emphasis). Class, in the sense of socio-economic status, is related to new social movements, however, in that much of their membership is drawn from the 'new' new middle class – that is, the educated, socially aware elements of the middle class who grew up within the economic security of the old politics and found employment within the institutions it created (that is, in administration, health, education, etc.). The 'new' new middle class may be distinguished from the 'old' new middle class of lower-level, white-collar workers. Such groupings have politicized, not on behalf of a class, but around the wider issues addressed by new social movements: 'New middle class politics, in contrast to most working class politics, as well as old middle class politics, is typically the politics *of* a class but not *on behalf of* a class' (Offe 1985b: 833).

These academic debates relating to politics, it must be remembered, were taking place at a time in which (particularly in Britain), left-of-centre political parties endured successive electoral defeats (the Conservative government was in power from 1979 to 1997). A major feature of 'New Labour' has been its conscious attempt to distance itself from 'old politics', in particular the major representatives of 'class politics' such as the trade unions. Indeed the transformation of Labour politics might itself be seen as yet another instance of the increasing lack of relevance of 'class' in contemporary political debates.

As argued in our above discussion of changes in employment, and the employment relationship, the collectivities of 'class' are probably not a particularly significant source of social and political identity in 'Western' societies. The erosion of the linkage between employment class and voting behaviour might be seen as a manifestation of a more general tendency which, as we have seen, has always been a feature of critical commentaries on class – that is, the absence of a link between 'classes' and consciousness and action of a class nature (where voting is considered as an expression of a 'class' identity). The identification of a class structure has often been associated with the (implicit or explicit) assumption that class interests may be identified corresponding to their structural location, and likely class action then derived from these interests. For example, Erikson and Goldthorpe (1988) have written of the need to investigate the conditions under which a 'class in itself' becomes a 'class for itself', that is, 'the conditions under which individuals who hold similar class positions do actually come to define their interests in class terms and to act collectively – for example, through class-based movements and organizations – in their pursuit' (cited in Muller 1990: 308). Goldthorpe's analytical reasoning from class structure→demographic class formation→socio-political class formation did indeed reflect this linkage of structure→consciousness→action (S→C→A; Pahl 1989), although his more recent (Goldthorpe 2000) adoption of 'rational action theory' (RAT; see chapter 7) represents a decisive break with this kind of reasoning.

The supposed shift from 'class' to 'identity' politics is also linked with the thesis of increasing individualization, as, it is argued, 'alternative' sources of social identity are becoming more important than class. This begs the question, of course, as to whether a consciously articulated collective class identity was ever in fact a widespread phenomenon (Savage 2000: ch. 2). Nevertheless, as we have seen in previous chapters, in the work of authors such as Beck and Giddens, 'increasing individualization' and 'the end of class' are inextricably bound together. Moreover, it is often suggested that these changes, together with others linked to globalization and technological change, constitute a 'societal shift' – that is, a radical, and fundamental, change in the organization and functioning of human societies as a result of which concepts such as 'class' are simply irrelevant.

Farewell to class societies?

An influential strand of debate suggests that contemporary social changes – including those we have discussed – are truly 'epochal' (Urry 2000b). For example: 'epochal change is based on the fact that the guiding ideas and core institutional responses of the first modernity no longer appear self-evident or even convincing . . . The West's guiding ideas about modernity . . . are in the process of falling apart' (Beck 2000a: 23–4). Thus Beck argues that the 'work society' or 'first modernity' – that is, industrial societies organized around full-time, stable, 'breadwinner' jobs – is in the process of being transcended. It is being replaced with 'second modernity', in which work as employment is fluid and transient, the nation state has to a considerable extent lost its regulatory capacities, and risk is universal. Beck argues that the old certainties can never be recovered, and new ideas and institutions must be developed.

These changes have come about as a consequence of globalization, that is, the increasingly interconnected and interdependent ways of life, and economies, across the world. Globalization can be cultural, as evidenced by world brands such as Disney or McDonald's, as well as media such as television and film. Globalization is financial, as global financial institutions, operating on a twenty-four-hour basis, shift resources between nations and organizations. Non-financial services and manufacturing are globally organized as production and employment are moved and co-ordinated around the world. These developments have been facilitated by the development of wireless and electronic communications such as the Internet and hand-held computers. People, as well as ideas, information and resources, have become increasingly mobile. Political and economic migration has increased, many employees of global companies are constrained to move between different sites in the course of their work, and holidays to 'exotic' locations have become commonplace.

These dramatic changes are not being denied, nor are they irrelevant to the concerns of class and stratification analysis. The key question is whether they represent an 'epochal shift', and whether sociology as a consequence requires a completely new set of intellectual tools (and the abandonment of old ones) for their analysis. It will be suggested that yes, new approaches can generate new insights as far as new problems are concerned. Castells's analysis of the 'network society' (2000) and Urry's (2000a) advocacy of a 'mobile sociology' are examples of this kind of thinking. Nevertheless, a degree of caution should be exercised as well. It will be argued that it is more useful to see contemporary social change as being a consequence of the growth of neo-liberalism and the intensification of capitalism, rather than as an 'epochal shift'. Moreover, some elements of 'globalization thinking' have, to put it mildly, been overdone. In particular, arguments to the effect that these changes have rendered the nation state an irrelevance as far as sociological thinking is concerned are not particularly helpful. This supposed 'decline' relates not simply to the political and economic autonomy of the state, but also to the governance of its populations. Urry, for example, sees the major function of the contemporary state as regulating mobilities (of people, information, etc), rather than 'organising the rights and duties' (2000b: 188) of its citizen population. Again, there is ample evidence to suggest that even though mobilities may have indeed increased, the nation state has by no means abandoned efforts to provision and influence its citizenry, whose 'life chances' are to a substantial extent dependent on state policies and as a consequence vary dramatically.[10]

One theme that characterizes postmodernist arguments that there has been an 'epochal shift' in global societal functioning is the assertion that cultural consumption has itself become a (if not the) driving force in postmodern society (see chapter 2). Kumar's useful summary statement puts the argument thus: 'In the late capitalist stage, culture itself becomes the prime determinant of social, economic, political and even psychological reality . . . Culture has become "a product in its own right"; the process of cultural consumption is no longer merely an adjunct but the very essence of capitalist functioning' (1995: 115–16). This assertion of the primacy of culture and consumption, therefore, would seem to be in direct contradiction to the assumption that in *class* societies, the processes of economic production and the market serve to delineate interests, identities and action. If broadly materialist explanations are to be rejected, can it be argued that we are, any longer, living in class societies?

Lash and Urry's (1994) discussion of current and future trends suggests that a profound societal transformation is, indeed, taking place. They describe a four-stage model of capitalist development: first, locally competitive liberal capitalism, which prevailed in the nineteenth century, followed by (in the twentieth century) 'organized' capitalism. 'Organized' capitalism was nationally based, and describes, in broad outline, the development of large bureaucratic firms, together with labour union organization and governmental strategies of economic management – that is, the set of societal arrangements that have been described as 'Fordist' (see above). 'Disorganized capitalism'[11] describes the 'post-Fordist' breakdown of 'organized capitalism'. It is characterized by fragmented and flexible production systems, in which capitalism itself becomes global as 'the various subjects and objects of the capitalist political economy circulate not only along routes of greater and greater distance, but also . . . at ever greater *velocity*' (1994: 2). Lash and Urry argue that out of this third stage there is developing a global 'economy of signs and space', characterized by an increasingly significant 'reflexive' human subjectivity, arising out of a process of detraditionalization in which social agents are 'set free' in order to be self-monitoring and reflexive.

Flows – of people, of information, of ideas, of images, of technologies, of capital – rather than structures dominate economies of signs and space. These flows are evident in global capital markets, controlled from head office sites in global cities, and in globalized popular culture, as well as in mass tourism and migration. Production, as well as the workers in it, has itself taken on a 'reflexive' character, as information systems become increasingly central. The worker, argue Lash and Urry, is increasingly no longer circumscribed by the constraints of 'structure', but is responsible for its transformation (1994: 122). The massive growth in both services and cultural production only serves to reinforce this reflexivity. In 'socio-economies' it is culture, rather than economic position, that gives meaning to social practices, and it is consciousness or reflexivity that determines class (i.e. occupational) structure. Often, Lash and Urry's tone is a positive one, for example describing the 'reintegration of conceptualisation and execution' in the circumstances of information-rich, reflexive, production systems. However, they also identify the simultaneous expansion of 'wild zones', such as the 'collapsing empires' of state socialism, as well as the areas and localities into which are concentrated the very poorest or 'underclass', that is, those who have lost out following the decline of unskilled jobs that pay a living wage (these jobs *were* available during the Fordist/corporatist compromise). As noted above, Urry (2000a; 2000b: 189) has further developed a manifesto for a 'mobile sociology', to supersede the 'old' sociology bounded by class and nation state.

Lash and Urry's argument is dense and complex, and a detailed critique will not be developed here. However, before we consider the broad implications of their arguments, we will review in brief a very similar, and more explicit, set of claims that 'class is dead' in 'postmodern' societies. In a similar fashion to that of Lash and Urry, Pakulski and Waters (1996; see also Waters 1996) periodize capitalist development, but into three phases, rather than four. The term 'economic class' society they largely reserve for capitalist industrialism in the eighteenth and nineteenth centuries (the competitive liberal capitalism identified by Lash and Urry). During this phase, they argue, interest groups were *economically* determined (bourgeoisie, proletariat, etc.), and this was reflected in patterns of domination and conflict. Culture was also class-divided. The next phase they identify is the 'organized class' or 'corporatist' phase, which is paralleled by Lash and Urry's 'organized capitalist/Fordist' description. 'Classes' are politically organized, and 'the cultural realm . . . unified under the state umbrella . . . It can thus be turned into an industrialised or mass culture' (Waters 1996: 73). The third (and currently emerging) phase is that of 'status conventionalism', in which stratification emerges from the sphere of culture and its consumption.

Pakulski and Waters employ a definition of 'class', and 'class society', which is both comprehensive and specific, and which is modelled on Marx and Engels' more economistic formulations. Class, they argue, describes the primary causal role of capital and labour market capacities in structuring material interests and social relationships; thus it should give rise to the most important social groupings in society; these groupings (classes) give rise to the most important and persisting bases for consciousness, identity and action outside the arena of economic production; and they are also the principal 'makers of history' (Pakulski and Waters 1996: 10; it may be noted that on this definition, only very brief periods of history – if indeed, any at all – would correspond to the definition of an economic class society). Pakulski and Waters argue that emergent status conventionalism is under way because of the increase in individualism brought about by changes in the nature of employment, together with the declining capacity of the national state – the key actor in organized class society – to control the economy. In part this is because of economic globalization, but it is also a result of increasing pressures on the state from different interest groups, articulated by 'identity politics'. In 'post-class', postmodern, status-conventional societies, occupation becomes a badge of status, together with other dimensions of status that have become 'value infused, symbolicized and reflexive . . . Identity is . . . not linked either to property or organizational position. Under conditions of advanced affluence, styles of consumption and commitment become socially salient as markers and delimiters' (Pakulski and Waters 1996: 156). Thus, they argue, culture and consumption practices have emerged as significant causal forces in the 'multiple mosaic of status communities' (Waters 1996: 80) that characterize 'status-conventional' societies.

Above we have briefly reviewed two ambitious attempts to develop what are, in fact, new postmodern 'meta-narratives' which, the authors argue, will enable us to better grasp the rapid social changes and developments associated with 'late', 'reflexive' or 'post'modernity.[12] Both Lash and Urry, and Pakulski and Waters, argue that a 'societal shift' is under way in that *consumption* and its associated practices have become the driving forces of post-modern societies. Both emphasize that instability, fragmentation, individualization and social fluidity have become more prevalent in postmodern societies, in contrast with the collectively organized 'class' stabilities of the 'Fordist' era. Both, moreover, are explicit that 'economies of signs and space' or 'multiple mosaics of status communities' are characterized by conflicts and inequalities – Lash and Urry, in particular, devote considerable attention to the question of the 'underclass'.

Because both sets of arguments are extremely complex, it is not too difficult to make criticisms of various points of detail. Lash and Urry's discussion of the 'collective reflexivity' of Japanese production systems, for example, makes little mention of the great majority (around 80 per cent) of the Japanese labour force who are not employed by the major firms offering these conditions – and more generally, Lash and Urry's description of changes in the nature of employment pays little attention to the explosion of routine, low-level, service work. The Alford index, which Pakulski and Waters use to describe the decline of 'class politics', has been widely criticized as not taking into account the significance of shifts in the occupational structure (Heath 1981). More generally, the point may be made that the trends these authors emphasize are not particularly new but, rather, represent the continuous development of features which have always been present since the advent of capitalism.

Debates about 'postindustrialism' are not new either (see Bell 1973). Sayer and Walker have argued at some length that the supposed economic and occupational shift to services has been much exaggerated. Many jobs labelled as 'services', they argue, are in fact productive activities: 'A legal brief or an environmental impact statement is simply intellectual craft applied to paper, as a chair is woodcraft applied to lumber' (1992: 63); similar arguments, they suggest, might be applied to many financial 'services', transport and information services such as computer packages. They argue that the 'transition to the service economy' is in fact better conceptualized as a 'widening and deepening' of the social and technical divisions of labour, itself a part of the more general process of industrial evolution and capitalist development. Complex hierarchies have evolved, and the division of labour has become extended, as in, for example, pre-production design and marketing, resulting in the growth of 'indirect labour' in respect of the production process. Thus Sayer and Walker insist upon 'certain indelible continuities with the past, continuities which the theory of services denies' (1992: 57) – in short, they insist that *productive*, rather than consumption, activities are still most important in contemporary societies, and the concepts developed to analyse production remain the most significant explanatory tools.

The explanatory primacy of consumption, therefore, remains a contested topic. However, there is a more general point of criticism that concerns an important underlying assumption made by both Lash and Urry and Pakulski and Waters. This is the assumption of what Waters describes as the 'perfectionalisation of the market'. To put the point in its full context: 'The force of detraditionalisation might be better expressed as the "perfectionalisation of the market"' (1996: 82). To make the same argument in another way, one of the reasons why consumption achieves explanatory primacy is because consumers (with resources) are increasingly able to get what they want; one of the reasons why consumers are able to get what they want is that information has become increasingly available because all kinds of markets have been 'detraditionalized'. For example, Lash and Urry (1994: 286–8) describe the transformation of the financial markets of the City of London from a closely packed square mile which used to operate on the basis of proximity and close personal ties into a deregulated, unconstrained, detraditionalized arena.

'Detraditionalization' means that everything has become 'marketized', the postmodernists argue.[13] Niche marketing and fashion shapes the choice of the 'neo-tribe', 'reflexive consumer' and 'status communities', rather than the preferences shaped by place and traditional 'belonging'. Individual rewards are increasingly separated from the 'closed' arrangements of status traditions and organizational hierarchies, and Waters (1996: 83) argues that the cultural economy is becoming a measure of individual worth; this may be described as the marketizing of the personality. However, the extent to which markets have in fact been 'perfectionalized' (or indeed, may ever be so rendered) may be seriously questioned. Indeed, the systematic problematizing of market rationality has formed the bedrock of the sociological critique of economics. As Durkheim argued nearly a century ago: 'All that is in the contract is not contractual' (1968); that is, contracts invariably incorporate *social* as well as economic or rational considerations (consider, for example, the labour contract). Markets cannot function in the absence of a parallel structure of social relationships. It is not simply that due regard has to be given to the cultural context of market relationships (for example, there are considerable cross-national variations in the extent to which they are expected to be accompanied by gift-giving), but rather, that the market itself is a social construct that is embedded in constructs of social relations (Granovetter 1985; Granovetter and Swedberg 1992). Moreover, economic relations are by no means co-ordinated entirely (or even largely) by markets, but also by custom, coercion and democratic negotiation (Sayer and Walker 1992).

In short, to the extent that the thesis of detraditionalization rests upon the parallel thesis of the perfectionalization of the market, then there are considerable problems in making this case. Indeed, it is somewhat paradoxical that the economic success of many of the nation states whose emergence has been identified as central to the process of worldwide 'globalization' (including Japan, and the 'tiger economies' of South East Asia) is grounded in firms and organizations structured along both actual family and quasi-family principles, and characterized by extensive recruitment (of key personnel) along these lines. Rather than the market having been perfectionalized, it may be suggested that there have in fact always been fluctuations in the extent to which market principles have been adopted as a mode of societal regulation, both *de jure* and *de facto*.

More particularly, it may be argued that recent developments may be interpreted not as a shift towards the primacy of the consumer and a detraditionalization of the market, but rather, as a conscious and deliberate attempt at change in a neo-liberal direction. Neo-liberalism is 'a theory of political economic practices that proposes that human well-being can best be advanced by liberating individual entrepreneurial freedoms and skills within an institutional framework characterised by strong private property rights, free markets, and free trade' (Harvey 2005: 2). Harvey argues that neo-liberalism grew out of the apparent failure of Keynesian economic management and the accompanying 'stagflation' (described above) of the 1970s and 1980s. According to Harvey (2005: 16), neo-liberalization 'was from the very beginning a project to achieve the restoration of class power'. The mid-twentieth-century social compromise had seen a shift of economic resources from the top to the lower echelons of society (Hills 2004), and inequalities had declined. In the situation of economic growth that followed the Second World War, this redistribution seemed a small price to pay for economic stability and continuing expansion, but: 'To have a stable share of an increasing pie is one thing. But when growth collapsed in the 1970s, when real interest rates went negative and paltry dividends and profits were the norm, then upper classes everywhere felt threatened' (Harvey 2005: 15).

As we have already seen, neo-liberalism has included the deregulation of financial and labour markets (often including the removal of labour protections such as the Wages Councils in Britain), and the privatization of state enterprise – even in basic commodities such as energy and water. Even those services that remain in the public sector – such as health and education – have been opened up to the pressure of 'market forces'. Tariff barriers have been brought down, and transnational corporations (TNCs) have flourished. With the advent of neo-liberalism, inequalities grew rapidly, and the ability of TNCs to switch production and employment has contributed to rising employee insecurity. There can also be little doubt that amongst many other changes, there has been a deliberate attempt to shift everyday discourse into the language of neo-liberal individualistic consumerism. Changes in the management of employees have already been discussed above. In Britain, the privatization of the railways has been accompanied by the disappearance of the 'passenger', to be replaced by the 'customer', and even police chiefs speak of their need to communicate with their 'customers' rather than 'the public'.

It is being suggested, therefore, that rather than understanding globalization and its associated changes as an 'epochal shift', requiring 'new' concepts and theories for its analysis, as Beck, Lash, Urry, etc. have argued, what we have in fact witnessed is the 'intensification of capitalism' (Crouch 1999). This has been accompanied by quite deliberate efforts to encourage individualism and consumerism. Moreover, the politics of deregulation does not mean that the market has been 'set free' (or 'perfectionalized') but rather that alternative, neo-liberal regulatory mechanisms have been introduced (for example, local authorities in Britain have been directed to introduce 'best-value' policies that have often resulted in the outsourcing of services once carried out 'in-house'). To repeat a previous point, 'markets' cannot function in the absence of a parallel system of social relationships, and the neo-liberal concept of a 'self-regulating' market is in fact a myth (Granovetter and Swedberg 1992; Polanyi 1957). Moreover, as Polanyi has argued: 'To allow the market mechanism to be the sole director of the fate of human beings and their natural environment . . . would result in the demolition of society' (1957: 73).

As many have argued, extreme capitalism, associated with liberal political and economic policies, characterized the early decades following the Industrial Revolution in Britain (Seccombe 1993). Polanyi's account of the end of mercantilism (where states and guilds controlled production and exchange) describes liberal attempts to set up 'one big self-regulating market' (1957: 67) in the late eighteenth and nineteenth centuries. However, whatever the gains of the Industrial Revolution, they were, as Polanyi puts it, 'catastrophic' for many of the 'common people' (artisanal producers, agricultural workers) whose livelihoods were removed by technical and social change alongside the removal of customary protections. Vast fortunes were made, but poverty and starvation were rife. In Polanyi's (1957: 76) account, in the nineteenth century:

A blind faith in spontaneous progress (ie, economic liberalism) had taken hold of people's minds, and with the fanaticism of sectarians the most enlightened pressed forward for boundless and unregulated change in society. The effects on the lives of the people were awful beyond description. Indeed, human society would have been annihilated but for protective countermoves which blunted the edge of this self-destructive mechanism.

Polanyi argues that as a consequence of the destructive excesses of early capitalism, there developed a 'double movement'; even as economic liberals were attempting to create a 'self-regulating market' so counter-moves against economic liberalism and *laissez-faire* – reform of the Poor Law, factory acts, limitations on working hours – were instituted: society in essence 'saved itself' from the destruction of the market. In the final chapter of this book, we will examine possible examples of these counter-movements against extreme capitalism in contemporary societies, but for the moment, we will review some of the responses to these various arguments that have announced both the 'end of class' and the end of class societies.

Where do we go from here?

It has been demonstrated that two interrelated arguments have been associated with assertions as to the 'end of class'. First, it has been argued that societies – indeed the world – have changed so much in recent decades that old theories and concepts, such as those associated with the analysis of 'class', are simply no longer adequate to understand the new reality. Second, as has been seen in this and previous chapters, it has been argued that 'old' class theories and concepts were in any case inadequate to start with. That is, despite apparently claiming to do so, these theories and methods did not, in fact, resolve the tensions between 'structural' and 'action' explanatory frameworks (Pahl 1996; Bottero 2005). Moreover, they laid an excessive emphasis on the *economic* determinants of 'class', leaving no space for other elements – gender, race and age, as well as cultural and behavioural factors – that shape the inequalities found in concrete 'classes' (see discussion, pp. 51, 70).

It is true that there have been massive social changes. As summarized above, changes in the structure and location of paid employment, together with changes in the management of employees, have eroded the presumed bases of collective, class-based identities and action. Increases in women's employment not only created unmanageable difficulties for employment-aggregate class analysis, but have also underlined the significance of non-class inequalities (which would include race and age as well as sex) in employment. The declining political relevance of class would seem to contribute further to the case for the irrelevance of the concept. However, it has been argued above that it is premature to assert that an 'epochal shift' has taken place, and that the phenomena associated with what may loosely be described as 'globalization' may best be understood as reflecting the resurgence of neo-liberalism and the intensification of capitalism. It is important not to underestimate the significance of the changes that have occurred, but their significance should not be overestimated either.

The second strand of criticism relates to the adequacy of class and stratification concepts more generally. As discussed in chapter 2 (p. 17), these difficulties are not only associated with class and stratification analysis, but reflect fundamental tensions within the social science enterprise as a whole. The position taken here is that debates about the nature of social science (the conflict between positivism and hermeneutic understanding) and the duality of the social world (the explanatory conflict between structure and agency), as well as the relative significance of the 'economic' versus the 'cultural', are incapable of any synthesis or accommodation within a single, overarching theory. Nevertheless, the study of class and stratification requires us to work across what are often conflicting perspectives. These arguments will be further developed in later chapters, but for the moment, we will examine a range of differing sociological responses to the problems of class and stratification analysis described in this chapter.

A number of broad categories of responses can be identified. First, the continuing practical relevance of 'class' can simply be reasserted in the face of all criticisms (Goldthorpe and Marshall 1992). Alternatively, new, improved theories, models and approaches have been developed (Bradley 1996; Anthias 2001, 2005; Bottero 2005). Finally, as we have seen, for many authors, the irrelevance of class has been accepted as given, and new (and by implication more relevant) axes of differentiation or sources of identity have been identified and investigated.

It is not difficult to demonstrate the persistent inequalities of class as revealed by occupational measures. 'Professional and managerial' class groupings earn more money, live in better housing, are more likely to gain higher-level qualifications and go to university, have a greater life expectancy, and are much less likely to have a long-term limiting illness (Reid 1998). In their defence of 'class analysis', Goldthorpe and Marshall (1992) laid much emphasis on the continuing class differences in opportunity revealed by studies of education and social mobility. The empirical persistence of occupational class inequalities is an important fact that should continue to be repeated and emphasized. The research programmes associated with disputes over measures of class may have ended, but this is no justification for not continuing to use these measures. Alternative measures incorporating consumption indicators are unreliable and unstable. However, this approach to 'class analysis' is relatively narrow. It does not incorporate other major dimensions of occupational inequality such as sex, age and race. More fundamentally, perhaps, the most common analytical tool that is used to demonstrate the persistence of class – occupational measures – do not adequately incorporate 'cultural' dimensions which are also vital in the production and reproduction of class inequalities.

Occupation and culture were famously linked in Lockwood's 1996 article that sought to demonstrate how different occupational groupings – traditional workers in mining and heavy industry; 'affluent' workers in large factories (Goldthorpe et al. 1968, 1969, 1970), and other, more isolated employees (e.g. Newby 1977) developed, as a consequence of their workplace and community experiences, varying working-class 'images of society'. As we have seen, this S→C→A model, as Savage (2000: 28) has put it, 'ultimately came unstuck' under the charge of economic reductionism. Goldthorpe, who in the 'affluent worker' research of the 1960s was very much associated with this position, has progressively distanced himself from any attempt to incorporate the cultural dimension of class and indeed now expresses considerable hostility to 'culturalist' perspectives on class. Again, methodological consistency has been achieved at the cost of rendering 'class' as a unidimensional, economistic concept.

New and revised approaches

Not surprisingly, therefore, a number of attempts have been made to broaden the scope of class and stratification theory and analysis both to incorporate the varying dimensions of inequality and to give due regard to cultural factors. Bradley seeks to 'pull together classical or modernist approaches to understanding inequalities with the newer perspectives inspired by postmodernism and post-structuralism' (1996: 3). Her attempt at synthesis, and/or providing a 'better version' (1996: 204) of modernist theory, contains many valuable insights. Nevertheless, ultimately it emerges as a series of descriptive statements relating to the interaction of class, gender, race and age, rather than a new theory as such. It is indisputable that the inequalities associated with class, gender, race and age *are* related to each other. However, rather than attempting to integrate 'modern' and 'postmodern' accounts of these phenomena, it is preferable to recognize that the theories in question not only give different versions of the same reality but also focus on different *aspects* of the whole. Thus, as argued in chapter 2 (see Wright 2005), 'class analysis' has to be seen as addressing a series of different *topics*, as well as reflecting a variety of theoretical perspectives.

Similarly, Anthias's (2005) major concern is to look at the non-class factors in social differentiation and inequality, and, in particular, divisions of gender and race/ethnicity. She identifies three models of stratification, 'reductionist', 'identity' and 'intersectionality'. She rejects both the 'reductionist' model, which is associated with attempts to reduce gender and ethnicity to class relations, and the 'identity' model, which is associated with trends in postmodernist theory. In place of these, she allies herself with a modified variant of the 'intersectionality' model. According to this model, people must be seen as occupying multiple and overlapping social positions which may be either reinforcing or contradictory in their effects on both inequality and collective identity. Anthias argues that a recognition of this 'translocational positionality' of social inequality must not focus on the purely descriptive, but must highlight the processes through which such multiple positions are reproduced. In arguing this point, she develops an unacknowledged reformulation of Lenski's (1966) argument on 'status inconsistency' in multidimensional systems of social stratification. The notion of 'intersectionality' makes the (sensible) point that inequalities persist along a number of different dimensions, and that individuals and groups in 'hybrid' social positionings (e.g. black working-class women) may experience multiple disadvantage. However, to recognize the complexities of inequality does not, in itself, represent a 'new' theoretical approach.

Another recent proposal for a multidimensional approach is to be found in Scott's (1996) reformulation of Weber's approach to class and stratification. Scott identifies class, status and command (power) as being 'systematically interrelated in the way that they shape people's life-chances and are involved in the formation of large-scale collectivities that stand in hierarchical relations to one another' (1996: 191). Scott's formulation closely follows that of Weber (see chapter 3) and will not be repeated in detail here. The boundaries between strata are delineated by mobility rates – that is, groups of occupations characterized by frequent mobility and interaction. These include the 'breaks' in the occupational structure across which intergenerational mobility is difficult or infrequent (e.g. Goldthorpe and Llewellyn 1977), as well as the social interactions of friendships and households. Scott's position is in fact quite close to that of Bottero (2005: 147), who has similarly theorized stratification as a social space of relationships, constituted through the clustering of economic, social and cultural relations.

Although in general terms the stance taken by Scott and Bottero is unexceptionable (and has many similarities with the arguments developed in this book), there are nevertheless difficulties in taking either as representing a new (or reconstituted) totalizing theory or approach. One example would be the question of measuring social class. Scott argues (1996: 203) that occupational classifications should not be rejected, but rather, refined as a consequence of his arguments. However, as has been argued in this book, multidimensional measures are extremely difficult to construct and maintain, particularly for 'everyday' use. It is argued here that for most practical purposes, the most appropriate strategy is not to continue with the endless task of creating or locating a universally applicable 'best' measure of occupational class (as Scott would seem to be suggesting), but rather, to continue to use the measures available whilst remaining conscious of their limitations. Of course, measures can be and should be improved where possible, and some measures are more appropriate to particular research topics than others. Nevertheless, as has been demonstrated above, the occupational class classifications available are highly intercorrelated and would appear to be measuring similar phenomena.

In a similar vein, Bottero has been closely associated with the development of the Cambridge occupational scale, which is a measure of lifestyle advantage. It is derived from a factor analysis of the occupations of an individual's closest friends and reflects the social choices people make about their way of life (Prandy 1991). Again, the Cambridge scale may be argued to be an 'improvement' as it encompasses social as well as economic dimensions, but it is rather problematic to maintain for general purposes. Another difficulty with the approach proposed by Bottero is her insistence on the indivisibility of structure and action. As a consequence, she argues that the causal model that has underpinned class analysis, in which economic structures give rise to social and cultural formations, should be abandoned. As we have seen, there are in fact many problems with the S→C→A model, but on the other hand, to abandon it completely might mean 'throwing the baby out with the bathwater'.

Put simply, to abandon attempts at causal explanation (as noted in chapter 2, p. 25 this is an explicit feature of the 'cultural turn' in sociology) means that sociologists effectively abandon the tools that might be used in policy (and other) debates relating to the amelioration or reduction of class inequalities. Moreover, although 'structure' and 'action', 'culture' and 'economy', *are* intertwined in empirical reality, it should be possible to recognize that in particular instances, a structural explanation might be preferred over an action account, and/or a cultural explanation over an economic. That is, as has been argued in chapter 2, an 'analytical dualism' must be maintained in respect of sociological research and explanation (Crompton and Scott 2005).

Other attempts at reformulation include the drawing up of new 'class maps' so as to reflect changes in the occupational structure (for example, Runciman 1990). Grusky and Sorensen (1998) have argued that occupational groups remain a significant source of social identities, and that a more fine-grained occupational class analysis is required in order to explore these linkages.[14] Perhaps one of the most prominent arenas within which changes in the 'class structure' has been debated, however, relates to the emergence of a supposed 'underclass'. Saunders, for example, has identified the 'major fault line' in countries like Britain as being between 'a majority of people who can service their key consumption requirements through the market and a minority who remain reliant on an increasingly inadequate and alienative form of direct state provision' (1987: ch. 3; see also Murray 1984). This split, Saunders argues, is affecting 'the material life chances and cultural identities' of the people involved – that is, they are increasingly disempowered in respect of the ('normal') majority who can service their needs through the market. It should be recognized that the 'underclass' is a highly contentious concept (this will be discussed further in chapter 7). Some have argued that the term has been developed not in order to describe an objective phenomenon or set of social relationships but, rather, as a stigmatizing label which effectively 'blames the victims' for their misfortunes. Thus Dean has argued that ' "Underclass" is a symbolic term with no single meaning, but a great many applications . . . It represents, not a useful concept, but a potent symbol' (1991: 35). With the advent of neo-liberalism, social polarization has indeed been on the increase, and we will be returning to this topic in our final chapter.

The creation of improved 'class maps' will be an ongoing enterprise. The actual value of any particular map cannot be conclusively resolved, as it will depend on its explanatory efficacy as a descriptive exercise. Most introductory textbooks will include such an exercise (see, for example, Fulcher and Scott 1999: ch. 15). The heuristic value of such exercises is considerable, but they do not constitute a 'new direction' as such.

As we have seen, substantive 'new directions' have tended to focus either on extending the range of 'class analysis' so as to include other dimensions of inequality, or attempting to resolve the theoretical difficulties of structure versus action – or some combination of both. Savage (2000: 151) has made a bold attempt to develop a 'more fluid approach' via the argument that class identities (consciousness) emerge not from a sense of collective belonging, but rather, in the process of differentiation from others. The decline of the traditional 'working class' has led to the predominance of middle-class, individualized identities, generated by a continuous process of comparison 'up' and 'down'. Savage's work (2000: ch. 6) documents the changes in employment and organizations that have generated this shift in identity formation.[15] Savage (2000: 149) is also insistent that class analysis is a mode of *cultural* analysis, and concludes:

> The ambivalence of class awareness [i.e. the fragility of the S→C→A model] is not an embarrassing fact . . . but can be treated as an issue that points the way to telling issues of contemporary importance concerning individualised cultures, reflexivity, and the culture of ambivalence. Bourdieu's class theory allows us the best way of developing an appropriate starting point for this venture.

Savage's theoretical arguments, therefore, may be read as transforming 'class' from a set of social relations into an individualized, hierarchical structure. This is not, however, his intention, and his more recent work develops the CARs (capitals, assets, resources) approach. This will be discussed in the next chapter of this book, in which the work of Bourdieu will receive greater scrutiny.

Conclusions

As can be seen from the debates summarized above, although the 'end of class' has been endlessly predicted, class and stratification analysis still survives and, as we shall see in later chapters, in some respects has been rejuvenated. However, this rejuvenation has not been without costs. One is the fragmentation of the field, which is perhaps not surprising given the multifaceted nature of the 'class' concept, as described in chapter 2 (Crompton 1996a). Indeed, one theme that has recurred throughout this chapter is the relative failure of offerings that purport to be either the 'one best way' of carrying out 'class analysis' (e.g. Goldthorpe 2000), or totalizing accounts that attempt to encompass all dimensions of inequality. The approach taken in this book, therefore, has been to argue that particular approaches to 'class' may be very different from each other, but if they have a focus on different things, then they are not necessarily incompatible. As argued in a previous edition

(Crompton 1998: 203), the 'most fruitful way ahead in "class analysis" within sociology lies in the recognition of plurality and difference [i.e. between different approaches to 'class'], rather than forcing a choice from amongst competing positions, or attempting to devise a completely new or revised theoretical approach'.

Savage (2000: ix) takes up a similar position when he argues that 'The ultimate test for the future of class analysis is to see whether it can renew itself, not by defensive action from entrenched positions, but by being able to go out and speak to diverse currents of social enquiry.' Rather than developing 'new tools', therefore, we have to make better use of the ones already available. For example, the revived interest in cultures of class has available to it the tools developed by anthropologists in their quest to 'make analytical . . . categories through which people make sense of their everyday lives' (Evans 2006: 176). As represented by the hegemonic 'employment-aggregate' approach of the 1980s and 1990s, 'class analysis' was both economistic and determinist, and the cultural dimension of class was largely absent from the discussion. The revived interest in the role of culture in class formation and experiences has been followed with an increasing focus on the work of Bourdieu, and it is to these issues that we now turn.

CLASS AND CULTURE: THE ETHNOGRAPHY OF CLASS

6

Introduction

In previous chapters, we have identified two interrelated themes that have run through criticisms of 'class analysis' as constituted within sociology during the last decades of the twentieth century and into the early twenty-first: first, the problems occasioned by the apparent failure of class action, and second, the overly economistic (sometimes described as determinist) bias of much class and stratification analysis. In this chapter, our major focus will be on this second point of criticism and the responses that have been developed. It will be argued that class reproduction (i.e. of concrete 'classes') has both economic *and* cultural dimensions, and that a full account will necessarily draw on both.

Although, for the purposes of research and investigation, an 'analytical dualism' has been insisted upon throughout this book, it has equally been recognized that empirically, structure and action, economy and culture, are intertwined. That is, not only are economic inequalities buttressed by social ('cultural') inequalities, but culture (ideas, symbols, ways of being) plays an important role in maintaining and reproducing class inequalities. That is, economic inequalities are structured by non-economic, cultural mechanisms. 'Classic' theorists have always recognized this fact. For Weber, as we have seen, 'status' was an independent dimension of inequality. Although Marx has often been straightforwardly described as an economic determinist, even here, as we have seen in chapter 3, many interpreters of Marx have argued that he did not consider the ideological (or cultural) 'superstructure' to be a simple reflection of the economic 'base'.

Culture, therefore, is not just an effect of class location but also a central mechanism through which class positions are constituted. In this chapter, we will first re-examine the concept of status with brief reference to both the 'community studies' approach to stratification developed in the US and Britain, and the concept of 'citizenship' as developed by T. H. Marshall. Next we will explore the work of Bourdieu, whose approach has become increasingly influential in recent years. We will discuss recent discussions of the cultural construction of the 'new middle classes', and our review will also include recent examples of empirical accounts of the 'working class' influenced by Bourdieu's approach. In our conclusions, we will discuss the impossibility of a 'unitary' approach in which both the economic and the cultural are combined in a single 'theory', and the subsequent requirement for a 'positive pluralism' in approaches to class and stratification analysis.

Social status, social hierarchies and social citizenship

As we have seen in previous chapters, one of the major objectives of those who have developed sociological, 'relational' approaches to employment-based class analysis (i.e. through the use of class schemes) has been to distinguish their measures from prestige or status scales. In chapters 3 and 4, an account has been given of the manner in which, after the Second World War, sociologists who were actively developing the 'conflict' approach in the field of class and stratification theory and research sought to distance themselves from the prevailing tradition of stratification research in the United States. This tradition was represented in the many-volume *Yankee City* series, which drew upon anthropologically inspired community research which began in 1930 (Warner 1963). Warner defined 'social class' as follows:

> By social class is meant two or more orders of people who are believed to be, and are accordingly ranked by the members of the community, in socially superior and inferior positions. Members of a class tend to marry within their own order, but the values of the society permit marriage up and down. A class system also provides that children are born into the same status as their parents. A class society distributes rights and privileges, duties and obligations, unequally among its inferior and superior grades.   (1963: 36–7)

This description of 'social classes' closely resembles the first meaning of the class concept identified in chapter 2 (p. 15) – that is, 'class' as prestige, status or 'style'. Warner's study of 'class' had in fact focused largely on the prestige order. His definition emphasizes the cultural, rather than the economic, construction of class and corresponds more closely to the commonsense definition of 'class' in ordinary usage. Indeed, Warner's definition of the 'class structure' was constructed from accounts gathered from local residents. Theoretically informed sociologists were at considerable pains to dissociate themselves from this approach and, following Bendix and Lipset (1967a), were emphatic as to the importance of the Weberian distinction between 'class' and 'status'.

Thus in his defence of his version of 'class analysis' against feminist critics, Goldthorpe (1983) laid much emphasis on this distinction between the 'American' and the 'European' traditions of class analysis:

> In the mainstream American literature the dominant . . . form of stratification [is seen] in terms of *social status*: that is, as resulting from the differential evaluations of family units that are made by 'the community' . . . the term 'social class' [is used] where European writers would be more likely to use that of 'status groups'.   (Goldthorpe 1983: 466)

Similarly, when he came to develop his Marxist 'class map', Wright drew a sharp distinction between the status or prestige order and the analysis of occupational *class* (Wright

1979; chapter 3 above). He has argued that as status bears no relation to production, it has no place in class analysis (Wright 1985: 79).

Economic 'class' factors (such as the nature of market demand, and the extent and nature of control and authority relationships) *are* analytically separable from 'prestige' factors in the structuring of employment patterns, the allocation of people to jobs, and the determination of levels of material reward. However, in practice, it is exceptionally difficult to draw a clear distinction between them. That these two aspects are inextricably intertwined is demonstrated, for example, by the considerable extent of empirical overlap between 'class' and 'status' (or prestige) occupational classifications, as we have seen in the preceding chapters. However, the sharp distinction drawn between class and status in the development of the employment-aggregate approach has had a number of consequences, not all of which have been positive. These debates have had a tendency to identify status with *prestige* or social ranking. Nevertheless, prestige is only one dimension of the complex status concept, and it may be suggested that the attention given to this dimension has tended to overshadow the exploration of the other aspects of status. Additionally, the desire to separate class from status empirically has also tended to deflect attention from the investigation of their interrelations.[1]

In Britain a tradition of community studies emerged alongside the establishing of sociology as an academic discipline after the Second World War. However, it was influenced by anthropology as much as sociology (Frankenberg 1966). As in the US, teams of researchers would focus on a particular locale with the objective of delivering a fine-grained account of local ('community') systems of class, status and culture (e.g. Dennis et al. 1956; Stacey 1960; Littlejohn 1963; Young and Wilmott 1957) – in short, these interrelations were at the centre of these investigations and no attempt was made, as in the 'employment-aggregate' approach, to 'bracket out' cultural dimensions of class. Indeed, the empirical data gathered by this tradition of sociological and anthropological research was drawn upon by Lockwood (1996) in his influential article, 'Sources of variation in working-class images of society', which, as we have seen in previous chapters, was crucial in the embedding of the S→C→A model that has proved to be so contentious as far as 'class analysis' was concerned. This body of empirical work was sensitive to the economic as well as the cultural dimensions of inequality within the communities studied (Crompton and Scott 2005). The tradition came under criticism, however, as being too narrow in its focus, and as failing to make the linkages to the macro-social processes that shaped the social structures and relationships within the 'community' in question (Stacey 1969). Nevertheless, this model of investigation has been recently revived by researchers seeking to explore the processes generating class identities (Savage et al. 2001).

As with class, the concept of status is complex and relates to the overall structuring of inequality along a number of different dimensions. In particular, as noted in chapter 3, the Weberian concept of status may usefully be considered to have three dimensions: (a) referring to actual prestige groupings or consciousness communities; (b) more diffuse notions of 'lifestyle' or 'social standing' (these first two aspects will obviously overlap to a considerable extent); and (c) non-market-based claims to material entitlements or 'life chances'. The first aspect of the status concept identified above – prestige groupings – is, as we have seen, the aspect from which 'theoretical', employment-based 'class analysis' sought to differentiate itself most sharply. Such groupings are here described as *consciousness communities*: 'In contrast to classes, *status groups* are normally communities' (Weber 1948: 186; emphasis in original). 'Community' in this sense need not necessarily imply residential propinquity. Not surprisingly, Warner's *Yankee City* provides a good historical example of these kinds of linkages: 'When George Washington made his grand presidential tour of the new nation . . . he came not only

as the Father of his Country and leader of all his people, but as a visiting Virginia aristocrat
. . . when he arrived in Yankee City he was entertained in the great houses of the town by
people who knew him as an equal' (1963: 15). 'Community' in this sense describes associational
groups sharing common cultures (Crompton 1987). The material wealth and power of those
in the 'great houses' indicates their dominant *class* situation; such groupings, however, also
maintain their dominance through the manner in which they deploy their *cultural* resources.

In a similar vein, Scott (1991; see also Scott 1996) has documented the manner in which
the British ruling class is reproduced through a network of social activities including private
London clubs, the residual activities of the London 'season', attendance at major sporting
and social events, and so on. The British public schools, as well as Oxbridge, also serve to
inculcate the kind of 'correct' behaviour which is likely to facilitate recruitment to superior
positions: 'Without any need for a consciously intended bias in recruitment, the established
'old boys' sponsor the recruitment through their networks of contacts of each new generation of old boys' (Scott 1991: 117). Status as prestige, therefore, plays a central role in the
processes of class formation and reproduction.

The ruling-class 'consciousness communities' briefly described above are clearly associated with a distinctive lifestyle, as Weber argued: 'In content, status honor is normally
expressed by the fact that above all a specific *style of life* can be expected' (Weber 1948: 187;
emphasis in original). Whereas 'class' is concerned with the production of goods, status is
concerned with their consumption. This has been described by Turner (1988: 66) as including 'the totality of cultural practices such as dress, speech, outlook and bodily dispositions'.
'Lifestyle' categories need not necessarily correspond exactly to consciousness communities (although they might reflect an aspiration to join them), but the two are clearly linked
to each other. However, the topic of consumption and its relation to class and stratification
also raises a broader range of issues. As we have seen, rising living standards in the West
have brought issues relating to consumption into sharper focus, and it is increasingly argued
that an investigation of consumption-related concerns should replace an outdated 'productivism' in class and stratification analysis. Although these arguments will by no means
be taken on board in their entirety, consumption in this broader sense – to include issues
such as, for example, the consumption of the environment and the construction of self-
identities – may be seen to have an impact on class and stratification systems. Besides the
role of specific lifestyles in the reproduction of established groupings, therefore, 'lifestyle'
in this broader sense may be seen as contributing to the emergence of newly differentiated
groups, and supplying new focuses for the articulation of interests and concerns. In particular, these issues have been argued to be central to the emergence and identification of the
'new middle classes', a topic which will be explored at greater length later in this chapter.

The third aspect of the status concept which may be identified is its use to describe non-
market-based claims to material entitlements or 'life chances'. Thus the term may be used to
describe pre-industrial 'estates' in contrast to 'classes', or the traditional, religiously based
claims of a particular caste grouping. Weber described status situation, in contrast to the economically determined class situation, as 'every typical component of the life fate of men that
is determined by a specific, positive or negative, social estimation of *honor*' (Weber 1948: 187).
Even in contemporary capitalist societies, the occupational order is socially, as well as economically, structured. An instance which has already been explored at some length is that of
gender. Occupational segregation means that the 'life fates' associated with particular occupations have been crucially affected by the sex of the likely occupant. The occupational order
is also shaped by explicit status claims. One example would be that of professionalism. Many

professional groups (such as doctors or lawyers) rest a part of their claim to material rewards on their undertaking *not* to exploit their skills and knowledge to their full market advantage, and to practise 'institutionalized altruism' in respect of their clients (Crompton 1990a).

One of the most frequently employed uses of the concept of status as entitlement, however, has been in T. H. Marshall's development of the concept of *citizenship*.[2] In an oft-quoted phrase, he asserted that 'in the twentieth century citizenship and the capitalist class system have been at war' with each other (1963: 87). Marshall identifies three elements of modern citizenship: civil, political and social. Civil citizenship describes those rights necessary for individual freedom – 'liberty of the person, freedom of speech, thought and faith, the right to own property and to conclude valid contracts, and the right to justice'. Political citizenship refers to the right to participate in the exercise of political power, which in contemporary societies corresponds to universal suffrage, without such restrictions as property qualifications, and the right to hold political office. These two aspects correspond, broadly, to the liberal ideal of citizenship. To these basic rights of the individual Marshall added a third dimension, social citizenship, which he described as 'the whole range from the right to a modicum of economic welfare and security to the right to share to the full in the social heritage and to live the life of a civilized being according to the standards prevailing in the society' (1963: 74). These rights, he argued, are associated with the development of the institutions of the modern welfare state.

Marshall developed his arguments through an analysis of recent British history. Chronologically, civil rights in England began to be established in the seventeenth century and were largely accomplished by the eighteenth century, during which equality before the law was established and the last elements of servile status were abolished, leaving individuals free to enter employment, to make contracts, to change employers and so on. Political rights were progressively attained by increasing numbers of the population during the nineteenth century, although full political citizenship for adults, including women, was not achieved until the twentieth. The major achievement of the twentieth century, however, lay in the development of the welfare state and the growth of social citizenship. Another important development spanning the nineteenth and twentieth centuries was the growth and legal recognition of trade unionism, which Marshall describes as a 'secondary system of industrial citizenship parallel with and supplementary to the system of political citizenship' (1963: 98).

The major contribution of citizenship to class abatement lies in its social dimension. The incorporation of social rights into the status of citizenship creates a universal right to real income which is not proportional to the market value of the claimant. The rights of social citizenship incorporate:

> no longer merely an attempt to abate the obvious nuisance of destitution in the lowest ranks of society. It is no longer content to raise the floor level in the basement of the social edifice, leaving the superstructure as it was. It has begun to remodel the whole building, and it might even end by converting a skyscraper into a bungalow.   (1963: 100–1)

In short, the rights of social citizenship make a significant contribution to 'the modern drive towards social equality' (1963: 73). Thus Marshall describes the development of social citizenship – that is, the right of all 'citizens' to services such as education and benefits such as those provided by the welfare state – to be one of the most important developments to affect stratification systems in the twentieth century. In practical terms, the rights of social citizenship may be seen as a key element of the 'mid-[twentieth-]century social compromise' (Crouch 1999: 53).

The exploration of the *interrelationship* of class and status requires a particular method-ological approach, as suggested above. Large data sets and sample surveys have had, and continue to have, a central place in empirical investigations of the 'class structure'. However, the investigation of the *processes* of class structuring – which will include the examination of aspects of status – requires a rather different approach. Similarly, although large data sets may provide useful attitudinal data relating to topics such as class consciousness, the dynam-ics of the processes and organizations which shape this consciousness can only be explored using an approach which views the social unit (the neighbourhood, the trade union, the workgroup, the political party) as a whole – that is, the *case study*.

Many empirical investigations of class processes which have employed the case-study method have been carried out by sociologists who have self-consciously embraced a 'realist' approach to their empirical work (Bagguley et al. 1989; Savage et al. 1992). However, the methodology of the case study is not specific to realism, and indeed, is central to the disci-pline of anthropology. Indeed, it may be argued that the case study still remains as the bedrock of empirical investigation in the social sciences, despite the fact that, as a research method, it has been variously dismissed as unscientific, capable only of generating, not testing, hypotheses, prone to bias and arbitrary interpretation, and so on.[3] The method-ological issues raised by these criticisms are complex. They will therefore be simply stated as follows. (a) The case-study approach should not be taken as synonymous only with qual-itative methods, or ethnography. A case study may be quantitative, as was, for example, the early investigation of the 'affluent worker' by Goldthorpe et al. (1968, 1969, 1970). Case studies of particular occupations have also frequently incorporated extensive programmes of interviewing and the quantitative analysis of interview data – as, for example, in Newby's study of agricultural workers (1977). (b) Case studies are in fact the *only* method whereby action (collective or otherwise) may be explored in its context; they facilitate theoreti-cal/logical thinking and thus *causal* explanations.

Often, cases are judged on their 'typicality', but, as Mitchell (1983) has argued, they should be judged on the basis of the validity of their analysis, rather than their typicality. In any event, case studies are not immune to empirical evaluation. Besides the relatively ortho-dox strategy of replication, the theoretical reasoning developed in the context of a particu-lar case study may be subjected to empirical scrutiny through a process of comparison, particularly cross-national comparisons (Pickvance 1992; for examples see Lamont 2000; Crompton 2006b). These points are made in order to emphasize that to advocate the method of the case study should not be taken to imply a recourse to mere description, or to abandon any attempt at the rigorous investigation of the topics at issue. Not only methodological, but theoretical, issues are raised by the examination of the interpenetration of economic and cultural dimensions in the constitution of class. This is, therefore, an appropriate point at which to examine Bourdieu's influential approach to class and stratification.

Bourdieu

Bourdieu's work has already been identified (chapter 3, p. 48) as advocating a 'unitary' approach in respect of 'action' and 'structure' in relation to class and stratification. He also lays a simultaneous emphasis on economic and cultural inputs into class differentiation.

Thus Sayer (2005: 73) describes Bourdieu's (1973) descriptive account of the French class structure as utilizing concrete (rather than abstract) concepts, as 'attempting . . . to synthesise diverse forms of differentiation'. Bourdieu's conceptualization of social class, therefore, is rather general, going beyond both Marx and Weber, who both defined class in respect of the economy – notwithstanding their very real theoretical differences. Bourdieu has been influenced by both Marx's and Weber's theoretical work. However, as Brubaker has argued, 'The conceptual space within which Bourdieu defines class is not that of production, but that of social relations in general. Class divisions are defined not by differing relations to the means of production, but by differing conditions of existence, differing systems of dispositions produced by differential conditioning, and differing endowments of power or capital' (1985: 761). For Bourdieu, class analysis cannot be reduced to the analysis of economic relations; rather, it simultaneously entails an analysis of symbolic relations. These broadly correspond to the status groups identified by Weber (Weininger 2005: 84).

Bourdieu's sociology begins from the assumption that (class) inequalities are reproduced, sustained and modified through the daily activities of individuals. Individuals themselves in their daily activities produce inequalities. This is not to say that inequality can be reduced to individual actions: rather, there is an interplay between embodied practices and institutional processes which together generate far-reaching inequalities of various kinds. Devine and Savage (2005: 13–14) summarize Bourdieu's approach as follows:

> Bourdieu explores this broad issue [of inequalities] through his conceptual trinity of field, capital and habitus. The concept of field has some of the same property as structure in the conventional sociology of stratification. Fields 'present themselves' as 'structured spaces of positions (or posts) whose properties depend on their position within these spaces and which can be analysed independently of the characteristics of their occupants' (Bourdieu 1993: 72). . . . Fields only operate when there are skilful people, interested in the stakes that field can offer, who are prepared and able to make it work. People have to be competent to operate in these fields . . . People's competence to participate in fields is critically related to their habitus, and their socially and historically acquired dispositions.

For Bourdieu, capital may be economic (material resources, property, income, etc.), cultural (cultural knowledge, credentials), social (connections, networks) or symbolic (respect and reputation).[4] Various combinations of capital constitute a *habitus* – a set of acquired patterns of thought, behaviour and taste, that is, a system of dispositions (or competences) shared by all individuals who are products of the same conditionings – economic, cultural, social and symbolic – which together empower (or otherwise) agents in their struggle for position within 'social space'. Thus within the dominant class, for example, Bourdieu draws a distinction between the bourgeoisie – high on economic capital, relatively low on cultural capital – and the intellectuals – high on cultural capital, relatively low on economic capital.

Bourdieu's emphasis on the diverse and socially constructed nature of 'classes' leads him to describe class boundaries as like 'a flame whose edges are in constant movement, oscillating around a line or surface' (1987: 13). Although, therefore, Bourdieu employs aggregate occupational categories in his vast ethnographic study of the French class structure (*Distinction*, 1986), he does not consider these categories to constitute 'classes', even though he recognizes that occupation is generally a 'good and economical' indicator of position in social space, and provides information on occupational effects such as the nature of work, the occupational milieu and 'its cultural and organizational specificities' (1986: 4).

Nevertheless, the classes so identified are not 'real, objectively constituted groups' (ibid.). The commonalities of their location, their similar conditions of existence and conditioning, might indeed result in similarities of attitude and practices. However, Bourdieu argues that:

> contrary to what Marxist theory [he is here making specific reference to Wright's attempt to construct a Marxist occupational class scheme] assumes, the movement from probability to reality, from theoretical class to practical class, is never given: even though they are supported by the sense of one's 'place' and by the affinity of habitus, the principles of vision and division of the social world at work in the construction of theoretical classes have to compete, *in reality*, with other principles, ethnic, racial or national, and more concretely still, with principles imposed by the ordinary experience of occupational, communal and local divisions and rivalries.   (1987: 7)

That is, class 'boundaries must be understood in terms of *social practices* rather than *theoretical conjuncture*' (Weininger 2005: 85).

In *Distinction* Bourdieu uses the class concept, therefore, as a generic name for social groups distinguished by their conditions of existence and their corresponding dispositions. As described above, the conditions of existence identified by Bourdieu include economic capital, which describes the level of material resources – income, property and so on – that may be possessed by an individual or a group, as well as cultural capital, which is largely acquired through education, and describes the intangible 'knowing' which, amongst other things, can both secure and perpetuate access to economic capital. Thus his approach leads to an exploration of the *processes* of social differentiation which goes beyond the mere mapping of tastes. The exploration of these processes requires the interpretation of the aggregate-level association between occupational groups and patterns of consumption, as well as the development of cultural case studies which have also focused upon the uncovering of causal links.

Bourdieu's work, therefore, is primarily concerned with the active processes of class structuring, or class formation. The 'struggles of the field', as different groups position and reposition themselves, are not, however, necessarily deliberate or conscious, nor is the acquisition of habitus. Rather, people unconsciously align themselves with others in similar social positions, and particular tastes (in food, music, entertainment, etc.) are genuinely preferred to those of other groups. Nevertheless, the acquisition of a particular habitus is accompanied by the evolution of very real structures of social and economic advantage and disadvantage. For example: 'Middle-class children, by virtue of their upbringing, already have reserves of the knowledge (of "high" culture) and competences (abstract reasoning) which are rewarded in examination, and so are always likely to do better than equally bright, hard-working working-class children . . . class advantage is embedded in the reward system' (Bottero 2005: 152–3). In a similar vein, working-class parents may hesitate to send their children to schools they perceive as 'posh' or inappropriate, even though such schools may be academically successful (Reay 1998; class differences in educational achievement will be a major topic of our next chapter).

'Struggles of the field' are not just about the positioning of individuals and groups, but also about establishing *what* is to be valued, that is, symbolic capital (Skeggs 2004). Bourdieu (1991) argues that human communication (or discourse) is not simply about information exchange and mutual understanding, but also about the pursuit of symbolic profit – the 'symbolic economy' – through which particular characteristics are designated as being of particular repute and associated with particular groups (or classes). From this perspective, discourse is constitutive of social groupings, in that it not only represents and reproduces systems of belief and power, but also establishes and maintains structures of inequality and privilege as it defines the 'valuable' and the 'not valuable' – and 'not valuable' characteristics are invariably associated with 'inferior' social groupings. For example, Skeggs (2004: 4) describes how in the eighteenth and nineteenth centuries the bourgeoisie sought to distance themselves from both the 'decadent' aristocracy and the unruly hordes (or 'great unwashed') below: 'Dirt and waste, sexuality and contagion, danger and disorder, degeneracy and pathology, became the moral evaluations by which the working-class were coded and became known and are still reproduced today.' Thus 'symbolic power' (the capacity to define the good and valuable) can also constitute 'symbolic violence' via the 'dis-identification' of inferior groups.

Bourdieu's approach has been enormously influential across a range of different fields (no pun intended) in sociology and cultural studies (the sociology of the body, of art, discourse analysis, the media), as well as class and stratification. At the most general level, it is impossible to disagree with the approach he articulates. People *are* knowledgeable individuals whose behaviour is informed by the rules and strategies of the game (or field) they are playing. These rules *do* become codified and can operate as constraints – although, as they were created by humans in the first place, the rules can also be changed or modified. Individuals and groups *do* use these resources (economic, cultural, social and symbolic) in a continuing struggle for advantage that will also (in part) define what is to be seen as 'valuable'. These struggles *will* result in devaluation, and disadvantage, for some individuals and groups.

However, Bourdieu's approach has been criticized as being overly reproductionist, and indeed, reductionist and tautological (Calhoun 2003; Jenkins 1992). That is, advantages are generated through being in a position of advantage, and the dominant classes always win. Individuals and groups are described, in Bourdieu's analyses, as being locked into cycles of deprivation and disadvantage, as well as their opposite, and it might be argued that there can be little possibility of social change.[5] Moreover (and following from this), despite Bourdieu's apparent emphasis on the importance of transcending the binaries of action/structure, subjectivism and objectivism, his analysis ultimately reverts to the embedded structures of material and cultural inequalities and is thus in fact determinist. Habitus guides people to choose particular routes and rewards (for example, to turn down a place at a prestigious university; see Reay et al. 2001) even if it can be argued to be not in their 'best' interest. Moreover, habitus means that power is often 'misrecognized' – inequalities are not seen as a power relation, but, via the power of symbolic recognition, as legitimate demands for deference and obedience. The parallels between Bourdieu's concept of 'misrecognition' and the Marxist notion of 'false consciousness' are very apparent, and subject to similar kinds of criticism.[6]

Thus, it has been argued, despite Bourdieu's protestations, that he underestimates people's capacities for agency and reflexivity. That is, habitus involves resistance, as well as compliance. As Sayer (2005: 30) argues: 'it is possible for actors not only to deliberate on their situation and on what they have become, but to strive to change their own habitus'. Moreover, although it is true that individuals do struggle for advantage in the social field, these struggles are not invariably self-interested. Groups 'also struggle for things which they value for their own sake, regardless of whether they bring them advantage vis-à-vis others' (Sayer 2005: 100). Thus, as Sayer argues, the micro-politics of the social field include normative agendas – for example, feminist and anti-feminist, left-leaning and right-leaning – that are 'not merely about getting to the top of the pile but about changing the nature of the social order' (ibid.).

Bourdieu's perspective on cultural hierarchies, and what is valued, has also been criticized. His distinction between 'high' and 'low' cultures has been challenged (Bottero 2005: 155). People take pleasure in particular cultural items and practices for their own sake – as Sayer (2005: 109) has remarked, a BMW may be purchased in order to demonstrate that its owner has 'arrived', but: 'If BMWs were unreliable and awful to drive they would not bring their owners any distinction.' Mass cultures, aimed at the widest possible audience, are weakly differentiated and relatively non-hierarchical. Indeed, some have argued that the distinctions between 'high' and 'low' cultures have collapsed, and a cultural 'omnivorousness' is undermining hierarchical cultural rankings (Peterson and Kern 1996; this argument might be made in respect of the changing cultural significance of Association Football, as discussed in chapter 1). Against this view, it has been suggested that a capacity for cultural 'omnivorousness' is itself a reflection of the more extensive networks and knowledge of dominant groups (see the discussion of the 'new middle classes' below). Another argument against the fixedness of 'high' and 'low' cultures is the fact that cultural hierarchies also vary cross-nationally. Lamont's (1992) comparative work, for example, has argued that cultural boundaries and hierarchies are stronger in France than in the US, where there was far less agreement (amongst upper-class men) about what constituted 'acceptable' cultural behaviour.

Many critical commentaries on Bourdieu, therefore, suggest that the analytical frameworks he has developed are in fact as 'determinist' as the approaches to 'class analysis' he criticizes. What *is* distinctive, however, is his emphasis on the importance of cultural factors in the creation and reproduction of class inequalities – indeed, the simultaneous constitution of economic and cultural differentiation. In the rest of this chapter, therefore, we will, first, discuss the manner in which it has been argued that consumption practices have reconstituted the 'new middle class'. Second, we will briefly review contemporary work on the ethnography of the working class. One of the most important applications of Bourdieu's thinking has been in the sociology of education, and this will be discussed in the next chapter of this book.

The 'new middle classes'

As we have seen in previous chapters, shifts in the occupational structure (deindustrialization, technological change, the growth of the service economy) have resulted in an increase in those kinds of occupations which have always been categorized as 'middle-class' – particularly administrative, professional and managerial occupations – as well as the expansion of new occupations such as IT experts, call-centre workers and psychotherapists. Thus the term 'middle-class' encompasses a wide variety of occupational groupings. It might include relatively low-level service employees – such as, for example, first-line managers in the 'hospitality industry' (hotels and restaurants) – as well as the new service professionals – social workers, librarians, physiotherapists – associated with the growth and development of the welfare state.

This diversity of 'middle-class' occupations has been cited in arguments to the effect that the 'middle class' cannot be usefully regarded as a single entity, but is a multitude of fractions with (often) conflicting interests – between men and women, between public-service and private-sector employees (Duke and Edgell 1987; Savage et al. 1992). Such arguments would appear to be contradicted by the assertion, particularly by Goldthorpe (1980; 1987), that the 'service class' is in fact securing and consolidating its advantaged position, and is thus a source of societal stability. In fact, it is possible for both sets of arguments to be correct. As we shall see, there is much fragmentation and instability between the different groupings that go to make up the 'middle classes'. Nevertheless, it is also the case that the relatively privileged are in a better position both to defend their own interests, and to pass them on to their descendants. Thus it is not surprising that a nominally defined grouping of the relatively privileged – such as Goldthorpe's 'service class' – should prove, in aggregate, more efficient at passing on their occupational status to their children than the less privileged are at actually *improving* the occupational status of their offspring, as Goldthorpe's studies of social mobility have demonstrated (chapter 7). It is also not particularly unusual for the better-off to wish to defend the status quo.

The way in which different theorists have approached the topic of the new middle class(es) has reflected the occupational diversity within these groupings. Marxists (and those influenced by Marx's work, such as Abercrombie and Urry 1983) have distinguished between the routine, deskilled, non-manual workers and the upper levels of management; these higher levels would be located by Wright in the bourgeoisie, by Abercrombie and Urry in the 'service class'. Wright's distinction between 'skill' and 'organizational' assets corresponds to the established sociological distinction between 'managers' and 'professionals', and this has been taken up by Savage et al. (1992; see also Butler and Savage 1996). The categories of Weberian class analysis have distinguished between 'service', 'subaltern service' and 'intermediate' locations in the occupational structure (Goldthorpe 1980, 1987). A common feature of these established frameworks of class analysis, whether Marxist or Weberian, is that employment, production and/or market relationships are regarded as crucial to the placement of the 'class'. Thus implicitly the class placement of these newly emerging groups is decided with reference to conventional, *economically* derived criteria of class location, and much of the discussion relating to occupational and employment-based class schemes has been concerned with whether newly emerging occupations and jobs can be fitted into *existing* occupational classifications (Wright, for example, has explicitly identified this as one of the major foci of his research).

Approaches influenced by Bourdieu, however, are more focused on the new groupings emerging out of the struggle for position within the field or social space. As we have seen in this book, 'postmodern' theorists have argued that in the present era it is increasingly cultural, rather than economic, factors which determine societal structuring. Others have argued that, rather than 'culture' having become *more* significant, cultural discourses have *always* been significant in the constitution of classes (Skeggs 2004). In relation to the former stance, it is argued that there has recently been a 'general liberation of stratification from social-structural milieux so that it becomes precisely cultural rather than social, focusing on life style rather than life chances, on consumption rather than production, and on values rather than interests. The emerging pattern of stratification will be fluid and shifting as commitments, tastes, and fashions change' (Waters 1996: 80). Thus within the sociology of consumption, there have developed arguments to the effect that the growth of these 'new middle-class' occupational categories is not a response to the changing requirements of the economy. Rather, their rise to prominence should be seen as an outcome of the wider cultural changes which have created demands for the satisfaction of new needs. Those whose occupations are concerned with the satisfaction of these needs are also viewed as having taken an *active* role in both the identification of the needs and the manner in which they are met.[7]

'Bourdieuian' approaches to the new middle classes (Featherstone 1987; Lash and Urry 1987; Wynne 1990; Savage et al. 1992) draw heavily on Bourdieu's massive empirical mapping of tastes and behaviour in France (*Distinction*, 1986), first published in 1979. Within the dominant class, as we have seen, Bourdieu draws a basic distinction between the bourgeoisie – high on economic capital, relatively low on cultural capital – and the intellectuals – high on cultural capital, relatively low on economic capital. Tastes within these groupings differ; whereas the intellectuals have a preference for aesthetic modernism, bourgeois taste tends towards the baroque and flamboyant. The younger elements within the bourgeoisie, however, tend to be high on both economic and cultural capital – the bourgeoisie in France having retained their children's positions by, amongst other things, the strategic use of the Grandes Ecoles (elite universities) and the US business schools. Thus the new bourgeoisie, writes Bourdieu:

> is the initiator of the ethical retooling required by the new economy from which it draws its power and profits, whose functioning depends as much on the production of needs and consumers as on the production of goods. The new logic of the economy rejects the aesthetic ethic of production and accumulation, based on abstinence, sobriety, saving and calculation, in favour of a hedonistic morality of consumption, based on credit, spending and enjoyment. (1986: 310)

There is in this argument of Bourdieu's a clear parallel with those developed by Bell in *The Cultural Contradictions of Capitalism* (1976). Bell argued that contemporary American society is comprised of three distinct realms – the economic, the political and the cultural – each of which is governed by a different 'axial principle'. The culture of modernism sought to substitute for religion or morality an aesthetic justification for life, but in sharp contrast to this postmodernism has completely substituted the *instinctual*. Thus impulse and pleasure alone are considered as real and life-affirming. As a consequence, American capitalism has lost its traditional legitimacy, which was based on a system of reward rooted in the Protestant sanctification of work, and 'the hedonism as a way of life promoted by the marketing system of business, constitutes the cultural contradiction of capitalism' (Bell 1976: 84).

However, whereas the logic of Bell's arguments suggests the need for some kind of moral renewal, as we have seen, Bourdieu's analysis is more concerned with the way in which different groups struggle for position within the changing social space – a space which they are simultaneously creating. Bourdieu suggests that in their struggles to establish their dominance, the new bourgeoisie finds a natural ally, both economically and politically, in the 'new petite [petty] bourgeoisie'. This group 'recognizes in the new bourgeoisie the embodiment of its human ideal' – the 'dynamic' executive – and 'collaborates enthusiastically in imposing the new ethical norms (especially as regards consumption) and the corresponding needs' (1986: 366). Thus the new petty bourgeoisie is represented in occupations involving presentation and representation, and in all institutions providing symbolic goods and services, cultural production and organization. Such occupations would include sales, marketing, advertising, public relations, fashion, interior design, as well as journalism and other media employment, craft work, etc. Occupations concerned with bodily and emotional regulation would also be included – vocational guidance, youth and play leaders, sports and exercise experts, and quasi-medical professions such as dietitians, psychotherapists, marriage guidance counsellors and physiotherapists (1986: 359). These 'indeterminate' positions, argues Bourdieu, are attractive to those individuals endowed with a strong cultural capital (that is, superior family background) imperfectly converted into educational capital, or rising individuals who have not obtained completely the educational capital needed for the top positions, and lack the cultural and social capital required to make this final leap. Thus the new petty bourgeoisie is split between the *déclassé* and the upwardly mobile.

These 'need merchants', 'new cultural intermediaries', as Bourdieu describes them, act as a transmission belt to pull into the race for consumption and competition those from whom it means to distinguish itself (1986: 365). In a similar vein, Lash and Urry (1987) draw upon the insights of Baudrillard (1972) to argue that in contemporary consumer capitalism we no longer consume products, but *signs*; thus the 'new petite bourgeoisie' (for Lash and Urry part of the lower echelons of the 'service class') have developed as 'sign-producers', to some extent displacing the 'commodity-producers' of 'organized' capitalism. Such groups and individuals are using their cultural capital to establish new systems of classification which actively *create* the jobs to suit their ambitions. Featherstone (1991) emphasizes the rapid inflation in consumer tastes, as dominant tastes (or 'positional goods') are brought within the reach of an ever-widening circle of consumers. Foreign holidays, cheap champagne, designer sportswear – all these goods lose their relative cultural value as they become more accessible, and in the 'leap-frogging social race to maintain recognisable distinctions', the cultural producers, the 'specialists in symbolic production', come into their own (1991: 89).

Bourdieu has drawn a distinction between the *déclassé* and the upwardly mobile within the new petty bourgeoisie. Featherstone emphasizes the difference – which may be a source of conflict – between the 'economic' and the 'cultural' producers, differentiated by their relative possession of economic and cultural capital. Both of these groups may be upwardly mobile but, whereas the 'culturally' upwardly mobile have achieved such mobility through formal educational routes followed by entry into professional occupations, the 'economically' mobile may lack such qualifications, having 'made the grade' through work–life mobility, usually in the private sector. Wynne (1990) has described the differentiation of the lifestyles of these two groups, which broadly reflect the kinds of differences of taste which Bourdieu identified between the bourgeoisie and the intellectuals. The 'economic' petty bourgeois are described by Wynne as the 'drinkers', characterized by a leisure style which besides regular convivial drinking includes family holidays taken in hotel packages, eating out at steakhouses, entertainment preferences for musical comedy and large spectacle, and a preference for comfort and tradition in home furnishing. In contrast, the 'cultural' 'sporters' are more preoccupied with style, rather than comfort, and more likely to holiday in a *gîte* or make other personal arrangements, to join hobby clubs and voluntary associations, and to patronize avant-garde theatre and classical music concerts. Thus through their very different lifestyles, the economic and the cultural petty bourgeois are constructing and affirming their social position.

Work by Savage et al. (1992) has developed further this mapping of cultural (consumption) tastes on to different sections of the middle class. Public-sector professionals (whose tastes closely resemble those of the 'sporters' identified by Wynne) are revealed, by market research surveys, to have an 'ascetic' lifestyle which is characterized by sport, healthy living and a relatively low consumption of alcohol, combined with 'high-cultural' activities such as plays, classical music and contemporary dance. This group is high on cultural, but low on economic, capital. A further group identified by Savage et al. corresponds broadly to the 'drinkers' identified by Wynne. Managers and government bureaucrats, on the other hand, are characterized by 'undistinctive' patterns of consumption, having average or below average consumption scores on high culture and exercise alike, and showing a preference for a cleaned-up version of the 'heritage' or 'countryside' tradition in their consumption patterns. As Savage et al. note, this 'undistinctive' group is not identified within Bourdieu's framework, perhaps because of the anti-intellectualism which has characterized managerial groupings in Britain, in some contrast to France.

The third group of middle-class consumers identified by Savage et al. are the 'postmoderns', the cultural 'omnivores'. This postmodern lifestyle is characterized by an absence of a single organizing principle in respect of consumption: 'high extravagance goes along with a culture of the body: appreciation of high cultural forms of art such as opera and classical music exists cheek by jowl with an interest in disco dancing or stock car racing' (1992: 108). These patterns may be broadly associated with the 'hedonism' identified (and lamented) by Bell, as well as with the 'new petite bourgeoisie' described by Bourdieu. However, Savage et al. emphasize that these consumption patterns are found not just amongst the newer occupations centred upon the cultivation of the body and the emotions, but amongst professionally educated private-sector workers more generally: 'barristers, accountants and surveyors partake in the post-modern lifestyle as much as sex therapists or advertising agents' (1992: 128). Cultural assets have been commodified, and practices considered to have an 'auratic' (or 'special') quality by previous generations – opera, skiing holidays, historic housing (albeit a luxury conversion or newly built in a traditional style) – are now accessible to those who have the money to pay for them.

More recently, Savage and his colleagues (Le Roux et al. 2007) have carried out a very similar mapping of class and cultural practices in Britain to that of Bourdieu (1986) in France. Their data (which gathers information on tastes and preferences across a wide range of topics including music, art, film, television, reading, sport and other leisure practices) suggests a considerable distance, in cultural terms, between elements of the 'service class' (see table 4.2, chapter 4). In particular, lower managers, in terms of their consumption and leisure practices, are much closer to 'intermediate' groupings than to higher managers and professionals. Their findings lead them to suggest that, once the cultural dimension of class formation has been incorporated into the analysis, it is more realistic to identify a rather smaller 'service' class, of professionals and higher managers alone, within the occupational structure. Their analysis suggests that, with this adjustment, occupational 'classes' map quite closely onto cultural practices, thus confirming a 'Bourdieuian' perspective. This would be contested by Chan and Goldthorpe (2007).

The cultural fragmentation within the middle class, therefore, reflects the economic and spatial fragmentation within these groupings which had already been identified by those working within more orthodox frameworks of 'class analysis' (Savage et al. 1988, 1992; Crompton 1992). What those writers who have emphasized the significance of the development of 'postmodernism' and associated lifestyles argue, however, is that (a) culture should be regarded as an *independent* variable in the construction and consolidation of class position or 'habitus', and (b) the hyperinflation of symbols associated with the growth of consumer capitalism has, relatively, increased the significance of culture in the processes of class structuring. A major consequence of these changes is the development within the middle occupational stratum of a 'cultural mass' of symbol producers. These changes have also had political consequences which are succinctly summarized by Harvey:

The politics of the cultural mass are . . . important, since they are in the business of defining the symbolic order through the production of images for everyone. The more it turns in upon itself, or the more it sides with this or that dominant class in society, the more the prevailing sense of the symbolic and moral order tends to shift . . . the cultural mass drew heavily upon the working-class movement for its cultural identity in the 1960s, but the attack upon, and decline of, the latter from the early 1970s onwards cut loose the cultural mass, which then shaped its own identity around its own concerns with money power, individualism, entrepreneurialism, and the like.   (1990: 348)

These arguments are highly suggestive, but they raise important questions relating to both causality and the permanence – or otherwise – of their impact. Have cultural changes actually *caused* the neo-liberal turn to 'marketization' – of which the commodification of culture may be regarded as one aspect – which has taken place over the last two decades? Or might it be that a political emphasis upon the overwhelming legitimacy of 'market forces' has created a cultural anomie, a situation exceptionally favourable to the challenging and commodification of normative cultural judgements of all kinds? Savage et al.'s arguments (see also Savage 2000) suggest the latter interpretation. They argue that the significance of bureaucratic structures to middle-class careers is declining as firms increasingly use market mechanisms, rather than managerial hierarchies, to structure their activities, externalizing aspects of production, drawing on the labour of specialists and so on (the so-called 'flexible firm'). They also argue that in Britain, the role of the state in both legitimating cultural assets and providing direct employment to large numbers of professional workers has changed to one of underwriting market provision. These twin factors, they suggest, have changed the basis of the legitimation of cultural assets: 'Increasingly cultural assets can be legitimised through their role in defining and perpetuating consumer cultures associated with private commodity production. Those receptive to the post-modern lifestyle increasingly look to the market to legitimate and reward their cultural assets' (Savage et al. 1992: 215).

The middle classes, therefore, have been seen as becoming increasingly fragmented, and as a consequence even more unlikely to develop any kind of conscious *collective* social (or 'class') identity. However, it may be suggested that to the extent that the middle classes *have* manifested forms of collective organization, this has usually been in order to protect their individual interests – as in, for example, the activities of professional groups (Freidson 1986; Grusky and Sorensen 1998).[8] In recent years, feelings of employment insecurity amongst the middle classes have intensified – even though they have actually improved their earnings situation relative to the lowest paid. Much anxiety, nevertheless, centres on the bureaucratic career, as organizations downsize and 'delayer', and the ethos of the 'lean corporation' is promulgated (Womack et al. 1990). Industries which once were the locus of the classic (male) bureaucratic career, such as retail banking, have been transformed. The clearing banks[9] once provided a stable route for the reasonably qualified (GCSE-level) school leaver to progress from clerical to managerial level, and this state of affairs persisted into the 1980s (Crompton and Jones 1984). Today, however, these organizations have been transformed. Recruitment has been stratified according to educational level and, realistically, only those recruited to managerial trainee grades (requiring relatively high levels of pre-entry qualification) will get promoted to the higher levels. The old structure of hierarchical grades has been transformed, and job mobility is now as likely to be sideways (in order to enhance an individual's 'skill portfolio') as upwards (Crompton 1989a; Halford and Savage 1995; Crompton et al. 2003; see also chapter 8). As banks face a worsening financial climate, there have, increasingly, been redundancies associated with organizational restructuring.

Aggregate data suggests that job insecurity is not in fact on the increase (Nolan 2003). However, there is increasing evidence that work *intensity* has grown for those in 'middle-class' occupations (Burchell et al. 2002). Particularly in neo-liberal economic regimes, working hours can be extremely long in some managerial and professional occupations (Gershuny 2005). It is suggested that this reflects a culture of 'presentism', that is, the need to demonstrate a level of organizational commitment which both justifies continuing employment and indicates suitability for promotion. Increased competition and job mobility, both internal and external, are likely to lead to increasing individuation (as described by Beck 1992). It may be suggested that older generations of the middle classes had a collective interest in preserving the stable hierarchies which were important mechanisms in preserving their individual advantages. Indeed, the level of collective representation in the clearing banks – the 'aristocracy' of clerks – was in fact quite high, although it was not accompanied by any radical ideology (Lockwood 1958; Blackburn 1967). Contemporary organizational change and development, however, have reduced even further the likelihood that the expanding middle classes might be a source of radicalism – despite the hopes of left-leaning social scientists of the 1960s and 1970s (Crompton 1979; Gouldner 1979; Walker 1979).

The contemporary ethnography of the working class

Much research in this area has focused on the pain, injury and subsequent disidentification experienced by the negatively inscribed 'working classes', low in economic, cultural, social and symbolic capital (Rubin 1976; Sennett and Cobb 1973). From the nineteenth century, the working classes had been seen as internally differentiated between the 'undeserving' and 'deserving' poor, the 'roughs' and the 'respectables'. Whereas the former were seen as work-shy and bordering on the criminal, the latter were held up as examples of hard work, morality and sobriety. However, hard work, morality and sobriety do not necessarily prevent these negatively inscribed groupings from the painful consequences of their disidentification.

This perspective is prominent in one of Bourdieu's later books, *The Weight of the World* (1993, translated 1999, subtitled *Social Suffering in Contemporary Society*). It is composed largely of transcripts of interviews (in France) with respondents living in marginal locations or circumstances – low-income housing developments, 'difficult' schools, in temporary work, struggling with agricultural decline, facing old age and disability. Although these people do not necessarily experience the extremes of material deprivation, their 'positional suffering' (Bourdieu 1999: 4) is keenly felt – they know they occupy 'inferior, obscure' positions in a 'privileged universe'. Not all interviewees are working-class, and in these respondents' cases marginality stems rather from divorce, physical handicap or mental breakdown, or their political views.

The Weight of the World was a considerable popular success and was associated with Bourdieu's turn to radical politics in the 1990s. The book seeks to understand 'ordinary suffering'. Through this understanding, explanation is achieved. The interviewers' sociological insight 'allows one to perceive and monitor *on the spot* . . . the effects of the social structure within which it is occurring' (Bourdieu 1999: 608). Each interview is, in a sense, a case study of positional suffering. As in our discussion of the case-study method above, the interviewers' capacities to imagine themselves in the places of their subjects facilitates a theoretical reasoning (Mitchell 1983) that uncovers the structural causes of suffering (Bourdieu 1999: 628). This understanding is 'political' for both the sociologist and the interviewee. As Bourdieu (1999: 629) puts it:

> producing awareness of these mechanisms that make life painful, even unliveable, does not neutralise them . . . but . . . one has to acknowledge the effect it can have in allowing those who suffer to find out that their suffering can be imputed to social causes and thus to feel exonerated; and in making generally known the social origin, collectively hidden, of unhappiness in all its forms, including the most intimate, the most secret.

The 'structural causes of suffering' that Bourdieu seeks to uncover are those following upon the introduction of neo-liberal policies in France – during a period in which there was a nominally socialist president. As has been argued in previous chapters, the introduction of neo-liberal policies is indeed accompanied by widening inequalities (an issue to which we will return in chapter 8) – although it may be argued that in France, their impact was considerably less than in countries like Britain and the United States. However, and following Bourdieu's own approach, the 'positional suffering' he identifies is by no means simply a consequence of policy changes, as other ethnographies informed by Bourdieu's work demonstrate. Skeggs's (1997) research on white working-class women in Britain demonstrated that they were both 'lacking' in economic and cultural capital and acutely aware of their situation. Her research began at a time of high unemployment (the early 1980s), and was carried out amongst young women attending Community Care courses at a local further education college:[10] 'I couldn't get a job, it's as simple as that and this was the easiest course to get on without any qualifications the careers officer said, he gave me the form. It was something to do' (Skeggs 1997: 58). These young women were uncomfortable talking about 'class', and defined the 'working class' as 'rough', the 'poorest of the poor': 'They're rough. You can always tell. Rough, you know, the women are common as muck you know, always have a fag in their mouths, the men are dead rough' (Skeggs 1997: 75). Therefore, Skeggs argues, these women disidentified themselves as 'working-class' and made considerable efforts not to be recognized as the 'roughs' they so despised. What they sought above all was *respectability*, that is, *not* to be identified as lower- (working-) class. Simultaneously, they were also painfully aware of their own negative positioning and resented what they saw as negative (working-class) identifications by others: 'The women know they are being positioned as contagious, not-belonging or dirty . . . They do not believe they have the same entitlements, the access to the same rights' (Skeggs 1997: 93).

'Class' is central to Skeggs's analysis, but her arguments suggest that misrecognition in a sense 'denies' class rights to those at the bottom. Unlike the middle classes, they are unable to 'propertize' (i.e. give value to) themselves and their culture and are therefore without worth (Skeggs 2004: 176). In contrast, Lamont's (2000) ethnography of American and French working men concludes that class remains an important basis for collective identity amongst workers.[11] White American working-class men identify themselves as hardworking and straightforward (the disciplined self), distinguishing themselves from those above (the middle classes), who are seen as lacking in integrity and straightforwardness. Those below – black Americans – were often seen as lazy and therefore as holding the wrong values. African

Americans also see the middle classes as lacking in loyalty (integrity), but think of themselves as informed by a greater spirit of community and collectivity than whites (including the white working class). Working-class men used a rhetoric of class to talk about the differences between 'our kind of people' and others. Judgements were made on the basis of 'worth', and Lamont's interviewees certainly did not regard themselves as 'worthless', as might be implied by Skeggs's arguments.

Nevertheless, other ethnographies have demonstrated that 'those who cannot represent the nature of their own lives because they are excluded from the institutions of culture' (Charlesworth 2007: 4–5) do come to exist in a state of utter worthlessness. Charlesworth's interviews with unemployed (or sub-employed) men in South Yorkshire (a region devastated by the destruction of the mining industry in the 1980s) reveal that existences 'made asocial by a lack of value and the inability to find meaningful public relational forms through employment and status' (Charlesworth 2007: 9) force the individual into 'a privatised world that cannot be escaped': 'Nobody wants yer if yer an't got any money, 'cos yer no use to them, that's ahr it is.' In these blasted communities, drug-taking and criminality are rife, and the men interviewed by Charlesworth desperately attempt not to care, to want nothing, to be nothing and thereby be content with being nothing.

Our brief discussion has focused on working-class ethnographies. One feature they have in common is that 'class' remains a salient feature of everyday lives – even as it is sometimes denied. The difference lies in the conclusions drawn from these studies (and it should be remembered that they focused on rather different groups within the working class). Skeggs and Charlesworth (and to some extent Bourdieu) see 'working-classness' as a stigmatized identity that can result in the negation of 'identity' itself – the poverty of the habitus is such that, in the case of Charlesworth's respondents in particular, a sense of hopelessness prevails and capacities for agency and reflexivity are virtually non-existent. Skeggs (2004, 2005) argues that even though the working class is represented as having no value, it may nevertheless be plundered by middle-class cultural omnivores, as aspects of working-class culture (sexuality, the frisson of danger associated with criminality) are used as 'mobile resources' in middle-class careers (for example, in media representations; Skeggs 2005: 59–60).

In contrast, Lamont and others (see Devine 2004; Savage 2000) have drawn attention to the fact that amongst the working classes, habitus can be empowering. As Sayer (2005: 30) has noted, many of the interviews in *The Weight of the World* testify to the struggles of individuals to transform their circumstances, examples of which are also evident in many of Lamont's interviews: 'I went to one of my wholesale distributors yesterday . . . I saw all these guys coming in, that were wearing jeans and sneakers and everything else and I just thought that I used to be in that position. I used to be there and look at who I am now' (Lamont 2000: 98; the interviewee is now a salesman). More generally, working-class informants interviewed in other studies describe themselves as 'ordinary working people', somewhere in the middle, a perspective that continues to offer some positive evaluations of working-class identification (Savage 2000: 116).

A Bourdieuian approach, therefore, can illuminate resistance as well as reproduction, hope as well as hopeless misery. As has been noted, these findings will depend, in some large part, on the particular fraction of the 'working classes' that is being researched. However, the rather negative conclusions that have been drawn from some ethnographies have led to more general criticisms of 'culturalist' approaches to class analysis. If class reproduction is seen to be largely a consequence of a lack of aspirations, motivations, etc. deriving from the absence of cultural capital then this may be seen as endorsing 'culture of poverty' arguments, which effectively 'blame the victims' for their low aspirations and stunted lives (Walker 1990).

More generally, Fraser (2000) has argued that in 'culturalist' theories of contemporary society, within which economic inequality and cultural hierarchy are seen to be seamlessly fused, there is an all-too-present danger of 'displacement'. That is, economic inequalities are effectively subsumed within (displaced onto) cultural concerns, and within this model: 'to revalue unjustly devalued identities is simultaneously to attack the deep sources of economic inequality; (and) no explicit politics of redistribution is needed' (2000: 111). Such 'vulgar culturalism', Fraser argues, is nothing more than the mirror image of the 'vulgar economism' that saw cultural or status differences as deriving directly from economic inequalities. However, the current reality in capitalist societies is that the economic mechanisms of distribution are at least partially decoupled from cultural patterns. For example, if a white UK male loses his job because production is relocated to China, this is not because the owners and controllers of capital think of the Chinese as culturally superior (or inferior).

Fraser suggests that a rethinking of these theoretical tensions between redistribution and recognition politics may be resolved by returning to the Weberian distinction between 'class' and 'status'. Class involves relationships that are constituted in economic terms as specific 'market situations', while status relations involve 'socially entrenched patterns of cultural value . . . culturally defined categories of social actors' (2000: 117). For Fraser, social justice has to be seen, on this basis, as involving the two analytically distinct dimensions of distribution and recognition, that is, 'class' and 'status' (this position that has many parallels with that of Scott; see p. 90).

Fraser's solution, therefore, endorses an analytical dualism that has been consistently argued for in this book, a perspective that is rather different from that of Bourdieu (although his work is not consistent on this point; see Crompton and Scott 2005). These debates will be taken up in the next chapter of this book, on social mobility and educational opportunity. However, we will first, in our conclusions to this chapter, briefly discuss whether materialist and culturalist accounts of class can be synthesized – or, in other words, whether a 'unitary' account of class analysis may yet be a possibility.

Discussion and conclusions: a new synthesis?

In our discussion of Bourdieu, and his approach to class and inequality, we have returned to some of the issues in sociological theory that were raised in chapter 2 (p. 24) – that is, the distinctions between agency and structure, economy and culture, that have proved to be so problematic in attempts to develop a unified theory of class and stratification (or, for that matter, a unified approach within the social sciences more generally). Bourdieu nails his colours very firmly to the anti-positivist mast – referring with some scepticism, for example, to the 'positivist dream of an epistemological stage of perfect innocence' (1999: 608) – and insists that scientific 'facts' do not 'exist' outside of everyday practice. In this book, we have refused to take up either a 'positivist' or a 'humanist' stance. We have argued for a pluralist, not to say pragmatic, approach to the study of class and stratification. This has not been to argue that 'anything goes', that is, that all approaches to the topic are equally valid and there is no basis on which to choose between them. Far from it. Rather, it has been argued as follows:

- Broadly conceived, agency and structure, 'economic' and 'cultural' structures and processes, contribute to the production and reproduction of concrete class inequalities.
- Although empirically these factors are intertwined, nevertheless they can be separately identified for the purposes of investigation and research (a position described in this book as 'analytical dualism').
- Moreover, although authors such as Bottero (2005: 54) have described the history of social analysis as 'a graveyard of failed attempts to balance the terms of these binaries [i.e. agency and structure, 'economic' and 'cultural']. In practice, one side or the other has become dominant', *this 'failure' is not in fact problematic*. As inequalities have complex origins, it is perfectly possible that particular circumstances and cases might indeed be *primarily* explained by agency *or* structure, economy *or* culture.
- Therefore, as Wright (2005: 180) has argued (and as has been argued in previous editions of this book), different approaches ('theories') of class and stratification are more or less appropriate to the investigation of the range of different questions and topics that might be addressed within the broad field of 'class analysis'.

Two further points have also been argued:

- Class inequalities have a negative impact on human flourishing and increase suffering.
- If we wish to address these issues in policy terms, then it is important that we are able to identify their causes. These have to be established empirically.

This means working with frameworks and approaches which at times might seem contradictory, but are nevertheless necessary in order to understand the complex whole – hence the label of 'positive pluralism'. This position may be further illuminated via a discussion of a recent attempt to develop a 'unitary' approach to class reproduction that incorporates both 'economic' and 'cultural' dimensions – Savage et al.'s (2005) development of the CARs (capitals, assets, resources) approach.

Savage et al. (2005: 32) begin by noting that: 'since the 1980s defenders of class analysis have shifted their foundations away from [a] "macro" emphasis on the division of labour towards a more "micro" interest in how the effects of class are produced through individual actions drawing variously on "assets" . . . "capitals" . . . or "resources" '. These include Wright's use of game-theoretic Marxism in the reformulation of his class scheme (see discussion in chapter 4), Goldthorpe's embrace of rational action theory (RAT; this will be discussed in the next chapter of this book), and Bourdieu's elaboration of the different elements of 'capital' possessed by individuals, which has been discussed at some length in this chapter. Savage (2000), it will be remembered from chapter 5, had already made this theoretical move from 'macro' to 'micro' in his argument that class cultures and identities have been reformed around individualized axes. However, whilst not denying that this shift in 'class thinking' to the micro-, individual level has to some extent occurred (in part, it may be suggested, in response to the theses of individualization and the 'death of class' discussed in chapter 5), this does not mean that 'macro' structures, such as the organization of capitalist production and capitalist labour markets, have simply disappeared altogether. In line with the arguments developed in this book, although it is not particularly helpful to regard individuals as 'structural dopes' devoid of agency, neither do individuals operate independently of the wider social structures in which they are embedded.

Indeed, Savage et al. also hold to this view, and one of their objectives is to 'revive class analysis' through a capital, assets, resources- (CARs-) based approach that incorporates these wider processes. For example, in describing the accumulatory potential of economic capital, Savage et al. draw on Marx's M–C–M' (money–commodities–money') formula, in which money becomes capital only when it accumulates: 'In the capital–labour relationship it is the routine, daily, exchange of labour power for wages, and the relentless accumulation of capital, that defines the nature of this particular relationship' (Savage et al. 2005: 43). Nevertheless, they insist (2005: 31) that: 'how capital is distinctive [is] not in terms of distinct relations of exploitation, but through its potential to accumulate and to be converted to other resources'.

They argue that Bourdieu's approach offers the most fruitful 'way ahead', as his framework incorporates both economic and cultural dimensions, recognizes the institutional underpinnings of capital, and is focused on accumulation rather than exploitation, thus directing attention away from 'the rather sterile debate about exploitation and how certain groups gain relative advantage towards a focus on the accumulation and convertibility of capitals' (2005: 43).

> Bourdieu recognises that the economic cannot be isolated, even analytically, from other determinants . . . Cultural phenomena are integral to his understanding of social structure . . . He sidesteps the entrenched and ultimately unproductive debates about exploitation and relationality . . . and instead focuses on . . . the accumulation and convertibility of CARs. (Savage et al. 2005: 41–2)

However, as argued above, there are difficulties in taking up this kind of position. If the economic cannot be isolated 'even analytically' from other determinants, then this not only presents considerable problems as far as empirical research is concerned but would also seriously hamper attempts to uncover causes (Crompton and Scott 2005). More particularly, a focus on accumulation throws up new problems as to the manner in which the accumulation of different kinds of capital (in the Bourdieuian sense) is achieved.

This is because although the 'micro' shift identified by Savage et al. is described as having a focus on *individual* capacities for agency and accumulation, in practice, much of this accumulation is achieved not via the individual, but by the *family*. As previously argued, family relationships do not in and of themselves *create* classes and class relationships, but they play the major role in reproducing them, and the family is the major transmission belt of social advantage and disadvantage. Indeed, despite their differences, both 'economic' and 'culturalist' accounts of class reproduction are united in their recognition of the crucial role of the family (Crompton 2006). As Erikson and Goldthorpe (1993: 233) put it: 'The family is . . . the unit of class "fate" . . . the economic decision-making in which family members engage . . . is typically of a joint or interdependent kind. The family is, at the "micro" level, a key unit of strategic action pursued within the class structure.' Similarly, Bourdieu (1996: 145) writes of the 'reproductive strategies which privileged families produce, without consultation or deliberation . . . separately and often in subjective competition, and which have the effect of contributing . . . to the reproduction of existing positions and the social order'.

As families play a major role in the reproduction of advantage and disadvantage, a degree of circularity of explanation is inevitable given that the reproduction of both economic and

cultural capitals takes place over the life cycle of the family. Thus accounts of this reproduction are bound to be descriptive (a criticism that Savage et al. 2005 make of rational
action theory (RAT), and that might equally, as we have seen in this chapter, be made of
Bourdieu's approach). However, accurate descriptions of these processes and practices are
required in order that we may understand them. Such descriptions may be circular, but this
kind of evidence can identify causes, as well as questions that may be systematically investigated via further research, both quantitative and qualitative.

Most families will continue to do their very best to ensure the position of their children
within the limits of the resources they have available; thus the class structure has strong self-
maintaining properties. However, it is also important to remember that class reproduction
is not an inevitable process. Not all individuals from disadvantaged backgrounds remain
disadvantaged as adults, and not every child from a middle-class home becomes a manager
or professional. Nevertheless, given the self-maintaining nature of family reproduction, it
is likely that social change in the direction of more or less class inequality – and this is a
very important point – is likely to originate externally to the processes of family reproduction. Thus the nature and extent of class reproduction is overwhelmingly shaped by the
context within which it takes place, and as a range of empirical research has demonstrated,
the nature of class inequalities and their impact on individuals and families may be substantially modified, particularly via state policies. To take an example from this chapter,
Marshall's discussion of the institutions of social 'citizenship', which he describes as being
'at war' with class inequalities, can be seen as integral to the policies developed within the
mid-twentieth-century social compromise that were instrumental, within the 'Western
world', in reducing class inequalities for many decades after the Second World War.

However, states may also operate in a manner that serves to enhance the potential for
class reproduction via the family. For example, it will be argued in the next chapter that
recent policies in respect of education in Britain (developing a 'quasi-market', increasing
de facto selection, publishing 'league tables', etc.) have created a scenario in which middle-
class families have increased opportunities and enhanced strategies to achieve returns on
their cultural and material capital investments. Indeed, in general, the implementation of
neo-liberal economic and social policies, which seek to increase competition by changing
or removing the institutions of market regulation (or, in the case of education in Britain,
attempting to create a quasi-market), is likely to increase the extent to which families are
'forced' to rely on their own resources.

As Sayer (2005: 88) has argued:

> Capitalism requires private property in the means of production to be concentrated into the
> hands of a minority and the majority to be wage-labourers (whether they be cleaners or man-
> agers), but any individual can do these things, nobody is born a capitalist or worker or doctor
> or cleaner. Other mechanisms not intrinsic to the basic structure of capitalism may contingently
> influence who becomes a capitalist or a worker or workers of particular kinds, but from the point
> of view of what is necessary for capitalism to exist, anyone can find a place in its structures.

Thus abstractly, 'class' is primarily an economic concept, and class *locations* are largely
(although not entirely) generated by economic processes (see Fraser 2000; Sayer 2005; Scott
1996).[12] At this most abstract level, accounts of the reproduction of the 'class structure' *are*
economically reductive. However, if definitions of the 'class' concept are restricted to this
economic dimension (as Bottero (2004: 1000) has recently suggested), we run the risk of
sidelining the cultural dimension of class reproduction. Nevertheless, there is an important

distinction to be made in respect of these two dimensions. Although, in the most general sense, both economic and cultural capital may be said to be 'inherited', the *processes* via which economic and cultural capital are accumulated and transferred are not identical to each other.

It is true (as we shall see in the next chapter) that 'cultural capital developed in the parental home can be translated into the educational field so that children can do well in gaining educational qualifications, and thence these qualifications can be translated into advantaged jobs within the division of labour' (Savage et al. 2005: 44). However, the kind of 'cultural capital' to which Savage et al. refer rests with the individual concerned, and cannot be stored or passed on in any direct sense (educational qualifications cannot be inherited). Its transmission is dependent upon the successful transmission of identity (or habitus). Objectively, winning the lottery might transform an individual (and their family) into rentier capitalists, but there are no tickets available for lotteries in cultural capital. In short, it is being argued that economic (e.g. Marx's) and cultural (e.g. Bourdieu's) class concepts cannot be seamlessly combined in a single theoretical 'approach' (such as CARs). However, as they are not mutually exclusive, they may be used in combination with each other, and indeed, should be (Sayer 2005: 72).

'Concrete' conceptions of class (or stratification), it has been argued in this book, are many-sided, and accounts of this complexity will incorporate both material and cultural processes.[13] The processes of material and cultural reproduction are intertwined, but analytically, they may be treated as distinct. Concretely, much of the reproduction of social classes takes place with the family. Accounts of these processes, both economic and cultural, are bound to be circular and often 'merely descriptive'. What I want to argue, however, is that these kinds of criticisms are not fatal. In the next chapter, therefore, we will examine the closely related topics of social mobility and educational opportunity. We will see that both 'positivist' employment-aggregate investigations and interpretative, Bourdieuian-inspired culturalist ethnographies have much to contribute to these debates.

FAMILIES, SOCIAL MOBILITY AND EDUCATIONAL ACHIEVEMENT

7

Introduction: class and the family

In this book, we have described a range of contrasting approaches to class and stratification. With considerable oversimplification, as we have seen in the last chapter, one dimension on which they might be compared is as broadly 'economistic' as contrasted to broadly 'culturalist' accounts of class. These variations in emphasis are associated with apparently conflicting accounts of causal (class) processes. For example, a broadly materialist (or economic) account of class reproduction would suggest that the major explanation of class inequalities rests in the nature of access to and take-up of material resources and the institutions that govern such access – for example, higher education (e.g. Goldthorpe 2000: ch. 9). In contrast, a broadly culturalist account might suggest that the major explanation rests in the spoiled (or, conversely, enhanced) identities and behaviours generated by dominant and subordinate 'cultures of class' (e.g. Skeggs 1997).

However, as we have discussed in the previous chapter, one important feature that unites both of these apparently contradictory approaches is that class reproduction is seen as taking place largely through the family. In the West, 'the family' has been subject to recent and considerable change. From the second half of the twentieth century, there have been dramatic changes in family formation and behaviour. Rates of marriage have declined, divorce rates have risen, the numbers living in consensual unions have increased, and the average age at marriage has risen. These changes have been reflected in fertility rates, and in England and Wales, the total fertility rate (TFR) has fallen from 2.9 in 1964 to 1.7 in 2000. Births outside marriage have increased dramatically, from 7 per cent in 1964 to 40 per cent in 2000 in England and Wales (ONS data). These trends in fertility and family behaviour are taking place in all 'Western' countries (for a cross-nationally comparative empirical summary of these developments, see Crouch 1999: chs 2, 7). Some authors (e.g. Beck and Beck-Gernsheim 2002) have argued that changes in gender roles and the family are a significant factor associated with increasing 'individualization' in contemporary societies.

Processes of individualization within the family, it has been suggested, are a major factor driving the individualization of society more generally. For example, Beck and Beck-Gernsheim (2002: 86) argue that what was once a 'community of need' is becoming, increasingly, an 'elective relationship' (see also Giddens 1991). Traditional family arrangements, it is argued, were constituted in inequalities between men and women, as well as the 'feudal' division of labour that allocated domestic work to women and market work to men. Women's claims to equality have radically destabilized this traditional structure, as is reflected in the demographic changes summarized above. Women have themselves become individualized and increasingly able to exercise their choices. As a consequence, family relationships are in flux and 'there is no given set of obligations and opportunities, no way of organising everyday work, the relationship between men and women, parents and children, which can just be copied' (Beck and Beck-Gernsheim 2002: 203).

These kinds of arguments – and indeed, 'individualization' arguments more generally – seriously underestimate the continuing significance of within-family patterns of reciprocities and obligations (Finch and Mason 1993), as well as class-differentiated patterns of behaviour that serve to reproduce class inequalities. Class-differentiated patterns of behaviour are also systematically associated with class-associated variations in attitudes to family life (Crompton 2006a). The role of the family in the reproduction of class inequalities is nowhere more conclusively demonstrated than in the closely linked processes of social mobility and educational achievement, as we shall see in this chapter. An investigation of these processes will also enable us to demonstrate another argument that has been central to this book, that is, the requirement to draw upon a range of different theoretical and methodological approaches, which at times might appear to be in conflict, in order to comprehend the totality of class and stratification.

Social mobility

Research in social mobility measures the mobility of individuals between occupations and/or occupational origins, both between generations and over the life cycle. An interest in social mobility extends across the political spectrum.[1] Evidence of high rates of social mobility may be used to argue that the society in question is characterized by achievement rather than ascription, and that individuals reap their rewards according to their personal qualities, rather than on the basis of 'unfair' advantages such as inherited wealth, or personal connections – in short, that a true meritocracy is in operation. Besides the powerful legitimation of structures of occupational inequality which such arguments bestow, social mobility has also acted as an important 'safety valve' in advanced industrial societies:

> Mobility provides an escape route for large numbers of the most able and ambitious members of the underclass, thereby easing some of the tensions generated by inequality. Elevation into the middle classes represents a *personal* solution to the problems of low status, and as such tends to weaken collectivist efforts to improve the lot of the underclass as a whole. It has often been suggested that upward mobility undermines the political base of the underclass most seriously by siphoning off the men [*sic*] best fitted for leadership.   (Parkin 1972: 50)

This argument has been pithily – if unsociologically – expressed in the well-known ditty, sung to the tune of the socialist anthem 'The Red Flag': 'The working class can kiss my arse; I've got the foreman's job at last.' In a rather more serious vein, Marx wrote that: 'The more a ruling class is able to assimilate the foremost minds of a ruled class, the more stable and dangerous becomes its rule' (1974: 601).

In the United States, the study of social mobility has assumed particular significance because of its apparent association with what have been regarded as significant 'core values' of American society – that is, the belief that individual hard work, application and effort will eventually bring their rewards; that, regardless of social background or family connections, inherited wealth or aristocratic title, it is indeed possible for the suitably talented individual to rise from a log cabin to the White House (Devine 1997). The widespread popularity of such classic liberal ideas relating to individual opportunity was not, of course, confined to the United States, as nineteenth-century books such as Samuel Smiles's *Self-Help* (1859) indicate.

The extent of social mobility, therefore, has been widely used as a measure of the 'openness' of industrial societies, and high mobility rates seen as an indication that the liberal promise of equality of opportunity has indeed been achieved. Blau and Duncan's (1967) statistical investigation of a sample of nearly 21,000 men aged 20 to 64 (drawn in 1962) in the United States appeared to confirm that, even if this happy state had not yet arrived, the US was well on the way to it. Blau and Duncan used techniques of path analysis in order to explore (amongst a variety of other empirical associations) the effect of social origins, education and career beginnings on subsequent career success. The researchers concluded that, although social origins did indeed have an influence, educational background and training, and early work experience, had a more pronounced effect on chances of success (1967: 402).[2] They also demonstrated that rates of social mobility in the United States were high, and argued that this was a consequence of the 'advanced level of industrialization and education'. It was argued that other industrial countries would, in due course, catch up (1967: 433).

Thus, for Blau and Duncan, there can be little doubt that increasing social mobility is inevitable, as well as a Good Thing. The underlying optimism of their perspective is very evident:

> a fundamental trend towards expanding universalism characterizes industrial society. Objective criteria of evaluation that are universally accepted increasingly pervade all spheres of life and displace particularistic standards of diverse ingroups [and] intuitive judgments . . . The growing emphasis on rationality and efficiency inherent in this spread of universalism finds expression in rapid technological progress and increasing division of labor and differentiation generally . . . The strong interdependence among men and groups engendered by the extensive division of labor becomes the source of their organic solidarity, to use Durkheim's term, inasmuch as social differentiation weakens the particularistic ingroup values that unite men.   (1967: 429)

Blau and Duncan's work has been subject to extensive criticism. It was suggested that, far from being a source of integration, extensive social mobility might actually be a destabilizing element in industrial societies. Lipset and Bendix (1959) argued that through the process of mobility people lose their previous attachments to social collectivities which had contributed to their sense of self-worth and psychological stability, and the resulting 'status inconsistency' might be a source of social disruption. As the above extract from their work makes clear, however, Blau and Duncan's conclusions gave substantial support to the 'industrial society' thesis concerning the inevitability of increasing social stability, equality of opportunity, and societal convergence. These kinds of arguments, as we have seen (chapter 3), were strongly contested by those who emphasized continuing conflict and the persistence of *class* inequalities.

Blau and Duncan's model of mobility takes the occupational structure to be a finely graded hierarchy, into which individuals are sorted according to their (individual) attributes. However, as critics such as Crowder (1974) have pointed out, a substantial degree of the variance in status attainment is not explained by the Blau–Duncan model, and indeed the wide distribution of income *within* educational attainment categories suggests that the relationship between income and education is not linear. Crowder argued that the large residual paths of the model are not to be explained, as Blau and Duncan had suggested, by 'pure luck', but rather, are the outcome of systematic *structural* constraints which shape not only the occupational system but also processes of allocation within it. These structural constraints include the institutions of political power and private property, and material and ideological constraints which specify the extent of control and the 'appropriate' behaviour associated with particular positions – in short, 'class' inequalities.

These arguments are echoed by Goldthorpe, who, as we have seen, favours not a graded hierarchy of occupations (or status scale) but his theoretical, relational class scheme. The use of such a scheme attempts to incorporate explicitly the kinds of structural constraints absent from the Blau–Duncan model. Goldthorpe claims that his scheme encompasses the dynamics of class relations; it is *relational*, rather than gradational.[3] Advances in statistical techniques, in particular, log-linear modelling, made it possible to employ non-linear class schemes such as Goldthorpe's in social mobility research. In contrast, Blau and Duncan's statistical techniques (path analysis) presupposed a hierarchical (that is, gradational) ordering of the underlying categories (income, education, occupational status).

Log-linear models also offered a solution to other technical problems which have historically beset research in social mobility. Social mobility investigations record movement within an occupational structure at two (or more) points in time – but the structure itself is not stable. As industrial societies have developed, so there have occurred massive changes in the structure of occupations (and thus the 'class' structure), first from agricultural to industrial occupations, then, during the course of the twentieth century, from predominantly 'manual' to 'non-manual' occupations (chapter 5). For example, in Great Britain, non-manual workers increased from 18.7 per cent of the occupied population in 1911 to 52.3 per cent in 1981, with a corresponding decline in the proportion of manual workers (Price and Bain 1988: 164; by 2003, the proportion of those in 'semi-routine' and 'routine' occupations had declined to 23.1 per cent). Thus in any standard mobility tabulation comparing fathers' occupations with sons' occupations (research on social mobility focused entirely on men until the 1980s), the marginal totals will vary, reflecting the difference in the occupational structure at different times. In a simple 2×2 table comparing manual with non-manual, for example, there will be more manual fathers and, conversely, more non-manual sons. To put the point another way, given long-term changes in the occupational structure, a certain amount of 'upward' mobility is 'built in' or 'forced', given the undersupply of non-manual sons.

In Glass's study of social mobility after the Second World War (1954), this problem had been resolved by drawing a distinction between 'structural' and 'exchange' mobility.[4] The differences between the marginal totals in the mobility table are used to provide a measure of 'structural' mobility brought about through occupational changes. The further extent of mobility revealed in the table was described as 'exchange' mobility – that is, mobility net of structural effects.

There are a number of statistical problems associated with Glass's approach (Goldthorpe 1980; 1987: 74–5; Heath 1981). In consequence, approaches to the study of inequalities of opportunity have been developed which distinguish between 'absolute' and 'relative' mobility *rates*. 'Absolute' mobility describes the total mobility revealed in a mobility table, which would include the mobility brought about by changes in the occupational structure (or occupational 'upgrading' over time). 'Relative' mobility chances are calculated by comparing, for people from different occupational backgrounds, their chances of entering different 'classes'. This is described as a measure of 'social fluidity'; that is, as a measure of 'whether or not changes in the structure of objective mobility opportunities over time are being equally reflected in the mobility experience of individuals of all origins alike' (Goldthorpe 1980; 1987: 75). These chances are computed using odds ratios. These demonstrate the chance ('odds') of a service-class son being recruited to the service class, rather than to the working class, by comparison with the odds of a working-class son being recruited to the service class rather than the working class.[5]

Glass's (1954) research appeared to demonstrate that Britain was not a particularly 'open' society, in that long-range mobility (that is, from bottom to top, or from top to bottom) was relatively rare, and there was a high degree of self-recruitment to the 'elite' positions in British society. What mobility there was tended to be only short-range; that is, to positions more or less adjacent in the occupational hierarchy, from manual worker to supervisor, or clerk to lower-level manager. In particular, if mobility did occur across the boundary between manual and non-manual occupations (seen by many as representing the fundamental line of cleavage within the class structure), then this was highly likely to be only between adjacent classes – for example, from skilled manual to lower-level non-manual – within what has been described as the 'buffer zone' of the class structure overall (Glass 1954; see also Westergaard and Resler 1975; Goldthorpe 1980, 1987).

Goldthorpe's 1972–4 enquiry into social mobility revealed a rather different picture. It suggested that a considerable amount of *long-range* mobility had in fact occurred – for example, 28.5 per cent of those in class I in the 1972 survey were from class VI and VII backgrounds (Goldthorpe 1980; 1987: 45). The sheer extent of mobility which had taken place also served to undermine the 'buffer-zone' hypothesis. The extent of mobility revealed by the Oxford survey might, of course, have been anticipated, given the long-term changes in the occupational structure which have led to an inexorable expansion of the middle and upper 'classes'. As a consequence, the extent of upward mobility in the population is far in excess of downward mobility.

However, Goldthorpe argues that these results did *not* demonstrate that Britain had become a more 'open' society. This (apparently) contradictory assertion can be demonstrated by evidence using the distinction between absolute and relative rates of social mobility, employing the techniques of odds ratios as described above. The analysis of relative mobility chances, or patterns of social fluidity, within the Oxford sample demonstrated that, despite high rates of absolute social mobility, there were marked, and persistent, differences in the *relative* chances of men of different social backgrounds moving into higher-level occupations. Put simply, the data revealed a 'disparity ratio' of 1 : 2 : 4 for the chances of access to classes I and II for men from 'Service', 'Intermediate' and 'Working' classes (1980; 1987: 50). Thus Goldthorpe concludes:

> the pattern of relative mobility chances . . . associated with the British class structure . . .
> embodies inequalities that are of a quite striking kind: in particular, those that emerge if one

compares the chances of men whose fathers held higher-level service-class positions being themselves found in such positions rather than in working-class ones with the corresponding chances of men of working-class origins. Where inequalities in class chances of this magnitude are displayed – of the order . . . of over 30 : 1 – then, we believe, the presumption must be that to a substantial extent they do reflect inequalities of opportunity that are rooted in the class structure.   (1987: 328)

Goldthorpe's class scheme, together with the associated emphasis on *relative* mobility rates, has been developed in international comparisons of social mobility.[6] Comparative work allows for the testing of the 'industrial society' thesis of universally increasing openness and opportunity, which had been advanced in Blau and Duncan's work. However, different countries industrialize at different rates, and the process of industrialization does not always result in a uniform occupational outcome.[7] Such differences between the units of comparison have rendered cross-national comparisons highly problematic. Thus Featherman, Jones and Hauser (FJH) (1975) have advanced a modified version of the thesis of universalism. Absolute mobility rates may vary between different societies because of factors such as differences in the occupational structure, the size of the agricultural sector and so on, but nevertheless the underlying 'mobility regime' – that is, *relative* mobility rates – would show a basic similarity in all societies with market economies and nuclear family systems. This has become known as the thesis of 'constant social fluidity'. Using a version of Goldthorpe's class scheme, the international group of researchers associated with the CASMIN project (Comparative Analysis of Social Mobility in Industrial Societies) has carried out a series of comparisons of relative social mobility. Their results have largely confirmed the FJH hypothesis in that basic patterns of relative mobility chances proved to be similar between different countries (Erikson and Goldthorpe 1993).

What are the *consequences* of social mobility for stratification systems? One important feature of advanced industrial societies which the finding of constant social fluidity does demonstrate is that, despite legislative efforts (such as educational reform, etc.) to achieve greater 'openness' and equality of opportunity, this has not, as yet, been achieved. Although overall rates of upward mobility have risen, the different *relative* rates of class mobility prospects have proved remarkably resistant to change. All of the emphasis in the work of Goldthorpe and his colleagues, therefore, has been on the *stability* of relative chances, rather than on the changes in the occupational structure which have increased *absolute* levels of opportunity, and this has been the source of much criticism (e.g. Morris and Scott 1996).

Goldthorpe has also been accused of 'political bias' in the presentation of his data in respect of the British case. Saunders (1990a) has argued that Goldthorpe, as well as other 'left-wing' sociologists who have followed a broadly similar strategy in their analysis of contemporary British mobility patterns (in particular, Marshall and his colleagues at the University of Essex (1988)), have been excessively concerned with relativities rather than absolutes in respect of social mobility. In contrast, Saunders emphasizes the significance of the *absolute* increases in mobility rates which have been brought about by economic expansion since the Second World War, and changes in the occupational structure. He also argues that presumptions as to the lack of 'openness' in British society are founded upon the unwarranted assumption that the different talents, aptitudes and abilities which shape 'life chances' *are* randomly distributed within society:

> Goldthorpe and many other contemporary sociologists effectively end up denying that . . . natural inequalities can have any importance in influencing people's destinies. If, for example,

the working class accounts for half of the population, then for Goldthorpe and for the Essex researchers we should expect half of all doctors, managers and top civil servants to have originated in the working class. If we find, as Goldthorpe did, that only one quarter of such groups are from working-class origins, then according to this reasoning we are justified in assuming that the 'shortfall' is entirely due to social barriers and that British society is therefore just as class-ridden and unjust as its critics have always maintained. In the idealised world of John Goldthorpe and other 'left' sociologists, people's destinies should be randomly determined because talents are randomly distributed. British society is thus found wanting because people of working-class origins are not in the majority in all the top jobs. This argument is ludicrous, yet in modern sociology it is all too rarely questioned.   (Saunders 1990a: 83)

Saunders states a clear political preference for the neo-liberal argument, developed by economists such as Hayek (2001), that a relative lack of regulation, together with its associated inequalities, within the capitalist marketplace is more dynamic than its 'regulated' alternatives and thus of more material benefit to the population as a whole. Goldthorpe has stated an equally clear preference for a degree of market regulation or 'corporatism' (Goldthorpe 1984a). There are theoretical arguments, and empirical evidence, which would be supportive of either perspective, but ultimately, judgements as to the superiority – or otherwise – of the alternatives on offer are unavoidably political.[8]

Saunders's arguments also incorporate the neo-liberal assumption that an absence of regulation will allow the 'best' to achieve the most. That is, the greater the level of competition, the more likely it is that a true meritocracy will be achieved. That the greatest share of the available rewards do go to the 'best' or 'functionally most important' is, as we have seen, in chapter 2, a central argument of 'functionalist' theories of stratification. The functional theory of stratification has argued that social inequality is an 'unconsciously evolved device' whereby the most important positions are filled by the most qualified persons. If occupational class is taken to be an indicator of the importance of a position, and education is taken as an indicator of level of qualification, then functional theory would anticipate that those who achieve superior class positions will have higher levels of qualifications and, moreover, that education will be *more* important than class origins in getting higher-level jobs (as we have seen, this was, indeed, Blau and Duncan's argument). However, Marshall and Swift (1993; Marshall et al. 1997) have shown that individuals' class of origin has a substantial influence on whether or not they eventually achieve a 'service-class' position – regardless of the level of qualification obtained.

For example, their data show that 43 per cent of men of service-class origins but with only middling levels of qualification (above GCSE- and up to A-level) reached service-class occupational positions.[9] However, only 15 per cent of men of working-class origins, with the *same* level of qualifications, reached service-class positions (Marshall and Swift 1993). There has been a general increase in the numbers of people gaining qualifications, but class differences in access to education have been maintained. Nevertheless, there does seem to have been some weakening of the 'class effect' over the last twenty years, in that, 'Given the same level of educational attainment, the odds of a man reaching the salariat from a class I or class II background have been approximately halved, relative to those for a man from an unskilled manual background' (Marshall et al. 1997: 129).

In contrast, Saunders has argued that ability and effort, rather than class background, are the most important features leading to occupational success (1996, 1997). Saunders uses evidence from the National Child Development Survey, a longitudinal survey based upon an initial panel of over 17,000 children born during one week in 1958. This survey carried out an intelligence test when the children were 11; Saunders's analysis uses a further survey carried out when the same subjects were aged 33. His results (using the technique of logistic regression) show that measured intelligence (at 11), together with other individual attributes such as motivation and work attitudes, were the most important factors predicting whether or not people achieved higher-level occupational positions. Thus he concludes that Britain is indeed a meritocracy, rather than a class-ridden society.

We have here, therefore, two positions which are apparently in complete contrast with each other. Marshall and Swift argue that class origins override educational levels, Saunders that ability and effort are more important than class background. However, it may be suggested that both of these apparently conflicting sets of arguments have some validity. Class inequalities will continue to give many an 'unfair' advantage, but in a society such as Britain, able and hard working people (of whatever class origin) are more likely to be occupationally successful than those who possess neither of these characteristics.[10] Indeed, both 'sides' of this particular argument produce evidence that might be used to support the other's case. We have seen that Marshall et al. have suggested that the 'class effect' on occupational attainment has declined somewhat over the years, suggesting a move in the direction of greater meritocracy (although, as we shall see, this trend has ceased). Saunders's evidence shows that private schooling is important for class I/II children in avoiding downward mobility, 'suggesting that the private schools may offer middle-class parents some means of insuring their less able offspring against downward mobility' (1997: 273). In respect of this particular debate, therefore, there are good grounds for taking a 'both/and' rather than an 'either/or' position.

In this section, therefore, we have used the topic of social mobility in the manner of a 'worked example' in order to illustrate a number of themes we have been developing in this book. We have demonstrated the continuities with a series of important debates in the social sciences concerning the explanation and origins of inequality, including conflict versus consensus approaches, and functionalist (liberal) versus radical (class) accounts of social inequality. We have seen that, although the level of social mobility has increased, relative rates of mobility remained remarkably stable for many years. However, an important point to emphasize is that the overwhelming emphasis on constant social fluidity (i.e. the stability of *relative* chances of social mobility depending on class of origin) to be found within the 'Nuffield' approach has had the effect of suggesting that nothing has 'really' changed; for example, 'British society is no more open now than it was at the time of the First World War' (Marshall 1997: 1). Nevertheless, the enormous increase in *absolute* mobility rates (or structural mobility) means that the opportunities of upward mobility for children of working-class parents have in fact expanded dramatically. As far as people's lived experiences are concerned, this absolute increase will have had more impact than the stability of relative rates.

A similar argument may be developed in respect of women and class analysis. The energies of those associated with the Nuffield programme have been largely devoted to demonstrating that *relative* mobility rates for women are similar to those of men, that a woman's partner's occupational class gives a better account of her political attitudes than her own, and so on.[11] That is, all of the emphasis has been upon the *lack* of change in gender, and gender relations, in relation to 'class' as defined within the Nuffield programme. However, the entry of women into paid employment has had a considerable impact on both individuals and families, particularly within the middle classes. The experiences of children growing up with two working parents will be very different from those of children who grew up in a 'male breadwinner' family. The entry of women into higher-level occupations appears to be leading to new cleavages within the middle classes, in that women tend to be disproportionately concentrating in *particular* professional, and managerial, occupations (Crompton 1998: 159). This restructuring is projected back into the family itself, as women in managerial occupations are less likely to have childcare responsibilities (and have fewer children) than professional women (Crompton and Harris 1998). Even more important, perhaps, as discussed in chapter 5, is the increase in social and economic polarization brought about by the widening gulf between two-wage and no-wage households (Gregg and Wadsworth 2001).

Declining social mobility

In recent years, however, discussions of social mobility have been dominated by the fact that in Britain, social mobility is actually in decline. In part, this is a consequence of changes in the occupational structure, particularly as far as men are concerned. The decline in skilled manual jobs, and a slowing of growth in professional and managerial employment, resulted in a decline in *absolute* levels of male mobility during the last decades of the twentieth century (Goldthorpe 2004). An increasing amount of cohort data, however, is now available, and this suggests that *relative* mobility rates are also widening. Cohort studies typically take all children born in a particular week and resurvey this cohort at fixed time intervals as they age (these resurveys are known as 'sweeps' or 'waves'). Cohort studies track individuals over time, and are therefore very robust measures of the associations between parental background, income, cognitive abilities and educational and occupational achievement. Moreover, comparisons of different cohorts allow the differing class 'fates' of individuals born at different times to be investigated – that is, a comparison of mobility experiences for people of different ages.

The major British sources of cohort data are the National Child Development Study (NCDS; see above), commencing in 1958, the British Cohort Study (BCS), which began in 1970, and the Millennium Cohort, whose participants were born in 2000–2. In addition, the British Household Panel Survey (BHPS), a longitudinal household survey which began in 1991, may be used to generate cohorts.

Levels of education are closely correlated with subsequent occupational achievement. During the 1980s and 1990s, there was a massive expansion of higher education in Britain (see below), and by the year 2000, participation had risen to the level of one in three of the 18–19-year-old age group. However, comparisons of cohort achievements over time show that, comparing the NCDS, BCS and BHPS cohorts, at age 23 (which would have been reached in 1981 (NCDS), 1993 (BCS) and 1999 (BHPS)), whereas the proportion of children of the highest 20 per cent parental income category getting a degree had risen from 20 per cent to 46 per cent, for the 20 per cent lowest-income category, it had risen only from 6 per cent to 9 per cent. That is, the relative odds of wealthy children achieving a degree as compared to poorer children had risen from 3.3 to 5.1 (Machin and Vignoles 2004: 116–17). Moreover, the gap between richer and poorer students of a given ability has widened, particularly for girls. The relative odds of high-ability girls from high-income backgrounds getting a degree (compared with high-ability girls from poor backgrounds) increased from 1.6 to 2.7 over the three cohorts (Machin and Vignoles 2004: 120). Machin and Vignoles (2004: 126) conclude, therefore:

the links between parental income, parental social class and eventual higher education achievement have strengthened over time. Family background, rather than a person's early ability, played a more important role in determining how well someone does for those born in 1970 than for those born in 1958. Furthermore, our analysis . . . shows parental income mattering even more in recent times.

Parents, therefore, are playing an increasingly crucial role in social mobility in Britain, and the better-off have benefited disproportionately from increased educational opportunity (mobility levels in Britain are lower than in Canada, Germany and the Nordic countries; see Blanden et al. 2005). However, what are the processes that ensure the growing success of class reproduction via the educational system?

Secondary and higher education in Britain

Before we discuss the answers to the rhetorical question posed above, the background to these debates will be briefly sketched via a summary of the changes that have taken place in British secondary and higher education since the Second World War.[12]

The 1944 Education Act introduced universal, and free, secondary education to Britain. However, this was organized in the 'tripartite' system of grammar, technical and secondary modern schools. Grammar schools were for the academically most able, technical schools for those with 'technical' rather than academic abilities, and secondary moderns for the less able children. Selection was on the basis of an intelligence test at the age of eleven. Private schools (the best in the secondary sector are rather misleadingly called 'public' schools) educated a minority of children whose parents could afford to pay. Tripartism came under criticism from the beginning. Secondary modern schools were seen as providing an inferior education, and grammar schools were unevenly geographically distributed, with many more places available in some areas than others. The intellectual basis of selection at eleven was challenged, and the test was class and gender biased (many more middle-class children passed the eleven-plus examination).[13] As a result of these pressures, there was a growing interest in 'comprehensive' (i.e. non-selective) education, and in 1964 the Labour government instructed all local authorities to prepare plans for the abolition of selection and the introduction of comprehensive schools, catering for children of all abilities. These policies were supported by the Conservatives (including Margaret Thatcher during her period as Education Secretary in the 1970s). Some grammar schools remained, however.

The comprehensive ideal came under increasing pressure from right-wing critics for 'failing' educational standards, and 'setting' (or tracking) by ability was widely introduced. With the election of the Conservative government in 1979, there began the explicit process of creating a 'quasi-market' in education. Parental choice was instituted in 1980, and in the 1988 Education Reform Act, open enrolment was introduced and schools were funded on a predominantly per capita basis. Schools were encouraged (forced) to compete for pupils – the logic being that this would improve school performance. However, this resulted in the better schools becoming oversubscribed, and poorer schools losing pupils. An increasing number of schools brought in some form of selection (e.g. by parental interview or pupil testing). Competition was further encouraged by the introduction of school 'league tables' (based largely on examination results) from 1992 onwards. A national curriculum was introduced and the Office for Standards in Education (OFSTED) was created in 1992 (replacing the Schools Inspectorate). OFSTED began a process of school inspections that were widely seen to be punitive, identifying 'failing schools' and allocating responsibility for educational failure to the quality of teaching.

This introduction of a 'quasi-market' has to a considerable extent eroded local authority control over schools. The election of a 'New Labour' government in 1997 did not markedly change these policies (retaining OFSTED, league tables, etc.), and 'parental choice' remains the keystone of education policy. The system is still nominally comprehensive, but a whole new range of schools has been introduced (or the schools' provision extended) – for example, faith schools, specialist schools, foundation schools, city academies, voluntary aided schools. To varying degrees, these schools have control over their budgets and control over the entry of pupils.

Higher education in Britain was a minority (and elite) pursuit until the 1960s. Following the Robbins Report in 1963, there was an expansion of higher education that included the construction of 'greenfield' new universities and the upgrading of a number of existing colleges of advanced technology. There also existed an almost equal number of polytechnics and higher education colleges serving local communities that received public funding (administered by local authorities) but did not have 'university' status. By 1991, the number of students enrolled in polytechnics and colleges equalled that of students in universities (in the 1990s, polytechnics were allowed to expand rapidly by taking 'fees only' students at marginal costs). Polytechnics and colleges had a major focus on teaching, rather than academic research. This 'binary' system was ended in 1992 when the Conservative government, at a stroke, increased the number of university places by upgrading the polytechnics to 'university' status, and all 'universities' were brought together under the same funding umbrella. The same funding body distributed funding for research, which is allocated via a competitive research assessment exercise. In practice, the 'old' and the first generation of 'new' universities continue to be of higher status and are the major recipients of research funding.

Explaining class differences in educational achievement

The professed objective of educational reforms and changes has been to raise the standards of education as well as increase educational participation. However, as we have seen in our discussion of social mobility, despite numerous attempts at reform, educational achievement, so vital to occupational success and social mobility, has remained class differentiated. Even when there is no difference in levels of measured academic achievement, working-class children are less likely to gain higher-level qualifications than middle-class children. In explaining educational differentials, there are competing accounts available, both 'economic' and 'cultural'. Our aim will be to demonstrate that *both* accounts are required in order to understand class reproduction.

Goldthorpe (2000: chs 8, 11) draws upon rational action theory (RAT) in order to explain persisting class differences in educational attainment.[14] In brief, Goldthorpe argues that middle-class families not only see education as necessarily required in order to maintain the advantages of their children, but also, given that they can afford it, as a desirable 'consumption good'. They can also make further investments in cases of failure. In contrast, relatively speaking, working-class families (given their limited resources) take a greater risk in bearing the costs of higher education for their children, and in any case, are not beset by the same 'status anxiety' as the middle classes as their children have less distance to fall in relation to mobility. Moreover, the costs of failure (in higher education) are greater in terms of income forgone and other opportunities missed. Thus, argues Goldthorpe, class-related choices are determined by the costs and benefits of different courses of action, and 'disadvantaged families require greater assurance of benefits for more costly courses of action to be pursued in comparison to advantaged families' (Devine 2004: 7). This persistence of 'rational' choices (and actions) ensures the persistence of class inequalities in educational achievement, despite the fact that educational opportunities are free and open to all.

In making this argument, Goldthorpe is emphatic that rational economic explanations should be preferred over the more 'cultural' explanations of educational attainment offered by Bourdieu (see preceding chapter). It is the differing mix of opportunities and constraints available to 'middle-class' and 'working-class' parents that explains, in aggregate, the choices they make on behalf of their children, rather than any 'cultural' factors. These cultural factors would include the 'dominant' culture embodied in the educational system, which, it has been argued, excludes working-class children who have not been socialized into it and therefore do not possess the appropriate cultural capital or 'habitus' (Bourdieu 1973). In rejecting culturalist explanations of educational achievement, Goldthorpe is sensitive to the fact that such arguments can result in 'blaming the victims', that is, as seeing working-class parents as having a 'poverty of aspirations' and in some way responsible for their failure to instil the 'correct' values, as far as educational success is concerned, into their children (as we shall see, his caution in this respect is well founded). Moreover, he argues that culturalist arguments are circular, and simply do not take into account the considerable amount of upward mobility that has, in fact, taken place (see also Halsey et al. 1980).

Another point made by Goldthorpe in his arguments against culturalist explanations relates to the stability of class differentials: 'although class differentials appear in general to have been little reduced, there is no evidence from any modern society that these differentials have appreciably *widened*, which is the consequence of expansion [i.e. of educational opportunities] that theories invoking the reproduction of class cultural divergence would lead one to expect' (Goldthorpe 2000: 170). However, as we have seen, there is substantial recent evidence of a widening of class differentials in educational achievement. In the light of this widening, we will examine accounts of class reproduction that examine the role of cultural and social capital (see the discussion of Bourdieu in chapter 6) in more depth. Before we do this, however, the important point must be made that our objective is not to demonstrate that Goldthorpe is 'wrong' in his identification of the material calculations and choices that lead to the reproduction of educational inequalities. Rather, our aim will be to emphasize the significance of 'economic' *as well as* 'cultural' and 'social' factors and processes.

Critics of Goldthorpe's explanation of the persistence of class inequalities in the educational sphere, therefore, do not reject his materialist account but argue that cultural and social processes should be examined as well: 'The error RAT makes is to *counterpose* rational choice to culture, rather than seeing it as one element in a culturally-shaped repertoire' (Hatcher 1998: 16; see also Devine 2004). Indeed, it may be argued that the (quasi-)marketization of public (i.e. state) education in Britain has increased opportunities for the effective use of economic capital by increasing the opportunities for it to be used. Housing in the catchment areas of 'good' state schools can cost tens of thousands of pounds more than housing that is not so advantageously located, and there is increasing evidence that residential school segregation is occurring. Parents with economic resources available can pay for tutors to prepare their children for vital entrance tests to the better schools (Ball 2003: 94–5), as well as tutoring in individual subjects to keep their children in the higher streams. Parents in low-income households face great difficulties in sending their children to schools outside the immediate area, but this is not seen as a problem by middle-class parents (Ball et al. 1997). Economic resources, therefore, bring advantage in the state school education market in Britain. More particularly, parents in Britain can buy a private school education for their children (examination results in the private sector are better than those in state schools, and private (public) school students are over-represented at the more prestigious universities, particularly Oxford and Cambridge; see Adonis and Pollard (1997). Only a small minority of British secondary school children are privately educated – just under 10 per cent – but numbers are rising, despite a decline in the relevant age grouping.

There can be no question, therefore, that economic capital plays an absolutely crucial role in the reproduction of class differences in educational achievement. What, however, of the role of cultural and social capital? As we have seen in the preceding chapter, Bourdieu has argued that combinations of economic, cultural, social and symbolic capital together constitute a habitus which is virtually 'instinctive' and therefore not consciously deployed by individuals (it is this argument that has led many to argue that Bourdieu's approach is overly determinist and reproductionist). Moreover, if habitus is internally constituted, how are its aspects to be reliably identified for the purposes of sociological investigation? This relates to another criticism of Bourdieu developed in the previous chapter, that is, his insistence on the inseparability of the economic and the cultural.

Not surprisingly, therefore, definitions of what constitutes cultural capital have been diverse and wide-ranging. Sullivan (2001) has used a quantitative measure based on 'cultural' activities, knowledge and language (reading, television watching, etc.), but this definition is rather narrow and perhaps too closely tied to notions of elite 'culture'. Most studies of the impact of cultural capital on educational success have been case based and qualitative. For example, Lareau (1997) studied parental activity (i.e. responses to school requests for parental involvement) in schools in two US communities, one white working-class and one professional middle-class. Her methods included classroom observation, and interviews with parents and teachers, rather than a questionnaire study. She found that parental responses were highly conditioned by cultural capital. Working-class parents valued education no less than middle-class parents, but depended on the teacher to educate their child. Middle-class parents, however, had no such deference to professionals, and saw education as a shared enterprise: 'Middle-class parents, in supervising, monitoring and overseeing the educational experience of their children, behave in ways that mirror the requests of schools. This appears to provide middle-class children with educational advantages over working-class children' (Lareau 1997: 714). That is, the schools' definition of the proper family–school relationship was geared to the cultural capital of the middle classes.

Lareau's approach to cultural capital, therefore, focuses on 'ways of behaving' rather than (in contrast to Sullivan) cultural consumption or knowledge in the formal sense. Her basic finding – that the cultural capital of middle-class parents renders them in general more effective (as far as their children's academic outcomes are concerned) in dealing with schools and teachers has been endlessly repeated (e.g. Gewirtz et al. 1995; Connell et al. 1982; Evans

2006). In such studies, establishing the impact of cultural capital has usually depended upon a close 'ethnographic' analysis of actors' accounts and rationales of their behaviour and the choices they make. In relation to the contemporary emphasis on choice in education, a frequent conclusion of this research is that normative (i.e. official) constructions of parental 'choice' are based on middle-class, not working-class, choice-making (Reay et al. 1997).

Working-class parents tend to go along with their children's preferences, which are conditioned by locality and friendship, whereas middle-class parents are more strategic and craft carefully chosen options for their child, in which academic success is paramount. Working-class children tend to go to local schools – even if these are widely regarded as bad or 'demonized'. They often are aware that 'good' schools tend to be outside their locality and sometimes attempt to 'choose' them. However, very few get selected for these 'better' schools – indeed, it may be questioned whether these children actually have a 'choice' – and the 'unselected' children work hard to come to terms with their (virtually inevitable) allocation to local schools (Reay and Lucey 2003). Moreover, many working-class parents are reluctant to choose high-reputation schools because of a fear of humiliation or rejection:

> They can go through the school for nothing, but then we thought . . . well I felt . . . Richard would be . . . the children there are paying children . . . they would not be Richard's sort . . . maybe he might feel out of it.

> I thought mine wouldn't get in anyway, because my cousin's little girl, no, my sister in law's little girl is very clever and she didn't get in so I thought, well there's no hope for mine.   (Reay et al. 1997: 43)

In contrast, middle-class parents deploy their cultural and social capital in the active shaping of a school choice for their child. They need 'sufficient cultural capital – the information and specific competence – to decode the local market; to make judgements about the state of the market often five or even ten years into the future' (Reay and Lucey 2003: 122). The introduction of a quasi-market in education and the presence of academic league tables means that secondary schools are in competition for those children likely to be the highest achievers – the middle class. Parents use their networks of contacts to search out suitable schools for their children:

> we spoke to teachers in the schools, spoke to other parents, and spoke to my friends who are scattered across the borough and where their children went to and what they thought about it.

> somebody I know from work hailed me across a meeting and said 'they're going to stream at Milton, they're going to do something about the brighter child, you know, you must think about sending Todd there'.   (Ball 2003: ch. 4)

Parents are concerned not only about the school, but the families of other children likely to be going there: 'these parents are looking for other "parents with similar ambitions" (Mrs Cornwell), or "the likelihood of finding kindred spirits I think", who have certain "social and cultural skills" (Mrs Symons)' (Ball 2003: ch. 4). On the basis of these kinds of researches, middle-class parents set limits to the choices available to their children, which reflect the kind of education they are aiming for:

> In the end it was her final say but we decided on the schools we would look at first, so she was given a limited amount of choice to look at.   (Mrs Little, white middle-class mother)

it was her final choice . . . yes . . . but there were schools that we didn't look at because I . . . said that I didn't want her to go to . . . so we didn't look at those, so that wasn't an option that they had . . . but apart from that . . . yes anywhere in London . . . any school they wanted really (Mrs Manor, white middle class mother).   (Reay et al. 1998: 438)

These examples also illustrate the manner in which social capital (networking, contacts, etc.) has been employed in order to secure a good (i.e. academic) secondary education for middle-class children. Similar deployments of cultural and social capital take place at the point of transition to higher education. As described above, there has been a massive expansion of higher education in Britain but the sector is increasingly stratified: 'While more working class and minority students are entering university, for the most part they are entering different universities to their middle class counterparts' (Reay et al. 2001: 858). Working-class and ethnic-minority students tend to go to the second generation of 'new' universities – that is, the upgraded polytechnics. This is partly for reasons of expense, as students can live at the parental home, and travel costs are also an issue: 'Yes, I live near Putney Bridge, and Roehampton, for locality Roehampton appeals, because I can go home for tea. And I also thought about being a poor student and I thought well, it's about 90 pence on the bus' (Reay et al. 2001: 861). Working-class students also rejected more elite universities on the grounds of potential discomfort that might be felt at these institutions: 'What's a person like me going to do at a place like that?' (Reay et al. 2001: 864). On the whole, middle-class students feel no such inhibitions and, what is more, are able to draw upon their established contacts: 'I've been for a week at Oxford, following around my cousin, doing physiology. And a week at a vet's. A week at a doctor's clinic, which was really good' (Ball 2003: 84).

On the basis of her ethnographic research in Bermondsey (a working-class area of London), Evans (2006: 7) summarizes the situation as follows:

problems are more likely to arise, at school, for working class children not only because the schools they go to are more likely to be failing and their parents are less likely to be either well-off financially or well educated themselves, but also because the form of participation that is required of them at school doesn't closely match the one that is required of them at home and in their immediate surroundings. Educated middle class parents, in contrast, tend to be better off, better educated and require of their children at home a form of participation that matches more closely what is expected of children at school. This means that compared to their middle class peers, working class children tend to be at a disadvantage when they get to school where they first have to learn all about a new form of learning, which is called education.

In this section, we have discussed contemporary research that seeks to explain the persistence, and even widening, of class differences in educational achievement. Material or 'economic' explanations, such as RAT, clearly have much to contribute, and indeed, RAT-based explanations could usefully be employed to interpret many of the qualitative research findings we have summarized above. However, it is equally clear that class-based endowments of cultural and social capital also play a significant role in the reproduction of class-based educational disadvantage. These findings leave us with two (difficult) questions. First, how can these rather different explanations help us to understand the widening of class differentials (and decline in social mobility) in Britain? Second, if increasing inequality is seen to be a problem, what can be done about it? (And it should be remembered, of course, that some would argue that increasing inequality is not a problem, as increased competition will ensure that it is only the best who get to the top.)

What is to be done?

Declining social mobility (particularly for men) is in part attributable to shifts in the occupational structure, as noted above. Deindustrialization in Britain in the 1970s and 1980s was associated with the decline of 'good' working-class jobs in industry, and the shift to the service economy meant that gaining formal academic qualifications became even more important. At the same time, the traditional craft apprenticeship system in Britain, which was heavily reliant on firms to provide on-the job training, collapsed as firms cut costs in a worsening economic climate. Since the 1990s, 'modern apprenticeships' have been introduced but funds have been largely directed at private-sector 'training providers' focused on meeting targets rather than responding to local skill needs, and there is a high drop-out rate. Apprenticeship in Britain is not a legally defined entity, standards vary considerably, and the system is characterized by 'chronic information failure'. A recent review concludes that 'apprenticeship in Britain, judged as a programme, falls short of that provided elsewhere in Europe on every important measure of good practice' (Steedman 2001: n.p.).[15] Structural changes, therefore, such as this decline in 'good' working-class craft employment, will contribute to the widening of class differentials.

However, the creation of a market in education will also widen class differentials as it makes the possession of economic, cultural and social capital even more vital for success in this market. Of course, many working-class children do well, but the odds are stacked against them and the research summarized above, quantitative and qualitative, suggests the situation is getting worse, rather than better.

Public policy in Britain is committed to the reduction of educational inequalities. However, the government's preferred strategy has been to focus on individual children and families. Much of this effort is directed at the early years of childhood, via programmes such as Sure Start.[16] Much attention is directed at parents: 'Parents will have to show a determination to lift their aspirations and those of their family. The poverty of aspiration which is commonplace must be replaced by a new determination to succeed' (Murphy 2006: 13). To remedy this situation, it is argued, resources must be directed at the very young, living in the poorest and most deprived areas. In this model, the problem lies with the person; change the people, problem over. In short, make middle-class cultural capital a universal attribute by 'catching them young'. As Evans (2006: 7) has commented:

> If we were to go with a social deprivation model the resolution of the problem would be simple: all we would have to do would be to provide increased opportunities for working class people to learn the forms of participation that middle class people take for granted . . . Exactly this kind of logic lies behind the government drive to get working class children away from their parents as early as possible . . . into nurseries and centres of early learning.

The parallels with the Victorian tradition of 'self-help' are unmistakable, but current policies do not rely on individual improvement alone. The government aims to reduce child poverty, and to improve education and health resources in deprived areas, increase parental employment, and reform the tax and welfare system. No one wishing to reduce inequalities could argue that the direction of public resources towards those most in need is not a positive step. However, there are problems with this strategy. Even if working-class people could be 'educated' (and this is most unlikely) so that they were no longer 'deficient' in middle-class cultural capital, they would still lack economic and social capital and therefore be at a disadvantage in the education quasi-market.

More particularly, there is the question of the nature of employment – that is, the kinds of jobs available. It is true that rates of employment in Britain are relatively high. This has been argued to be a consequence of the relatively unregulated nature of the labour market in Britain – itself a consequence of neo-liberal policies (as we have seen, however, this assertion has been extensively contested; see Taylor 2002). However, it is also true that income inequalities from employment have widened considerably since the 1970s (Hills 2004). Moreover, it is also the case that many newly created jobs in the expanding service sector are often of low quality, and poorly paid – and this is not simply a case of 'McJobs' (a term coined to describe low-level jobs in the fast food industry; see Ritzer 1996).

Take, for example, childcare workers, who are largely women. As we have seen, the British government is committed to a substantial increase in childcare provision, and this is a rapidly expanding occupation. However, the wages of childcare workers are low, and there are few opportunities for career progression. Childcare workers earn only two-thirds of the average female wage, and in 2006 average hourly pay for unqualified nursery workers was £5.02, and for qualified (NVQ level 2 and above) £5.80.[17] These rates are just above the minimum wage. There are efforts under way to improve the qualifications of childcare workers, but a substantial minority (40 per cent) have either no qualifications, or up to NVQ level 2, and only a very small minority (under 10 per cent) are qualified beyond NVQ level 3 – that is, beyond GCSE level. The major expansion of childcare that has taken place in Britain in recent years has taken place in the private sector, and childcare is big business. The day nursery market is worth £3.26bn and during 2004 grew by more than 20 per cent (Vincent and Ball 2006: 31). This expanding sector of employment, therefore, is largely staffed by low-paid, poorly qualified employees. A similar situation prevails in other countries with a largely private childcare market. For example, as Hochschild (2000: 144) notes, in the US, dog catchers and traffic meter collectors are better paid than childcare workers. This is in some contrast to the Scandinavian countries, where childcare is state provided, universal, and of high quality, and childcare workers are highly educated and well paid (Nyberg 2006: 99).

In summary: the focus of British government policy in respect of class differences in educational achievement is to focus on the perceived inadequacies of children and families and their lack of competitiveness in the education market. This focus on the individual meshes with neo-liberal thinking and extends to other areas of social and welfare policy. For example, as Sayer (2005: 93) has remarked: 'the British government (and many others) prefers to treat unemployment as a problem of the identity of individuals who are unemployed and their inability to make themselves marketable, rather than of the inability of the economic system to provide sufficient employment'. Although the government seeks to improve school standards 'across the board', by its very nature a 'quasi-market' in education is going to create 'winners' and 'losers' amongst schools. 'Choice' in education has become a mantra, but it may be suggested that many, if not most, parents would be willing to forgo 'choice' if a good, well-funded, local school was universally available.

Moreover, the eventual destinations of young adults have to be considered. There will always be those with fewer qualifications than others, and the future for those with no or few qualifications appears to be particularly bleak at the moment (McDowell 2003). Not only education but also job quality (and this would include pay) need to be upgraded across the board (as in the example of childcare workers discussed above). In short, rather than just, as at present, a primary policy focus on equipping the individual for market competition (whether in schooling or employment), it may be argued that class inequalities can only be addressed if the structures within which these individuals are embedded are changed as well. To paraphrase Marshall (chapter 6, p. 98), in respect of employment, we should think rather more about the possibilities of transforming a skyscraper into a bungalow.

Conclusions

In this chapter, we have examined debates and evidence relating to class differences in social mobility and educational achievement. In relation to these persistent inequalities, the major transmission belt is the family. Thus class inequalities have, as many authors have observed, strong self-maintaining properties. To repeat, in a capitalist society, families do not *create* the 'class structure', but they play a vital role in ensuring who gets what positions within it.

Social mobility (or rather, opportunities for social mobility) plays a key role not only in determining 'life chances', but also in the justification of continuing inequalities. If everyone has an equal opportunity in the competition for the best jobs that society has to offer – to realize their 'capabilities' (Sen 1999) – then this might persuasively be argued to be fair, and the pattern of rewards in society might come close to reflecting ability and effort.[18] However, as we have seen in our discussion of class-related differences in educational achievement, this is not the case, despite numerous attempts at reform. Indeed, it is likely that the creation of a quasi-market in education in Britain has actually made upward mobility more problematic, as the middle classes are so much better equipped to compete in the education market. As a consequence, social mobility in Britain is in decline. It has been argued that directing resources so as to bring working-class children and parents 'up' to 'middle-class' standards cannot be the answer, even if it were possible. Of course, it is important to improve schools, healthcare and social and economic infrastructure in the areas of greatest need. However, it is equally if not more important to address the question of employment – putting it crudely, the 'class structure'. As a teacher in a Bermondsey school interviewed by Evans (2006: n.p.) put it: 'These kids don't know they're working class; they won't know that until they leave school and realise that the dreams they've nurtured through childhood can't come true.'

This chapter has also served to illustrate the need for a multifaceted, pluralist approach to the question of class and class reproduction. In understanding social mobility and educational achievement, we have drawn on quantitative as well as qualitative research, and argued for the significance of cultural and social, as well as economic, capital, and that individuals are constrained by structures but nevertheless empowered to act. These binaries may be contrasted as shown in figure 7.1.

'Structure'	'Action'
'Economy'	'Culture'
'Quantitative'	'Qualitative'
'Facts'	'Values'
'Class'	'Status'

Figure 7.1 Interdependencies in 'class analysis'

Nevertheless, the important point is that although these binaries are useful in helping us to understand the complex processes of class reproduction, in both theory and practice, *these are not binaries but, rather, interdependencies.* To return to the conclusions of the previous chapter, we need to preserve an analytical dualism in order to facilitate empirical research, but to emphasize one of these interdependencies to the exclusion of the other (as, for example, in Goldthorpe's rejection of the significance of cultural capital in educational achievement in his development of RAT) runs the danger of excluding a range of issues vital to our understanding of class inequalities.

In terms of the distance from 'top' to 'bottom', class inequalities are increasing in Britain. In our concluding chapter, therefore, we will examine some of the reasons for this increasing social polarization.

WIDENING INEQUALITIES AND DEBATES ON 'CLASS': DISCUSSION AND CONCLUSIONS 8

Introduction

In this chapter, we will draw out further a number of the themes that have been developed in this book. It will be argued that although the last few decades have indeed been characterized by rapid global and social change, it is nevertheless rather misleading to take this uncritically as evidence of an 'epochal change' or a major 'societal shift'. Rather, it will be argued that what we have witnessed is a sustained turn to the economic and political ideas of neo-liberalism – an ideology (and practice) with a long pedigree.

This assertion will of course be contested. After all, there has been a 'centre left' government in office in Britain since 1997, and the centre left has also been in power for substantial periods in many other European countries. As a consequence, many commentators would argue that there has been a shift in ideology, and policy thinking, from neo-liberalism to the 'third way' (Giddens 2001). A concise definition of the 'third way' is impossible, but crudely, it attempts to steer a course between neo-liberalism and 'top-down' socialism, between free markets and state controls, between 'left' and 'right' in politics. In the 'third way', the state will still provide, but it will not necessarily organize and deliver this provision. Thus services paid for by the state are contracted out to private (profit-making) providers (as in the example of nursery care discussed in the last chapter), and 'quasi-markets' are developed in sectors that cannot be privatized. Examples would be education, as discussed in the last chapter, as well as policies such as 'best value' in local government.[1]

As we have seen in previous chapters, besides a generalized preference for private sector organization, and the value of 'market forces' as organizing mechanisms, these kinds of policies emphasize the importance of 'choice' and individual 'empowerment'. An emphasis on individual rights may be bound together with the necessity for state intervention – as, for example, in the concept of 'stakeholding' (Kelly et al. 1997). 'Stakeholding' argues not for redistributive equality, but rather for equality of opportunity; that is, all 'stakeholders' (citizens) should be guaranteed a minimum endowment of capabilities and opportunities (training, education, job opportunities, etc.). Thus *inclusion* in society, rather than absolute equality, is the key concept. At the same time, it is argued that the market by itself is not sufficient to provide opportunities, and thus a wide range of institutions – employment organizations and financial and political systems – will have to be reformed in order that the majority might be included. Proponents of 'stakeholding', therefore, are laying a major emphasis upon the necessity for the *individual* to achieve the practical capacity to achieve citizenship rights through skills, education and job opportunities.

A similar individualist theme emerges in the recent governmental equalities review (*Fairness and Freedom*, HMSO 2007: 16). Equality is defined as follows:

> An equal society protects and promotes equal, real freedom and substantive opportunity to live in the ways people value and would choose, so that everyone can flourish.
>
> An equal society recognises people's different needs, situations and goals and removes the barriers that limit what people can do and can be.

This definition is derived from the 'capabilities' approach developed by Sen (1999). This approach shifts attention from inequalities in resources, outcomes and opportunities to inequalities in capabilities, that is, the 'real freedom' a person has to be or to do what she or he has reason to value. As described in the review:

> this approach focuses on what matters to people (the important things in life that people can actually do and be), recognises that people have different needs and some people may need more or different resources to have access to the same outcomes as others, places emphasis on the barriers and constraints people operate under, and recognises that people have diverse goals in life.   (HMSO 2007: 126)[2]

The equalities review has developed a list of capabilities, ranging from health and standard of living to employment and social life.[3] Progress towards equality, it is argued, can be achieved by a combination of measurement, targeting, encouragement and enforcement.

In short, tackling inequalities means giving individuals the capacities (capabilities) to develop into what they want to be. As an ideal, this has much to commend it. However, there are problems with this approach. First, the opportunity structures – particularly the labour market – within which individuals attempt to realize their capabilities are taken as given. Yes, organizations have to ensure non-discriminatory policies, organizations and individuals need to be helped to achieve these ends, and the law has to be enforced – but in the equalities review, the inevitability of occupational polarization (for example) is taken for granted (HMSO 2007: 43). Second, embedded normative constraints, which have an important impact on what is 'valued' by individuals, are largely ignored in this approach.[4] For example, the normative assignment of caring and domestic work to women means that many women will put a high value on these activities, and may, indeed, 'choose' to prioritize them. However, in practice this inhibits their 'agency freedom' to realize their capabilities in respect of employment (Crompton et al. 2007a). In short, an individually based approach to the reduction of inequalities may give the state the duty to do what it can to provide for and nurture these individuals, but ultimately, the responsibility lies with the individual. As the equalities review (HMSO 2007: 45) argues: 'A large part of what will unseat entrenched inequalities will lie in what communities and families do for themselves', and 'barriers to aspiration' must be removed. Although, therefore, the policy emphasis in respect of inequality has markedly shifted under 'New Labour', a number of underlying assumptions, particularly the emphasis on the individual, remain the same as in the 'Thatcherite' era. In the next section, we will explore these arguments further via debates on the 'underclass'.

From the 'underclass' debate to social exclusion

As we have seen in our discussion above, recent policies have stressed the necessity for the inclusion of the individual via a minimum endowment of capabilities, for which the state has a major responsibility. However, the right-leaning originators of the 'underclass' debate argued that individuals have been excluded from the societal mainstream *because* of the granting of the entitlements and welfare rights of social citizenship as described by Marshall (see chapter 6).

Neo-liberals have argued that the welfare benefits available to the poorest members of society have played an important part in increasing inequality via their role in the creation of an 'underclass'. In chapter 2, we have discussed in brief the neo-liberal argument that attempts to achieve equality of outcome through, for example, programmes of affirmative action for disadvantaged groups might undermine legal or formal equalities (see p. 12). In a similar vein, libertarian critics of welfare-state provision have argued that the *compulsory* redistribution of income should be kept at a minimum, and that individuals should be free to determine the nature and extent of their own welfare provision. These arguments do not imply that those without resources should be left to starve, but they do indicate the targeting (that is, means-testing) of the benefits which are available in any 'minimalist' system of provision (Peacock 1991). As Plant (1991) has argued, neo-liberals have stressed the value of negative liberty – that is, the absence of intentional coercion – as against positive liberty – that is, the actual possession of powers, resources and capacities to act. A further twist to these arguments is developed by those who suggest that collective provisions have actually had the effect of undermining individual capacities. Thus state provision for the economically disadvantaged is argued, by some right-wing theorists, to be making an active contribution to the problem it is trying to solve, through the creation of 'welfare dependency' and thus the development of an underclass.

We have already encountered variants of these arguments in previous chapters. As we have seen in chapter 5, Saunders has identified a major division, in countries like Britain, between the majority in employment and a minority who remain reliant on an 'increasingly inadequate and alienative form of direct state provision' (1987: ch. 3), which, he argues, increasingly disempowers this minority as well. In a similar vein, Murray has written of the 'Great Society' welfare reforms in the United States in the 1960s that 'The first effect of the new rules [i.e. increases in welfare] was to make it more profitable for the poor to behave in the short term in ways that were destructive in the long term. Their second effect was to . . . subsidize irretrievable mistakes. We tried to provide more for the poor and produced more poor instead' (1984: 9). The notion of the 'underclass' proved to be a highly contentious concept, and it has been argued that the term has been developed not in order to describe an objective phenomenon or set of social relationships but, rather, as a stigmatizing label which effectively 'blames the victims' for their misfortunes.

In fact, the notion of an underclass has a long history, although the same label has not always been used. Marx, for example, described the 'lumpenproletariat' of the nineteenth century in terms which closely resemble twentieth-century accounts of the 'underclass'. In the most general terms, the concept describes those in persistent poverty, who are not able, for whatever reason, to gain a living within the dominant processes of production, distribution and exchange. In one sense, it might be suggested that the existence of such an underclass is in fact normal in a competitive capitalist society, which will inevitably produce losers as well as winners. As we have seen in chapter 6, social citizenship has been regarded as enabling (entitling) the (relative) 'losers' to participate in society, hence its role in 'class abatement'. Perhaps because the underclass has been defined with respect to its *lack* of direct structural relationship to the dominant processes of production and exchange, there has been a constant tendency to conceptualize it with respect to its supposed characteristics, rather than with respect to its relationship to other classes. These characteristics have usually been negative. It is, therefore, in the explanation of poverty – or why some people are losers whilst others are not, whether the causes of poverty are primarily structural or primarily cultural – that the 'underclass' concept assumes its contentious aspect.

As we have seen in previous chapters, a frequent explanation of individual inequality is that some people are simply more talented, and ambitious, than others; that they deserve, therefore, to succeed. It is perfectly possible to hold to this meritocratic view, however, without designating the less talented and less ambitious as 'worse' – as in the phrase: 'There's always got to be a bottom brick.' Bottom bricks may be bottom bricks, but they are essentially the same bricks as the top ones. It is but a short step, however, from recognizing talent and ambition in the more successful to the argument that the more fortunate are in fact better, and therefore *morally* superior to the losers. Nineteenth-century debates on poverty linked such arguments to wider economic questions; charity was seen not only as destroying incentives amongst the poor but as jeopardizing the nature of the capitalist enterprise itself. As economic liberals argued: 'Hunger must be permitted to do its work so that labourers are compelled to exert themselves. Otherwise they will reduce their efforts and destroy their only safeguard against starvation' (quoted in Bendix 1964: 58) – and not only the labourers, but the enterprise as a whole, will suffer. Parallel with these arguments, Malthus added his theory of population: the poor have a natural tendency to increase their numbers beyond that sustainable by the available food supply; this improvidence results from ignorance and a lack of moral restraint. Nothing less than a new set of moral values, therefore, will serve to improve the lot of those in poverty.

We may see, therefore, that arguments which hold the poor to be, in varying degrees, responsible for their own plight have a long history, as have arguments to the effect that charity (or welfare) simply stops the poor from helping themselves. It is not surprising, therefore, that such arguments resurfaced with the increasing influence of 'New Right' neo-liberal perspectives on welfare in the 1980s and 1990s – although the intention of these brief remarks has been to suggest that they are not, in fact, so 'new'. Murray (1984) argued that the 'Great Society' welfare reforms had created an 'underclass' in the United States. Murray identified the underclass amongst particular groups of the poor – unmarried single mothers, labour-force drop-outs (the unemployed) and those engaged in criminal activities – and attempted to demonstrate that all of these activities have been positively encouraged by welfare reforms.

Murray argued, for example, that changes in the benefits systems associated with Aid to Families with Dependent Children (AFDC) in the US had made unmarried parenthood, without employment, a more attractive option for *both* parents. He also argued that the decline in rates of arrest had increased the possibility of getting away with criminal activity, and thus its economic attractions. Welfare reforms had taken away the incentive to work. Thus for those in the black ghetto (in the United States, these arguments have focused almost entirely on the problems of poverty amongst urban blacks) there had been, with these changes in incentives, a change in attitude. The black 'underclass' was demoralized, the capacity for self-help in the community had been cumulatively undermined by the policies of well-meaning white liberals. Although Murray developed his empirical arguments largely in the US context, he also argued that such an 'underclass' was developing in Britain, and for similar reasons: 'Britain has a growing population of working-aged, healthy people who live in a different world from other Britons, who are raising their children to live in it, and whose values are now contaminating the life of entire neighbourhoods.' There were two steps, therefore, in Murray's explanation (see Murray 1990: 4; 1994): first, well-meaning reforms exacerbate the problem they are trying to solve, that is, poverty. Then the poor develop a moral stance which effectively removes the will to effort and further deepens the cycle of poverty.

Much of Murray's case, therefore, lay in his attempts to demonstrate the individual moral and cultural inferiority of the least well-off members of society. It is not accidental that his later work *The Bell Curve* (Herrnstein and Murray 1994) argued that low intelligence was the principal cause of poverty.[5] His empirical evidence has been widely contested. Wilson argues that, if Murray's thesis was correct, trends in black joblessness and family dissolution should have gone into reverse when the real value of welfare programmes (to the recipients) declined sharply during the 1970s; in fact, they continued to increase. Similarly, the number of single-parent families grew during the same period, when the value of AFDC benefits was going down.[6]

More generally, Murray's arguments have been systematically criticized by those who have emphasized the political and structural reasons for the increase in persistent poverty, and other 'social pathologies' such as single parenthood, in the black ghettos of the US North-West (Wilson 1987, 1993). These accounts, therefore, have focused upon the *processes* which have generated increasing social and economic polarization. Wilson argues that in the US the loss of manufacturing employment during the economic restructuring which followed upon the crisis of the 1970s had a particularly significant impact upon the inner city. Rising unemployment had been accompanied by a fall in the real value of wages, and thus an increase in poverty. The pattern of migration flows kept the age structure of the ghetto disproportionately young (and therefore more likely to have children), and the real decline in employment opportunities meant that young black women were confronting a shrinking pool of marriageable – that is, employed – men. The very success of Equal Opportunity and Affirmative Action programmes created an increasing black middle class who, given the long-term decline of overt discriminatory practices, have moved out of the ghetto – leaving those behind as the 'truly disadvantaged'. Thus vital elements of the black infrastructure, once provided by black professionals, have been removed, and with them the role models for the next generation.

Wilson, therefore, is not concerned to deny the increase in crime, poverty, single parenthood and so on which has occurred in the urban ghettos of America. He is, however, concerned to emphasize the macro-structural factors which have brought about such changes, and his analysis suggests that only macro-structural changes can alter the situation. The problems of the truly disadvantaged, he argues, require *non-racial* solutions. Macro-economic policies are needed to promote growth and tight labour markets, and there should be increased resources devoted to education and training, in combination with universalist child support programmes and access to childcare. In short, Wilson advocates the integration of social policy and economic policy.

An important feature of Wilson's argument is its emphasis upon the *spatial* dimension of the concentration of poverty. The spatial concentration of poverty, he suggests, means social isolation from the societal mainstream, exacerbated by factors such as poor and expensive public transport.[7] Wilson accepts that the combination of poverty, weak labour-force attachment and isolation from other groups of different class and/or racial backgrounds may lead to the more ready adoption of ghetto-specific practices such as 'overt emphasis on sexuality, idleness, and public drinking' (1993: 5). However, he is careful to draw a distinction between these associations and 'culture of poverty' arguments, which had suggested that the way in which the poor adapt to poverty (fatalism, the acceptance of anti-social behaviour and so on) are transmitted between the generations, locking the poor into a 'poverty cycle' (Lewis 1959). As Wilson points out, cultural practices alone cannot be held to account for 'unemployment, underemployment, low income, a persistent shortage of cash, and crowded living conditions' (1993: 4). In a similar vein, Merton's (1965) analysis of the conflict between societal or cultural goals and the institutionalized means through which they could be achieved provided a framework through which 'deviant' responses might be understood. Thus, when the goal of economic success is dominant but the individual lacks the means through which to achieve it, 'innovation' (illegal activity) is a possible response. This argument, of course, is perfectly compatible with Murray's underlying logic. However, as Merton emphasized: 'These categories [such as 'innovation'] refer to role behavior in specific types of situations, not to personality. They are types of more or less enduring response, not types of personality organization' (Merton 1965: 140).

A similar position has also been forcefully argued by British critics of Murray, who have emphasized the similarities between Murray's arguments and previous theories which have stressed the significance of the 'culture of poverty' in contributing to 'cycles of disadvantage' (Walker 1990). Empirical work in Britain on 'cycles of disadvantage' had failed to demonstrate its malign and enduring effect: 'At least half of the children born into a disadvantaged home do not repeat the pattern of disadvantage in the next generation. Over half of all forms of disadvantage arise anew each generation' (Rutter and Madge 1976).

The spatial dimension of poverty has also been emphasized in British research. Morris's research on Hartlepool (1994, 1995) demonstrates how a town once dominated by heavy industry (construction, shipbuilding, engineering and steel) had, by the 1990s, become an area in which male unemployment stood at 20 per cent. Morris's study included the long-term unemployed as well as those with very fragmented employment histories – both of these categories having been incorporated into definitions of the 'underclass'. However, Morris found there were substantial differences between the long-term unemployed and the insecurely employed. The latter were more likely to be skilled (although not apprenticed) workers, whereas the long-term unemployed were overwhelmingly unskilled. This, argues Morris, should be seen as the *source* of their vulnerability, rather than corresponding to their 'class' position. However, differences in skill did not differentiate between insecurely employed men and those who were securely employed. Insecurely employed men were no less likely to be skilled but they were likely to be younger. Unlike the long-term unemployed, they had access to networks of contacts, but these contacts were themselves likely to lead to insecure jobs. Like Wilson's, therefore, Morris's work points to the significance of social contacts – or their absence. Her work demonstrates the complexity of circumstances amongst the very poorest households, and she suggests that the 'underclass' concept is in any case not sufficient as a description of contemporary poverty: 'the notion of the under-class is an oversimplification, contaminated by its use as a tool of political rhetoric, which has been too readily applied to complex social phenomena' (1995: 74).

Discussions within the 'underclass' debate, therefore, have tended to stress the need to move away from the 'structure versus culture' (or individual morality) debates. They have, therefore, focused upon a careful unpacking of the various social processes which have gen-erated extremes of poverty. Not surprisingly, much of this discussion and research has been grounded in case-study research, through which these dimensions have been identified. However, arguments (such as those of Murray) that the lot of the very poor (or 'under-class') lies in their individual characteristics, including low intelligence, inferior morals and/or disinclination to work, may also be usefully examined via the methodology of the large-scale sample survey, characteristic of the 'employment-aggregate' approach and its variants. Gallie and Vogler's analysis (1993; see also Gallie 1994) found that the unem-ployed were actually *more* likely to say that they would continue in employment even if there was no financial necessity than were the employed (77 versus 66 per cent). That is, they appeared to be more 'committed' to the idea of work. Marshall et al. (1996), using survey data gathered in both Britain and the US, found that individuals living in poverty were *not* significantly more likely to express 'fatalistic' attitudes (supposedly an important element of the underclass 'culture of poverty') than those who were better off. This kind of evidence, therefore, demonstrates that the behavioural *consequences* of a supposed 'under-class' location are not, in fact, as would be predicted by Murray and 'culture of poverty' arguments.

The evidence presented in the 'underclass' debate, therefore, provides us with a useful example of the way in which different methodological approaches, which are characteris-tic of different approaches to 'class analysis', may be brought to bear on the same topic. Both the case-study investigation of social processes and survey evidence of the conse-quences of poverty and unemployment for individual attitudes have made important con-tributions to the empirical refutation of Murray's arguments. This fact helps us to appreciate an important point relating to the need to use a variety of methodologies in order to investigate complex phenomena.

For example, Morris has been very critical of the employment-aggregate approach, arguing that, in her exploration of the social changes that have accompanied the shifts in employment in Britain (including the 'underclass' debate): 'It has been something of a puzzle for me that social class, the concept which most overtly and directly addresses issues of structured inequality, has seemed of little relevance to this work' (1996: 184). She criti-cizes the employment-aggregate approach for its inability to accommodate the growing numbers of long-term unemployed (as we have seen in chapter 4, the long-term unem-ployed have now been included in the ONS-SEC classification), for the fact that it is static, providing no indication of an individual's career, and for failing to give any indication of household circumstances – all features which she found to be central in her own investiga-tions of the 'underclass'. By its very nature, the employment-aggregate approach tends to emphasize stability, rather than change; thus it is hardly surprising that Morris should find it wanting.[8] These kinds of criticism would seem to be particularly appropriate when employment-aggregate practitioners such as Marshall et al. assert that as the non-employed have similar attitudes to the employed, they can be treated as 'displaced class actors'. Thus 'there is little to be gained by incorporating into the research programme of class analysis those individuals without employment' (Marshall et al. 1997: 93).

However, both of these apparently contradictory positions have some substance. As Morris argues, the employment-aggregate approach (most particularly, the categories of the Goldthorpe class scheme) is inadequate as far as an exploration of the *processes* of 'underclass' formation are concerned. Marshall et al. are not interested in these processes (i.e. the investigation of these processes lies outside the scope of their 'research programme' of class analysis as they see it); rather, their interest lies solely in particular features of the *consequences* of social location. Yet again, we are witnessing the apparent failure of the practitioners of different approaches to 'class analysis' to recognize the different, but complementary, nature of each other's positions.

To return to broader sociological themes: it is not particularly helpful to attempt to deny the capacity for autonomous action amongst those in poverty. It is important, however, that this capacity is not linked automatically to arguments like Murray's to the effect that it is the *peculiar* nature of the poor's capacity for action – in particular, their lack of moral values stemming from a 'culture of poverty' – which explains their material circumstances. Murray would argue (as would other right-wing sociologists such as Saunders) that he wishes to *restore* the capacity for action to a population which has been deprived of it by the excesses of bureaucratic state welfare. As he has written:

> Government cannot identify the worthy, but it can protect a society in which the worthy can identify themselves. I am proposing triage of a sort, triage by self-selection. In triage on the battlefield, the doctor makes the decision – this one gets treatment, that one waits, the other one is made comfortable while waiting to die. In our social triage, the decision is left up to the patient. The patient always has a right to say 'I can do X' and get a chance to prove it. Society always has a right to hold him to that pledge. The patient always has the right to fail. Society always has the right to let him.   (1984: 234)

'The right to fail', however, has a chilling echo of the nineteenth-century arguments of Thomas Malthus:

> A man who is born into a world already possessed, if he cannot get subsistence from his parents on whom he has a just demand, and if the society does not want his labour, has no claim of right to the smallest portion of food, and, in fact, has no business to be where he is. At Nature's mighty feast there is no vacant cover for him. She tells him to be gone, and will quickly execute her own orders.   (Malthus cited in Bendix 1964: 65)

However, in more recent discussions the 'blame the victim' discourse associated with the identification of the 'underclass' has been substantially moderated. Debates about poverty persist, but the need for 'positive liberties' is emphasized, and blame is no longer squarely placed on the individual. For example, the equalities review argues that: 'the lack of a capability indicates a failure on the part of society to provide real freedom for people; it does not indicate anything deficient about the individuals themselves' (HMSO 2007: 126). Rather than the emphasis on 'moral turpitude' to be found in the 'underclass' debates, there has been a shift of emphasis towards the role of society and hence 'social exclusion': 'An individual is socially excluded if (a) he or she is geographically resident in a society, (b) he or she cannot participate in the normal activities of citizens in that society, and (c) he or she would like to so participate, but is prevented from doing so by factors beyond his or her control' (Burchardt et al. 1999: 229).

Social exclusion is seen to arise from a series of linked problems – unemployment, poor skills, low incomes, poor housing, high crime, bad health and family breakdown. The British government has set up a Social Exclusion Unit that has instituted programmes of urban renewal, 'Connexions' (a service that provides advice for teenagers about education, training and employment) and programmes such as Sure Start (discussed in chapter 7), as well as many others. However, as has been suggested in our discussion of the equalities review (and of contemporary education policies in the last chapter), these policy shifts retain a focus on specific individuals and groups, and on attempts to increase their range of choice and/or change their behaviour, rather than on any sustained effort to transform the wider structures within which these individuals and groups are embedded. For example, the equalities review (HMSO 2007: 32) recognizes the sharp rise in income inequality and job polarization in Britain in recent years, but does not acknowledge that rising income inequality and changes in the employment structure were themselves in part a consequence of deliberate changes in economic policy. However, as Wilson (discussed above) argued in his contribution to the 'underclass' debate in the United States, economic *and* social policies have to be linked in order to address inequalities as a whole. That is, although it is certainly a positive step to introduce policies that aim to develop the practical capacities for individuals to realize their 'capabilities', this does not mean that 'older' approaches to the problem of inequality, which had a focus on resources and outcomes, can simply be discarded. If we follow the usual convention of taking the occupational structure as a proxy for the class structure, then if this structure remains highly unequal, extensive inequalities will endure. In short, it is being argued that parallel efforts should be being made to improve the overall 'quality' of *employment*, as well as the 'quality' of the people taking up employment.

Widening inequality

As discussed in chapters 1 and 5, recent decades have witnessed an increasing turn to the political and economic ideas of neo-liberalism (Harvey 2005). Economic liberalism is not a new doctrine, as we have seen in our discussion of nineteenth-century attitudes to the poor. It is not being suggested that the neo-liberals of today would advocate actually leaving the poor to starve to death.[9] However, neo-liberal policies, particularly the deregulation of international trade, as well as of financial and labour markets, together with the removal of social protections, will increase inequality. As we have seen, this increase would be argued to be justified by increases in efficiency, productivity and profitability and thus total wealth. This wealth, however, is, increasingly, unequally shared.

After the election of the Conservative government in 1979, in Britain there was a rapid growth of income and wealth inequality in the 1980s. Between 1961 and 1979, as a whole all income groups benefited from rising incomes, with those of the lowest rising fastest. However, between 1979 and 1994/5, after housing costs, the incomes of the richest decile (the top 10 per cent of incomes) grew by over 60 per cent, while those of the poorest decile fell by nearly 10 per cent. From 1994/5, the growth in average living standards has raised the income of most groups with the exception of the poorest decile. Over the 23-year period from 1979 to 2002–3, for every £100 in additional net real income, £40 went to the richest tenth of the population (Hills 2004: 20ff). As Hills (2004: 28–9) emphasizes, the growth in income inequality in Britain was exceptional not only in British historical terms but also internationally. Amongst 'Western' developed countries, by the mid-1990s, inequality in Britain was greater than in any other country apart from the United States.

The 1979 Conservative government claimed that unemployment was caused by workers 'pricing themselves out of jobs'. Thus legislation was introduced which facilitated the payment of lower wages to workers who were often poorly paid in the first place. These policies included the removal of rights granted by the Employment Protection Act of the mid-1970s; the privatization of public-sector services, as a consequence of which those workers who did not lose their jobs were often rehired at lower rates of pay; subsidies to encourage low wage rates for young workers; and the removal of wages council protection in low-paid industries. At the same time, the abandonment of wage and salary controls allowed the incomes of the very highest earners to spiral up to previously unheard-of levels. As a consequence of these changes, as we have seen, the wages of the best-paid increased by more than 50 per cent, whilst those of the lowest-paid actually fell in relative terms. Sustained high levels of unemployment, together with legislation against trade union strategies such as picketing and the closed shop, further eroded the basis of collective action and thus the capacity to protect wage levels.

During the same period, direct tax cuts disproportionately benefited the better-off. Between 1979 and 1986, it has been calculated that out of the £8.1 billion in tax cuts, nearly half went to the richest 10 per cent and almost two-thirds went to the richest 20 per cent. As a result of rising unemployment, declining wage levels, and demographic changes such as the increase in households headed by single parents, the proportion of households dependent on social security benefits rose – social security payments accounted for a fifth of all income in 1992 and 1993 (Goodman et al. 1997). Since 1980, social security benefits have been indexed to prices, rather than wages. As wages (except those of the lowest-paid) have risen faster than prices, the value of benefits in relative terms declined.

It is clear, therefore, that the material impact of Conservative government policies, ostensibly designed to improve economic performance, disproportionately affected different groups – or classes – within the population. The Conservatives sought – and achieved – changes in the 'institutional filters' (welfare states, collective bargaining systems, education, employing organizations; see Esping-Andersen 1993) of class, particularly in respect of collective bargaining and the welfare state, and as a consequence inequality increased. The government's restructuring of other institutions increased inequality by opening up opportunities to 'earn' very high incomes. Amongst the most important examples here are the deregulation of the financial sector in 1986, together with the selling-off of state-owned utilities over the government's whole period in office. Financial deregulation (which was accompanied by 'sweeteners' such as encouraging individuals to cash in their occupational pensions and transfer to the private sector) resulted in an explosion of finance-related jobs, some of them very highly paid indeed.

Earnings of finance employees in the City of London hover around the £100,000 mark, and in January 2007, it was revealed that a City banker had collected £58.6m in earnings in less than a year and a half. In terms that sound familiar from chapter 1 of this book, the Bank of England's deputy governor argued in *The Times* that pay for such individuals 'is now being set in a world market'. Comparing the situation in private equity and hedge funds to the bumper pay packages for the world's football stars, he suggested that rewards for the financial sector's top cadres should be seen in a similar light: 'We have in the Premiership, as in the City, some of the best-paid people in an international industry which is developing very rapidly.'

It is important to emphasize, therefore, that increases in inequality have been a direct consequence of neo-liberal economic policies pursued by governments. However, it should also be emphasized that this is by no means the whole story. As has been noted in previous chapters, changes in the position of women have contributed to increasing class inequalities at the level of the household. Women's qualification levels have improved rapidly, and well-qualified women get better, higher-paying jobs. Such women tend to enter into partnerships with similar men, and are more likely to remain in employment when they have children (Crompton 2006a, b). These family behaviours contribute to widening inequalities. Other changes in social norms and family arrangements also have an impact. Increased family breakdown, and the growing number of single-parent families, make a substantial contribution to child and family poverty. As a consequence of these social changes, household inequalities have widened.

As described in previous chapters, globalization and technological change have had a significant impact on the structure of employment, particularly in the 'older' industrial countries. Besides the fact that many jobs in manufacturing have been moved overseas, technological innovation has meant that fewer people are required in order to achieve a rising level of manufacturing output. Thus it might be argued that the recent increase in social inequality is no more than some kind of 'natural' development, and that as the 'industrial' proletariat has declined, so a more disadvantaged 'service proletariat' has emerged. This important topic has been systematically investigated, through cross-national comparisons, by Esping-Andersen and his colleagues (1993). They argue that (national) institutional variations are of crucial significance in shaping stratification systems. As noted above, they argue that welfare states, education systems, collective bargaining systems and the modern corporation are decisive 'institutional filters' through which class (i.e. occupational) structures emerge. These also affect the nature of service jobs. Perhaps the best-known example here is that of the Scandinavian social democracies, in which the state-managed expansion of welfare services has led to a massive expansion of relatively low-level, but nevertheless reasonably paid and protected, service jobs.[10] Not only is state service provision for such groups as children and the elderly better in the Nordic countries, but the people providing these services are better paid, educated and trained.

In fact, Esping-Andersen concludes that unskilled service jobs do not constitute an emerging new service proletariat in the sense of 'a class imprisoned in a collectively shared, underprivileged, dead-end career' (1993: 231). This is partly because of the national institutional variations we have already mentioned, but also because the fluidity and mobility patterns around such jobs are simply too extensive for any significant social closure to occur (for example, many such jobs are held by young people, often students, who move on to better jobs). However, in the case of Britain Esping-Andersen concludes:

> The British unskilled workers are, as in North America, a sizeable stratum and mainly concentrated in private sector services. They are, however, clearly less mobile and when they do move it is much less likely to be in an upward direction. Indeed, for males the most likely move is to manual work . . . Hence, unskilled service workers in Britain seem to combine the worst features of the American and German model: large but relatively immobile – a potential proletariat. (1993: 233)[11]

Of course, the expansion of services generates not only low-level service jobs, but also an increasing number of professional and managerial jobs. However, in some contrast to the 'good' working-class jobs of the manufacturing era, men have to compete with women for these kinds of jobs. Moreover, as a consequence of this expansion, educational qualifications have become increasingly important in the job market. A 1990s Rowntree report (Joseph Rowntree Foundation 1995: 20) argues that the 'stakes have become higher for young people entering the labour market, with greater differences between those who do well (linked to high educational levels) and those who do not than there were twenty, or even ten, years ago'. Similarly, in his review of postindustrial service economies, Esping-Andersen concludes that: 'Access to educational credentials (and social skills) is clearly a potential catalyst of a new class axis' (1993: 236). Indeed, as we have seen in the preceding chapter, class differences in educational achievement are actually widening, and the introduction of a quasi-market in education has made things worse as far as class inequalities are concerned.

Nevertheless, it is not our purpose to deny that the processes of globalization and technological change *have*, with the growth of the service sector, contributed to occupational polarization and thus widening inequality. It is not accidental that many of these jobs – in marketized care work, retail and restaurants, for example – have historically been thought of as 'women's' jobs, in which wages were traditionally low. The first New Labour government introduced a minimum wage, which is a substantial step forward.[12] However, minimum wage rates are low. From October 2007, the rate for workers aged 22 and over is £5.52 an hour, for workers aged 18–21, £4.60 an hour, and workers aged 16 and 17, £3.40 an hour. These increases are in line with inflation, rather than average wages, and the minister rejected a recommendation that 21-year-olds should receive the full adult rate of £5.52 an hour, saying that such a move could damage their job prospects. Again, our objective is not to argue that it is not a positive move to establish minimum standards, but rather to argue that more should be done to improve the quality of the jobs available (as well as raising the level of minimum entitlements).

However, British governments have been notoriously reluctant to interfere with the employers' 'right to manage'.[13] Employment relations, as noted above, have been one of the major 'institutional filters' that shape the occupational (class) structure. Employment in Britain has always been relatively unregulated, with few protections. As described by Wilkinson and Ladipo, neo-liberals argue that:

> Left to itself, the market will establish equitable pay and conditions of work . . . Moreover, provided the labour market is working 'freely', everyone can find work so long as they are prepared to invest in the necessary skills and accept the real wage the market offers for their capabilities. And, if the government or trade unions try to interfere with this mechanism . . . they will undermine the productivity and 'competitiveness' of the economy upon which rests the health and security of the nation's workforce.   (Wilkinson and Ladipo 2002: 174)

Thus employment protections, whether of jobs themselves or the quality of jobs, are regarded with some suspicion. One feature of job 'quality' is career opportunities. In chapter 5 (see p. 76), we have briefly discussed the development of techniques of 'high-commitment' (also 'high-performance') management, in which the employee is encouraged to develop an 'entrepreneurial self'. One aspect of such management techniques has been the development of individualized promotion systems. As we have seen in chapter 4, Goldthorpe has argued that promotion opportunities are a key 'service class' characteristic. For much of the twentieth century, these opportunities were embedded in the organizational structures of service class employers. For example, banking was once the locus of the classic bureaucratic career (Lockwood 1958). Relatively well-qualified young men were carefully guided through the grade levels of a 'job for life'.[14] Banks held to a 'no poaching' policy (that is, they did not recruit employees from other banks), and promotion track positions were not advertised, either externally or internally. Rather, they were offered to individuals who had demonstrated good behaviour and commitment to the bank (Crompton and Jones 1984; Halford et al. 1997: 161). This usually involved getting the professional qualification supported by the banking industry (the Chartered Institute of Banking, CIB). Until the 1980s, career paths for men were preserved by the recruitment of young female school leavers, usually at lower levels of qualification than young men, who could be relied upon (or were required) to leave the bank at the birth of their first child (Crompton 1989a).

However, banks have now abandoned gender-discriminatory recruitment and promotion practices and, indeed, many are now at the cutting edge of equal opportunity employment. External recruitment is now practised, and in a bank which was studied in recent research, all jobs are advertised internally on a weekly basis.[15] The CIB examinations are no longer considered relevant; rather, employees prepare themselves for job progression by taking modules provided by individual banks. Job advertisements specify the characteristics (modules completed plus work experience) required, and employees are responsible for putting themselves forward for promotion.

These individualized promotion paths are open, transparent and 'fair'. It should be noted that they parallel other structural and policy trends that have similarly generated increasing 'individualization' in employment. However, at the same time as individualized promotion is being introduced and encouraged, opportunity structures within organizations are being truncated as a consequence of techniques such as 'delayering' (reducing the number of promotable grades) and 'outsourcing' (removing 'in-house' services; see Thompson and Warhurst 1998). For example, the bank discussed above had recently reduced the number of job grades from fourteen to seven. Managerial grades begin at G4, so a short hierarchy remains before management level. However, in the retail division of the bank, only 10 per cent of employees were management grade (G4) or above. As a consequence of the reorganization, employees had to reapply for their own jobs, and many chose to take redundancy packages.

Similar processes have occurred in other organizations within the service sector. For example, Grimshaw et al. (2001, 2002; see also Crompton 2006b: ch. 3) have demonstrated that a significant effect of recent changes in service-sector organizations has been to open up the 'gap' in the job ladder between lower-grade employees and the first step on the promotional ladder: 'the most direct effect of the flattened jobs hierarchy has been to remove the architecture necessary for career progression' (Grimshaw et al. 2001: 38). Making the transition to the first rung of the managerial ladder had become increasingly dependent on individual appraisals, and Grimshaw et al. argue that 'staff with ambitions to "move up" the organisation . . . know that they face an "all-or-nothing" effort in time and energy to make the transition to a mid-level post' (Grimshaw et al. 2002: 109).

It would seem, therefore, that competition for promotion is one of the factors associated with the increasing intensification of employment (Burchell et al. 2002). At all levels, individuals wishing to be promoted have to work long hours (working hours in Britain are amongst the longest in Europe, and are even longer in the USA). Other features of 'high-commitment' management include a culture of selling and target setting, and 'promotable' individuals are expected to overshoot these targets. Those wishing to be promoted are, invariably, expected to work full-time. These are just some of the reasons why women have (relatively) 'failed' to reach top positions within the occupational structure, even though formal barriers to employment and career progression have been removed. In general, women are still normatively assigned to caring and domestic work, and find it extremely difficult, if not impossible, to maintain the level of employment commitment required for promotion (Crompton 2006b).

Changes in the management of employees, therefore, have led to increased work intensity and feelings of job insecurity – even though aggregate-level data indicates that jobs have not, in fact, become more insecure.[16] The main point in this discussion of promotion and careers, however, is to suggest how changes in employer practices have contributed to increased inequality and social polarization. Another point to emphasize is that these changes are not simply a consequence of some kind of 'inevitable' process, but have been brought about by deliberate actions, and shifts in managerial strategy. Without wishing to subscribe to conspiracy theories, it cannot be doubted that the 'individualization' of employment is to some extent a consequence of the systematic dismantling and weakening of the institutions of collective representation (trade unions) that took place during the Thatcher era, and from which they have never recovered.

As with the example of the 'Nordic' expansion of state-regulated caring employment discussed above, cross-national comparisons suggest that 'neo-liberal' strategies of employment regulation are not the only, or even the best, way. As Wilkinson and Ladipo (2002) have argued, evidence from other countries (such as the Netherlands, Germany and Japan as well as the Nordic countries) suggests that statutory protections (against dismissal, during periods of technological change, of training, wage and safety standards, and of hours of work; in short, increased labour market regulation) are associated with both economic success and national recoveries from economic difficulties. Moreover, any labour process requires a minimum of co-operation to operate effectively (Edwards 2000: 144); thus, gaining the trust and loyalty of employees is essential. Individualized employment relations erode this trust.

In this section, it has been argued that the changes to the 'institutional filters' of class brought about by the implementation and enhancement of neo-liberal economic and social policies have played an important, even if not the only, role in the widening of class inequalities in Britain. Similarly, the promotion of individual 'choice' in areas such as education and welfare has been a quite deliberate strategy. It is somewhat paradoxical, therefore, that many social theorists write of 'individuation' as if it were some inevitable trend associated with the conditions of 'reflexive modernity'. It has been our purpose to argue that recent decades have seen not so much an unstoppable 'societal shift' as the intensification of capitalism associated with the increasing political and economic hegemony of neo-liberalism.

Some class theorists, notably Savage, have also argued for a shift in class analysis to the individual level:

> class 'rewards', in terms of claims to superior income, or advantaged positions in the division of labour, should not simply be seen as due to the working of an overarching class structure, or the rational workings of markets, but should be seen as the accomplishment of individuals, drawing on diverse resources . . . Class structures are instantiated in people's lives. (Savage 2000: 150)

However, in this chapter it has been argued not that we should necessarily reject this kind of perspective out of hand, but, rather, that at the same time we should not cease to maintain a focus on the pressures and processes that shape the structures within which individuals are embedded. These pressures and processes can be changed and reshaped – as Hills (2004: 261) argues: 'Policies matter, and we are free to choose between them.' To return to the conclusions of the previous chapter, it is being argued that as far as class analysis is concerned, 'action' and 'structure' are interdependent, and we have to retain a dual focus on both.

Back to definitions: the approach developed in this book

A major theme of this book has been that, despite the extent and rapidity of change that characterizes contemporary societies, we should not be too eager to discard or reject previous approaches to class and stratification. Both Marx and Weber, for example, were developing concepts for the analysis of societies that were in many respects very different from those we live in today, but nevertheless, their writings established a number of basic principles still relevant to contemporary class and stratification analysis. Thus occupation (employment) continues to be a significant indicator of both 'life chances' and economic class relations – for example, clear reflections of both Marx's and Weber's insights can be found in Goldthorpe's discussion of 'employment relations' in relation to ONS-SEC (figure 4.2, chapter 4). Both Marx and Weber, although in rather different ways, identified the irreconcilable (class) conflicts and tensions that are embedded in the structuring of market capitalism – conflicts and tensions that we still live with today. Weber also identified the significance of 'status' as a (relatively) autonomous dimension of stratification, an argument that has been fruitfully developed by contemporary political theorists (Fraser 2000).

Indeed (and in line with Marx's and Weber's arguments) in chapter 6, class has been described, at the most abstract level, as an economic concept (chapter 6 also provides a 'positional summary'; see p. 113). However, it has been simultaneously argued that this does not mean we should confine 'class analysis' to an analysis of the economic, as in the bracketing out of 'cultural factors' in Goldthorpe's (2000) rational action theory. Such a strategy will, as has been argued in the previous chapter, result in considerable lacunae in our understanding of significant processes associated with very important topics in class analysis – such as the persistence of class differentials in social mobility and educational achievement.

This characterization of class as, abstractly, an 'economic' concept (see chapter 6, p. 115) is one reason why this book does not include a systematic discussion of 'race'. Obviously, inequalities associated with race are important and enduring. However, whilst not wishing to insist on a 'correct' definition of 'class', the position taken in this book is that inequalities of race (and gender) are to a large extent a consequence of misrecognition and status subordination, rather than economic 'class' processes (Fraser 2000). 'Capitalism' as such is indifferent to the characteristics of the individuals who find places within its structures – although this assertion should immediately be qualified by noting that although 'capitalism' may be indifferent to these individual characteristics, employers and managers are not. Nevertheless, although race and gender are often crucial to this placement within structures, 'race' and 'gender' are not necessary for capitalism to exist.

'Misrecognition', as Fraser (2000: 113–14) has argued:

is not simply to be thought ill of, looked down upon or devalued in others' attitudes, beliefs or representations. It is rather to be denied the status of a full partner in social interaction, as a consequence of institutionalised patterns of cultural value that constitute one as comparatively unworthy of respect or esteem . . . misrecognition constitutes a form of institutionalised subordination.

Misrecognition means that the group so identified is prevented from 'participating as a peer in social life'. Redressing misrecognition, therefore, means changing the social institutions, and normative values regulating interaction, that impede parity of participation (Fraser 2000: 115). The entitlements of 'social citizenship' (see chapter 6, p. 98) also facilitate this participation. It might be argued that in many 'Western' societies, the misrecognition of women has gone some way to being redressed, in that women are no longer seen as inferior beings to men, and have achieved full civil rights. It is of course the case that deep-seated, gendered, normative beliefs still persist that impede 'parity of participation' – in particular the allocation of women to domestic and caring work. A parallel argument might be developed in respect of race – that is, that some progress has been made in achieving civil rights – whilst remaining fully aware of the persistence of race-based inequalities.

To argue that inequalities of race, gender and class have different antecedents is to say just that, and does not indicate any judgement as to which is 'more' or 'less' important as a topic of social science investigation. It is, however, one of the reasons why the argument has been developed, in chapters 5 and 6, as to the impossibility of a single, overarching, theoretical approach to class and stratification (or inequalities in general). Some class theorists would disagree with this argument. If 'class' is seen *primarily* as a social and cultural construction then class and race (and gender) are the same order of phenomena, and the failure to discuss race would be a serious omission. It may be suggested that Skeggs (2004: 3) takes up a stance that is very close to the position that 'class' is, in essence, 'cultural', for example arguing that: 'The discourses of the dangerous outcast, the urban mass, the revolutionary alien, the contagious women, the non-recuperable, came to produce what was known as class.' As discussed in chapter 6, Skeggs argues that 'misrecognition' is central to the creation and identification of 'class', and, moreover, 'misrecognition' translates into the 'economic' as the working classes are not able to 'propertize' themselves. However, the symbolic power of the middle classes enables them to 'propertize' working-class culture (Skeggs 2004: 176): 'Whilst the middle classes are busily propertising their accumulative, exchange value selves through the use of, attachment to, detachment from and experimentation with cultures not of their own making . . . the working classes make culture that is defined as deficit, their selves as abject, and their value as use-less.' Nevertheless, race and gender contribute to the 'making' of concrete (rather than abstract) 'classes'. In this book, the contribution of gender to this 'making' has been fairly extensively discussed, not least because of the importance of feminist criticisms of the 'employment-aggregate' approach to class analysis. Gender is, so to speak, embedded in the processes that generate concrete classes, particularly given the importance of the family as far as class reproduction is concerned. It could certainly be argued that race is 'embedded' in the same manner as gender. If the United States, rather than Britain, had been a major empirical reference point in our discussions, then again, the lack of attention paid to 'race' would have been inexcusable (see Devine 1997). Nevertheless, the relative absence of 'race' from our discussions may still be acknowledged as a relevant point of criticism.

Rather than seeking to develop an improved, more comprehensive or up-to-date approach to class and stratification, this book has argued that there is no 'one best way', and that those interested in the topic should rather focus on the particular concepts and methods already available that are appropriate to the issue at hand. As argued in the second edition of this book: 'the most fruitful way ahead in "class analysis" within sociology lies in the recognition of plurality and difference, rather than forcing a choice from amongst competing positions, or attempting to devise a completely new or revised theoretical approach' (Crompton 1998: 203). In a similar vein, it has been argued that, although it is important to recognize the very significant social, political and economic changes that have taken place over the last few decades, we should be wary of assertions that societies are now so very different that some kind of 'societal shift' has taken place, making 'old' concepts and ideas irrelevant and useless.

In this concluding chapter, we have argued that many of the changes that have been taken as evidence of such a 'societal' shift might in fact be understood as a consequence of the resurgence of political and economic neo-liberalism. In our closing remarks, therefore, we will undertake a brief (and perhaps risky) exercise, that is, to examine the possibility of the emergence of countervailing forces against these recent trends.

The possibility of countervailing processes

In Britain, as in many other 'Western' countries, the occupational structure has been 'upgraded' over the past half century – that is, relatively speaking, the proportion of 'routine and manual' jobs has declined, and there has been a corresponding increase in 'better' jobs. Thus for many – indeed the majority – these have been times of increasing material prosperity. It might seem perverse, therefore, to continue to emphasize the persistence of class inequalities (indeed, this is a feature of Saunders's arguments, summarized in the last chapter, concerning social mobility). However, as we have seen, the trend towards a decrease in class inequalities stalled in the 1980s, a decade that coincided with the introduction of neo-liberal economic and social policies. Following 'New Labour' reforms, the actual *increase* in inequality appears to have ceased as far as the poorest groups in society are concerned, but there is as yet no reversal. Other points of concern are that the 'class structure' appears to be becoming more rigid, as attested by the decline in social mobility and by an apparent reduction of opportunities for the less well qualified to 'work their way up' in organizations. As we shall see, Wilkinson (2005) argues that more inegalitarian societies (that is, societies with a wider income distribution) are also characterized by more intense class effects and psycho-social problems. Too much inequality, it would seem, is bad for society as a whole.

It might nevertheless be argued that the increase in social polarization in Britain that has been described above is a consequence of the linked factors of normative change (such as changes in gender relations and the family), technological changes (information technologies, global communications such as the Internet) and globalization. These changes, it is sometimes implied, are beyond the control of any single group, or any nation state. This position, however, tends to gloss over the fact that the *extent* of social polarization varies considerably between different nation states, and tends to be greatest in those countries where neo-liberal political and economic thinking has been most influential.

As noted above, income inequalities grew rapidly in Britain in the 1980s and 1990s, and by the end of the 1990s, data from the Luxembourg Income Study showed that amongst fifteen 'Western' countries, only the United States and Ireland had higher rates of poverty than the UK (Hills 2004: 57). The policies introduced by New Labour have improved the situation somewhat for those on the lowest incomes, and particularly for their children (Hills 2004: 230), but the continuing increase in incomes for those at the very top means that the gap between the top and the bottom has not closed appreciably, although the bottom has to some extent caught up with the middle.

It has long been recognized that class differences are systematically associated with a wide range of inequalities, and indeed, this has been one of the most common defences of 'class analysis' against its critics (e.g. Goldthorpe and Marshall 1992). In all developed countries, average life expectancy is between five and fifteen years shorter for those at the bottom of the social hierarchy than for those at the top. However, what is becoming increasingly apparent is that these differences are less extreme in more egalitarian countries (that is, those countries with a narrower income distribution) than they are in less egalitarian countries – that is, countries such as Britain and the US. People *at whatever level of income* have lower death rates if they live in a more egalitarian society (Wilkinson 2005: 134). Other negative social indicators, such as homicide rates, teenage pregnancy rates and child mortality rates, are also higher in less egalitarian societies (Wilkinson 2005; Gornick and Meyers 2003). People trust each other less in countries with a larger income difference, and the quality of social relations is poorer when income differences are bigger.[17] In short extremes of inequality, even in 'rich' societies, have a negative impact on the social fabric of society as a whole. These findings suggest, as has been argued above, that it is not sufficient to focus on improving the capabilities of the socially excluded, but that measures also have to be enacted to transform, or at least modify, the structures of social and economic disadvantage.[18] Cross-national comparisons, such as the empirical evidence (some of which has been summarized in this chapter) that some capitalist industrial societies are considerably more egalitarian than others, demonstrates that these modifications can, in fact, be achieved.

Wilkinson (2005: 300) has argued that: 'The combination of the market and inequality threatens . . . to undermine public-spiritedness and replace it with a tendency to regard other people simply as part of the material environment to be exploited for personal gain.' However, as we have argued in this book, policies influenced by neo-liberalism have done a considerable amount to encourage this sort of thinking. Employees are directed to become 'entrepreneurs of the self', quasi-markets have been created in public services (where public services have not actually been privatized), passengers on a train are now 'customers'. In the second chapter of this book, we have briefly noted Polanyi's argument that capitalist societies are characterized by a 'double movement'. That is, even as supporters of the 'self-regulating' market seek to eliminate all restrictions on its freedom to operate, so movements for reform seek to limit the effects of 'market forces':

> Not until 1834 was a competitive labour market established in England; hence, industrial capitalism as a social system cannot be said to have existed before that date. Yet almost immediately the self-protection of society set in: factory laws and social legislation, and a political and industrial working class movement sprang into being.   (Polanyi 1957: 83)

In Polanyi's account, counter-movements against the impact of market forces are described as being spontaneous (1957: 149–50):

The countermove against economic liberalism and laissez-faire possessed all the unmistakable characteristics of a spontaneous reaction. At innumerable disconnected points it set in without any traceable links between the interests directly affected or any ideological conformity between them . . . merely as a result of the increasing realisation of the nature of the problem in question . . . For if market economy was a threat to the human and natural components of the social fabric, as we insisted, what else would one expect than an urge on the part of a great variety of people to press for some sort of protection? . . . one would expect this to happen without any theoretical or intellectual preconceptions on their part, and irrespective of their attitudes towards the principles underlying a market economy.

There are, indeed, numerous contemporary examples of national and global pressures that argue for the urgent need to protect human societies against the unfettered workings of market forces. One obvious example would be the pressures being brought to bear by environmental movements (see chapter 5), against global warming in particular. A discussion of these movements is outside the scope of this book, but the influence of environmental arguments is having an impact at all levels of policy-making and behaviour.

Another example of possible pressures to reverse neo-liberal policies would be the increasing pressures within households, even in Western 'affluent' societies, which have emerged as a consequence of the increasing employment of women, particularly mothers. The 'problem' of human reproduction in capitalist industrialism was for a relatively brief period 'solved' by the allocation of women to unpaid domestic work. Indeed, it might be argued that the trade union fight for the 'family wage', which secured an income sufficient for a working man to support himself and his family, was in the late nineteenth and twentieth centuries an important example of one of the 'countervailing movements' identified by Polanyi (see Seccombe 1993). However, women's demands for the right to employment (and the increasing economic necessity for dual-earner households) have seriously destabilized this pattern. Many 'Western' countries now have falling fertility rates, and 'the family' has become an object of major political concern.

As discussed in previous chapters, in some countries (particularly the Nordic countries), the 'problem' of the increase in women's employment has to a considerable extent been met by the state's provision of caring resources. In other countries (particularly the US, and to a lesser extent in Britain), however, this has largely been left to 'the market'. However, Gornick and Meyers (2003: 107) have argued that: 'The results of the American experiment with market-based solutions [to the needs of dual-earner families] have been calamitous for many American parents and children.' In their twelve-country comparative study, the four Scandinavian countries (Denmark, Sweden, Norway and Finland) scored best on a whole series of indicators, including joint weekly working hours, child well-being and poverty, teenage pregnancy and many others. The three English-speaking countries (the United Kingdom, Canada and the United States) scored least well. Other European countries (Belgium, France, the Netherlands, Luxembourg and Germany) lay between the two extremes (Gornick and Meyers 2003: 258). European comparisons also demonstrate that fertility rates have declined less in those countries with good state dual-earner family supports (Fagnani 2007). As Gornick and Meyers (2003: ch. 9; see also Crompton 2006b) argue, therefore, statutory family-related supports of a material kind, together with regulation of employment relationships and individual employee rights, are required in order not only to combat deepening inequalities at the national level, but also to ameliorate the current forced tradeoffs, particularly in neo-liberal societies, between the interests of men, women and children. Statutory family-related supports would require increases in taxation, and a shift in resources 'downwards' rather than 'upwards'.

Thus these kinds of issues relating to family life and caring, which have historically been seen as 'women's' issues, are gaining in importance and recognition, both national and international. It is of some interest that although the material impact of these pressures is greatest as far as the working class is concerned, problems of work–life conflict are actually greater for managerial and professional employees, particularly in neo-liberal societies, where they tend to work longer hours (Lyonette et al. 2007; Crompton 2006b). One important way in which these pressures might be relieved would be to reduce work intensity (and working hours) – that is, to put limits on the employers' 'right to manage'. It is possible, therefore, that these kinds of pressures towards market (employment) regulation, which derive from pressures on the family, might come from across the social spectrum. As has been argued in this chapter, such employment regulation would also result in an enhancement in the quality of the jobs available – that is, an upgrading of the 'class structure' that would also improve lower-level jobs.

Particular examples of 'counter-movements', beyond those generated by the crises of the environment and the family, might be multiplied (for example, Local Economic Trading Systems (LETS), anti-IMF (International Monetary Fund) riots, campaigns against global poverty such as Live Aid). Some have argued that the tensions and contradictions of the world financial system point 'to the possibility of a major crisis within the heartland of the neoliberal order itself' – the United States (Harvey 2005: 188). Such a crisis, Harvey argues, might result in the consolidation of neo-conservative authoritarianism, but it simultaneously opens up the possibilities of alternatives to neo-liberalism.

Again, these issues lie outside the scope of this book. Modern history, as Polanyi (1957: 29) has demonstrated in his historical analysis of counter-movements against the 'utopian endeavour of economic liberalism to set up a self-regulating market system' in the nineteenth and early twentieth centuries, does suggest that self-protection might be achieved in the long run, and there is increasing evidence of social movements, and other pressures, that seek to do just this. In the short run, those with an interest in the reduction of inequalities (particularly class inequalities) can only continue to research and debate their origins, their impacts and what might be done about them. One of the major objectives of this book has been, hopefully, to provide contemporary researchers with the tools to do so.

NOTES

Chapter 1   Setting the Scene

1 'Liberalism' does not describe a single doctrine, and the term may encompass conflicting perspectives. For example, although all liberals would emphasize the importance of the rights and freedoms of the individual – whereas social liberals would argue that forms of support, usually provided by the state (education, welfare supports, etc.), are required in order that the individual may truly exercise these freedoms – economic liberalism argues that the inequality that arises from unequal bargaining positions (in the absence of coercion) is a natural outcome of free competition. Indeed, economic liberals would argue that the social supports advocated by social liberals interfere with market competition and should therefore be opposed or, at the very least, kept to a minimum. These kinds of debates and issues will be further explored in this book, particularly in chapters 2, 3, 4, 7 and 8.
2 So called after the economist J.M. Keynes. Keynes advocated a 'mixed economy' of public and private ownership, in which the state used its powers to smooth out market fluctuations. State intervention in the economy was also accompanied by the expansion of welfare policies and other market protections. In short (and in sharp contrast to classic economic liberalism or *laissez-faire*), Keynesian economics advocates direct state intervention in markets of all kinds.

Chapter 2   Approaches to Class and Stratification Analysis

1 The 'ideological' origins and nature of the caste system have been challenged, particularly by Marxist anthropologists (Meillassoux 1973). It is argued that in reality caste differentiation reflected degrees of material power and domination, rather than ritual purity.
2 Some categories of human beings, notably women, were initially excluded from this 'fraternal social contract'. See Pateman (1988, 1989).
3 As we shall see in ch. 3, Marx argued that feudal societies, like capitalist societies, were class-stratified. However, it may be suggested that the discourse of 'class' is peculiarly

modern, and this is the major reason why the term will be restricted to modern indus-trial societies in the subsequent discussion.

4 An obvious counter-argument to this view is that many of the goods and services created by innovators have not benefited either the environment or society in general. Tobacco and Thalidomide might be cited as examples.

5 Nevertheless, there remains the possibility that it might still be valid as an explanation in a particular instance – for example, the behaviour of the mineworkers during the General Strike in Britain in 1926, who remained on strike after others had returned to work, might be explained with reference to the nature of their work and community relations.

6 Here an exception must be made in the case of Marx, who argued that pre-capitalist soci-eties are 'class'-stratified. However, Marx's conceptualization of pre-capitalist 'classes' has many parallels with Weber's and Tonnies's status or *Gemeinschaft* groupings.

Chapter 3 Class Analysis: The Classic Inheritance and its Development in the Twentieth Century

1 It has to be said that, whatever Braverman's other strengths, his understanding of class analysis in sociology was rudimentary. His description was confined to a discussion of self-rated class, which he took to represent the investigation of class consciousness, and his discussion of Lockwood's work treats it as a historical, rather than a sociological, account of clerical work.

2 See, for example, Dawley (1979).

3 It is of interest that Giddens uses Willis (1977), a 'cultural' investigation of the 'class structure', as an example of the empirical application of 'structuration' (Giddens 1984: 289).

4 He has subsequently noted that the book has a 'somewhat "archaic" feel', and 'if I were to go over the same ground again today, the book would need thoroughgoing revision, and I would modify parts of it substantially' (Giddens 1990: 298).

5 See Kaye (1984: 23–5); also Gregory (1982).

6 Particularly that emanating from the Centre for Contemporary Cultural Studies at the University of Birmingham (e.g. Hall 1981; Willis 1977).

7 Examples include some of the arguments surrounding the relative significance of class and consumption sector. This became a debate as to the relative significance of employ-ment class versus house ownership in determining political attitudes and behaviour. Employment class remains most significant. See Hamnett (1989).

8 Note that Pawson (1989) has argued convincingly that although their critique may be valid, Keat and Urry's methodological prescriptions are essentially structuralist.

9 To avoid confusion, it should be pointed out that Bourdieu is here using the term 'realist' to describe those who, having determined empirically the properties and bound-aries of the class structure, argue that these are 'real' classes. These approaches will be discussed at length in ch. 6.

10 These are not the only offerings; see Archer (1982) on 'morphogenesis'. The diversity of theoretical approaches serves to emphasize the point that there exists no dominant theoretical paradigm.

Chapter 4 Measuring the 'Class Structure'

1 As an illustration of this anomaly, Nichols points out that in the British *Classification of Occupations*, 1951, the 'capitalist', the 'business speculator' and the 'landowner' were lumped into the same residual category as the 'expert' (undefined) and the 'lunatic (trade not stated)'.

2 The registrar-general's class index was devised and developed by the Office of Population and Census Statistics (OPCS), now the Office of National Statistics (ONS), but this was not the only government department in Britain collecting details of occupations. In particular, the Department of Employment (DE, which became the Department for Education and Employment (DfEE), now the Department for Education and Skills (DfES)), developed in the 1960s and 1970s a detailed classification of occupations (Classification of Occupations and Directory of Occupational Titles: CODOT), which was integrated into the 1980 Census Occupational Classifications. It was felt that the combination of OPCS and DE categorizations had not been particularly successful and, from the 1991 Census, these should be replaced by a new classification, the Standard Occupational Classification (SOC). This hierarchical classification assumed that occupations involve a set of typical work activities, which are then classified into major, minor and unit groups according to, first, the level of skill and qualifications involved, and second, the nature of the work activities (Thomas and Elias 1989).

3 Particularly the 'productive labour' definition employed by Poulantzas (1975). Wright's conceptualization, unsurprisingly, proved to be superior.

4 This impression will have been reinforced by the fact that Goldthorpe had worked closely with Lockwood on the 'Affluent Worker' project: see Goldthorpe et al. (1969). See also Breen (2005).

5 Goldthorpe has subsequently moved away from this position in his development of rational action theory (RAT), discussed in ch. 7 of this book.

6 The usual response to this criticism is that major wealth holders represent an extremely small grouping that would effectively be lost in aggregate analyses.

Chapter 5 An Untimely Prediction of Death and a Timely Renewal

1 Both Goldthorpe and Wright stress that their classifications rest on the attributes of jobs, rather than individual persons. Nevertheless, Ingham's argument still applies, given that individual jobs with similar attributes are being aggregated.

2 Within sociology, the employment-aggregate approach to 'class analysis' was still being described as 'hegemonic' in the 1990s (Savage et al. 1992).

3 The actual erosion of these associations has been contested. Heath and his colleagues have argued that the Goldthorpe class scheme is still the most appropriate measure for the analysis of patterns of voting behaviour in Britain (Heath et al. 1991; Sarlvik and Crewe 1983). They have also demonstrated that employment class seems to be particularly significant as far as *right-wing* voting is concerned, particularly amongst the self-employed.

4 This historical period has been described as one of 'Butskellism'; a term derived from the surnames of two 'moderate' party leaders of the contemporary left and right – Hugh Gaitskell and R. A. B. Butler.

5 It may be suggested, however, that the legislation which accompanied the 'social contract' – notably in respect of equal pay, and sex discrimination and equal opportunities – has proved to have far-reaching social consequences in extending 'citizenship' rights to these categories.

6 Private industry had not participated in the corporatist deal, and wages in the private sector had risen sharply as a consequence of inflation.

7 In other European countries, such as Finland, attempts to liberalize employment have recently been associated with an increase in less secure forms of employment such as temporary work.

8 Industrialization took place at different periods in different countries, a fact which has had important consequences for the development of class relations (see Ingham 1974; Therborn 1983). Women's employment in agriculture and family enterprises remained significant for much longer in some countries than others, and thus the 'male bread-winner' label may not always be appropriate. Indeed, it has been suggested that in some countries – such as Finland – the label may never have been useful: see Pfau-Effinger (1993).

9 There were and are, of course, many on the socialist left who had always maintained that the centrally planned regimes of the Soviet Union were not in fact 'socialist', but nevertheless, even such critical socialist analyses have suffered from 'guilt by association' as discredited regimes crumbled apace.

10 In teaching, a statistic I have regularly used to demonstrate the continuing relevance of nation states is the substantial variations in national fertility rates.

11 The title of Lash and Urry's previous book (1987) is *The End of Organized Capitalism*, and refers to this period.

12 As we have seen, the theoretical impact of poststructuralism and postmodernism is reflected in the rejection of the idea that a single 'organizing principle' or 'meta-narrative' that explained societal organization might be identified. Thus it might be suggested that neither Lash and Urry nor Pakulski and Waters are 'postmodern' theorists. However, Pakulski and Waters have themselves embraced the description. Lash and Urry have rejected the 'postmodern' label, but, as Kumar (1995: 139–40) has argued in an illuminating critique, they may nevertheless be described as 'closet postmodernists'. Rather than continue with a semantic debate, therefore, we will simply describe these authors as 'postmodern'.

13 It should be noted that, in this respect, Lash and Urry enter more caveats than Pakulski and Waters. Furthermore, others (and, rather confusingly, Lash 1994) have suggested that detraditionalization incorporates more complex processes than marketization alone.

14 Although Grusky and Sorensen's argument is persuasive in respect of some occupational groupings, particularly professionals, their strategy would be problematic in respect of others.

15 Savage's account is historical and British-based. He argues that in Britain, craft work (embodying the 'traditional' working-class identity) was associated with mastery and autonomy, but today, working-class jobs have been constructed as 'servile' work. In contrast, middle-class employees once 'serviced' their employers (hence 'service class') but such work has been reconstructed as requiring autonomy and entrepreneurship. This is an interesting, if contentious argument – for example, the actual predominance and role of the 'aristocracy of labour' (craft workers) within the trade union movement in Britain may itself be contested.

Chapter 6 Class and Culture: The Ethnography of Class

1 Marshall et al. do provide a suggestive mapping of the interaction of class and status (1988: 199). However, their substantive discussion is concerned to demonstrate the continuing salience of 'class' – as defined by employment aggregates. More recently, Goldthorpe has addressed this issue in his work with Chan. See Chan and Goldthorpe (2004).

2 It may be noted that T. H. Marshall's ideas on citizenship developed out of his earlier work on professionalism; see Crompton (1990a) for an account of this.

3 Goldthorpe's characteristically robust view of anthropological methods is described in his report of exchanges with Meyer Fortes (see Goldthorpe 2000: 75).

4 Economic and cultural capital are viewed as the most important resources.

5 Similar criticisms have been made of arguments relating to a 'culture of poverty' as described by Lewis (1959).

6 That is, to describe consciousness as false (or to argue that people 'misrecognize' their 'true' position) constitutes an effective denial of 'agency', and moreover, privileges the author's interpretation, which cannot, therefore, be disproved – i.e. be subject to empirical testing.

7 It might be noted – and this is a very important point – that middle-class groupings such as managers and professionals have always had an enhanced capacity to determine the needs which they supply.

8 The British Medical Association's (BMA) role in advancing and protecting the interests of its highly qualified membership has led to its recent characterization as 'the NUM [National Union of Mineworkers] in white coats'.

9 So called because they 'cleared' all cheques at the end of every day. They included Barclays, Lloyds, the Midland (now HSBC) and Natwest.

10 Respondents were reinterviewed through to the early 1990s.

11 None of Lamont's interviewees had college degrees, but all had school-leaving qualifications. See Lamont (2000: 341). Some were in lower-level 'white-collar' jobs.

12 For example, ceremonial positions associated with courts (royal and legal) and government are not 'economically' generated.

13 It should be clear that it is not the intention to reject the arguments of Savage et al. out of hand, and indeed, the position taken here might be seen as compatible with a relatively 'loose' CARs-based approach. Rather, it is being argued that CARs-based approaches do not offer 'a clear theoretical foundation for a revived class analysis', a negative possibility that the authors also consider. See Savage et al. (2005: 43).

Chapter 7 Families, Social Mobility and Educational Achievement

1 Goldthorpe (1980; 1987: 27). Ch. 1, 'Social mobility and social interests', provides an excellent account of the history and background of research and theorizing in the area of social mobility.

2 Blau and Duncan were at pains to emphasize the fact that their general findings were not applicable to the black population, and were very critical of the extent of structured racial inequality in the United States.

3 As we have seen in earlier chapters, it should be noted that Goldthorpe's scheme includes employment relations only and therefore not all of the structural constraints identified by Crowder.

4 Glass's original enquiry has been subject to extensive criticisms which have argued, amongst other things, that it underestimated the actual extent of mobility. See Payne (1987: ch. 6).

5 The statistical techniques used in social mobility research are extremely complex and impossible to summarize briefly. A useful description for the beginner may be found in appendix B of Marshall et al. (1997). The techniques used by Goldthorpe and his colleagues have also been criticized; see Saunders (1997) and Ringen (2000).

6 The CASMIN group was associated with the International Sociological Association's Research Committee 28 on Social Stratification. For a descriptive summary, see Marshall (1997).

7 One obvious example would be the case of the societies of what used to be referred to as the 'Eastern bloc'. For ideological as well as economic and organizational reasons, such societies have been more likely to designate particular occupations as belonging to the 'working class', and the size of the non-manual category is correspondingly reduced. Thus if 'occupation' is taken as an index of 'class', the 'class structure' of Eastern bloc societies is quite different from that of Western societies, although they are both 'industrial' societies (Parkin 1972; Goldthorpe 1967).

8 Goldthorpe's analysis has also been challenged on methodological grounds by Ringen (2000), who has argued that measurements derived from Gini indices are superior to odds ratios and, applied to the same data, demonstrate a greater openness in British society.

9 Marshall and Swift reanalyse the Essex survey; see Marshall et al. (1988).

10 The question as to whether this state of affairs is actually just raises another set of issues which are extensively discussed in Marshall et al. (1997).

11 In fact Wright (1989) suggests that this is not the case in Sweden.

12 In fact, this discussion applies to England and Wales, as the Scottish system of secondary and higher education was rather different. Historically, secondary students in Scotland have continued with a wider range of subjects ('Highers' rather than A-levels), and have entered university at a younger age. The undergraduate degree lasted four years rather than three.

13 More girls passed the test than boys, and there was a shortage of grammar school places for girls. As a consequence, the pass mark was set lower for boys than girls.

14 Savage (2000: 85) has argued that Goldthorpe's taking up of RAT-based approaches is a 'defensive attempt' to explain, given the absence (and decline) of class identities, how individuals act in class ways even when they lack class awareness.

15 This picture is in direct conflict with Goldthorpe's (2000: 175) RAT account of the choices available to working-class families: 'For working class families . . . the "best buys" for their children, despite places in higher education becoming more widely available, could still appear to be vocational courses, linked perhaps to on the job training, which would reduce the chances of relegation to the ranks of the unskilled or unemployed . . . while increasing those of relatively quick entry into skilled manual or technical or supervisory positions.'

16 Sure Start is a government-sponsored programme, developed since 2002, that 'aims to ensure delivery of free early education for all three- and four-year-olds; affordable, quality childcare and after-school activities in every area; and children's centres and

health and family support, particularly in disadvantaged areas where they are most needed. It works with parents to build aspirations for employment and for their children's education' (www.surestart.gov.uk). Sure Start is heavily imbued with the rhetoric of parental 'choice', together with the economic and social virtues of increasing parental employment, particularly that of mothers.

17 LFS (Labour Force Survey) data. NVQ = National Vocational Qualifications. These relate to 'knowledge, skill and understanding' of a particular vocational area, together with on-the-job experience.

18 It is of interest that, as we shall see in the next chapter, the government's recent report on inequality (HMSO 2007) has endorsed Sen's 'capability approach', which argues that all *individuals* should be given the resources to ensure their full 'flourishing'. Directing resources at individuals, however, may be argued to leave wider structures of inequality in place, and is compatible with a neo-liberal approach more generally. See Harvey (2005); also ch. 8 this book.

Chapter 8 Widening Inequalities and Debates on 'Class': Discussion and Conclusions

1 Local government in the UK has been instructed to provide services at 'best value'. This means that 'in-house' local government departments (e.g. refuse collection, computing) are forced to tender for contracts and compete with private-sector providers.

2 Putting the review in context, it should be noted that it was chaired by Trevor Phillips, chair of the Equalities Commission, and had a major focus on inequalities of gender, race, sexuality and disability. It was inevitable, therefore, that diversity and rights would be emphasized in the report.

3 The full list (HMSO 2007: 127–9) includes the capabilities to: be alive; live in physical security; be healthy; be knowledgeable; understand and reason, and have the skills to participate in society; enjoy a comfortable standard of living, with independence and security; engage in productive and valued activities; enjoy individual, family and social life; participate in decision-making, have a voice and influence; express yourself and have self-respect, knowing you will be protected and treated fairly by the law.

4 The normative handicaps associated with prejudices against gender, race and disability are recognized in the equalities review.

5 Herrnstein and Murray also argue that levels of intelligence differ amongst different ethnic groups. For a discussion and critique, see Devine (1997: 230ff).

6 Recent policies in the US have cut such benefits even further, but rates of teenage pregnancy and single parenthood are still high. See Gornick and Meyers (2003).

7 Lash and Urry (1994) also emphasize the growing problem of 'wild spaces' in 'reflexive modernity'.

8 In the British debate in particular, two factors have contributed to this emphasis on stability. First, cross-sectional 'longitudinal' studies of the 'class structure' have to assume that the occupational groupings they identify keep to their relative position(s) over time, otherwise comparisons are impossible. Second, as we have seen in the preceding chapter, the 'Nuffield programme' has emphasized the stability of *relative* opportunities, rather than the increase in *absolute* opportunities as far as mobility, educational opportunities, etc. are concerned.

9 However, it may be argued that the neo-liberal policies of institutions such as the World Bank have in fact had this effect. See Harvey (2005: ch. 4).

10 The entirety of Esping-Andersen's argument is simply too complex to summarize here. Much of the debate following his work has focused on women's employment in particular; see Lewis (1992) and Sainsbury (1994).

11 The reference to the 'German model' describes the highly regulated labour markets that emerged in 'corporatist' Europe, in which a lack of 'flexibility' was seen as a barrier to economic growth. See Crouch and Streeck (1997).

12 New Labour governments have also introduced a number of other policies to reduce poverty, particularly tax concessions and benefits for families with children. These are summarized in Hills (2004: 233ff).

13 For example, recent measures to improve work–life 'balance' have given the right to employees to 'request' flexible working – which may be refused. In contrast, in France (for example), employees have a *right* to switch to reduced hours working (in the same job) if they so wish.

14 Extract from interview with bank manager carried out in 1980: 'Every new entrant comes in on a four-month probationary period. After two months we do an interim report. Depending on their qualifications on entry, and how well they perform during their probationary period, it may be that we will decide to mark them potentially for accelerated promotion . . . Assuming that they join at 18: they've taken their A levels and they come in shortly before they get their results. They are going to be in grade 1 for say 12–15 months. They are probably going to stay in grade 2 then for another 18 months to two years . . . They may be in for as little as nine or ten months in grade 2. I would think that three years through the grades is probably . . . In the first year, regardless of whether it's accelerated training or not, they are not assessed and advised of their position. They are assessed, but it's just on our records at that stage.'

15 This section draws on evidence gathered during a case-study investigation of a major bank in Britain. See Crompton (2006b: ch. 3).

16 As Wilkinson and Ladipo (2002: 179) argue, one of the reasons why individuals *feel* insecure is because of the unrestricted operations of financial markets: 'one of the recurring themes in our case studies was of senior management looking over their shoulders to protect themselves from hostile takeovers whilst simultaneously seeking to make opportunistic gains through mergers and acquisitions. Thus, even when managers were unhappy with the pressures being brought to bear on their workforces, they often felt powerless to make real decisions over the internal running of "their" companies because of the external forces controlling their capital.'

17 Wilkinson's major arguments are directed against the socio-psychological problems of an extreme 'market society'. Thus many of his arguments are directed towards improving the quality of social relations, in which economic democracy and introducing a sense of 'real control' in the workplace play a large part.

18 Indeed, Wilkinson (2005: 284) argues that 'The substitution of equality of opportunity for equality of outcome as a political aim reflects a monumental failure even to begin thinking seriously about the causes of our society's problems.'

REFERENCES

Abercrombie, N. and Turner, B. S. 1978: The dominant ideology thesis. *British Journal of Sociology*, 29 (2), 149–70.

Abercrombie, N. and Urry, J. 1983: *Capital, Labour, and the Middle Classes*. Allen & Unwin: London.

Abrams, P. 1980: History, sociology, historical sociology. *Past and Present*, 87, 3–16.

Adonis, A. and Pollard, S. 1997: *A Class Act*. Hamish Hamilton: London.

Althusser, L. 1969: *For Marx*. Penguin: Harmondsworth.

Andrews, G. (ed.) 1991: *Citizenship*. Lawrence & Wishart: London.

Anthias, F. 2001: The material and the symbolic in theorizing social stratification. *British Journal of Sociology*, 52 (3), 367–90.

Anthias, F. 2005: Social stratification and social inequality: models of intersectionality and identity. In Devine et al. 2005.

Archer, M. 1982: Morphogenesis versus structuration: on combining structure and action. *British Journal of Sociology*, 33 (4), 445–83.

Archer, M. 1996: Social integration and system integration: developing the distinction. *Sociology*, 30 (4), 679–99.

Bagguley, P., Mark-Lawson, J., Shapiro, D., Urry, J., Walby, S. and Warde, A. 1989: *Restructuring Place, Class and Gender: Social and Spatial Change in a British Locality*. Sage: London.

Ball, S. J. 2003: *Class Strategies and the Education Market: The Middle Classes and Social Advantage*. Routledge Falmer: London.

Ball, S. J., Rowe, R. and Gewirtz, S. 1997: Circuits of schooling: a sociological exploration of parental choice in social class contexts. In Halsey et al. 1997.

Baudrillard, J. 1972: *For a Critique of the Political Economy of the Sign*. Telos Press: St Louis.

Bauman, Z. 1982: *Memories of Class*. Routledge: London.

Beatson, M. 1995: *Labour Market Flexibility*. Department of Employment: London.

Beck, U. 1992: *Risk Society*. Sage: London.

Beck, U. 2000a: The cosmopolitan perspective: sociology of the second age of modernity. *British Journal of Sociology*, 51 (1), 79–106.

Beck, U. 2000b: *The Brave New World of Work*. Polity: Cambridge.

Beck, U. and Beck-Gernsheim, E. 2002: *Individualization*. Sage: London.

Beck, U. and Sznaider, N. 2006: Unpacking cosmopolitanism for the social sciences. *British Journal of Sociology*, 57 (1), 1–24.

Bell, D. 1973: *The Coming of Post-Industrial Society*. Basic Books: New York.

Bell, D. 1976: *The Cultural Contradictions of Capitalism*. Heinemann: London.

Bendix, R. 1964: *Nation-Building and Citizenship*. John Wiley: New York.

Bendix, R. and Lipset, S. M. (eds) 1967a: *Class, Status and Power* (2nd edn). Routledge: London.

Bendix, R. and Lipset, S. M. 1967b: Karl Marx's theory of social classes. In Bendix and Lipset 1967a.

Benton, T. 1984: *The Rise and Fall of Structural Marxism*. Macmillan: London.

Berger, P. L. 1987: *The Capitalist Revolution: Fifty Propositions about Prosperity, Equality and Liberty*. Gower: Aldershot.

Blackburn, R. M. 1967: *Union Character and Social Class*. Batsford: London.

Blackburn, R. M. 1998: A new system of classes: but what are they and do we need them? *Work, Employment and Society*, 12 (4), 735–42.

Blanden, J., Gregg, P. and Machin, S. 2005: *Intergenerational Mobility in Europe and North America*. Centre for Economic Performance, London School of Economics: London.

Blau, P. and Duncan, O. D. 1967: *The American Occupational Structure*. John Wiley: New York.

Bottero, W. 2004: Class identities and the identity of class. *Sociology*, 38 (5), 985–1003.

Bottero, W. 2005: *Stratification: Social Division and Inequality*. Routledge: Abingdon.

Bottomore, T. 1991: *Classes in Modern Society* (2nd edn). HarperCollins Academic: London.

Bourdieu, P. 1973: Cultural reproduction and social reproduction. In R. Brown (ed.), *Knowledge, Education and Cultural Change*. Tavistock: London.

Bourdieu, P. 1986: *Distinction: A Social Critique of the Judgement of Taste*. Routledge: London/New York.

Bourdieu, P. 1987: What makes a social class? *Berkeley Journal of Sociology*, 22, 1–18.

Bourdieu, P. 1991: *Language and Symbolic Power*. Polity: Cambridge.

Bourdieu, P. 1993: *Sociology in Question*. Sage: London.

Bourdieu, P. 1996: On the family as a realised category. *Theory, Culture and Society*, 13, 19–26.

Bourdieu, P. 1999: *The Weight of the World: Social Suffering in Contemporary Society*. Polity: Cambridge.

Bowles, S. and Gintis, H. 1976: *Schooling in Capitalist America*. Routledge: London.

Bradley, H. 1996: *Fractured Identities*. Polity: Cambridge.

Braverman, H. 1974: *Labor and Monopoly Capital: The Degradation of Work in the Twentieth Century*. Monthly Review Press: New York.

Breen, R. 2005: Foundations of a neo-Weberian class analysis. In Wright 2005.

Breen, R. and Rottman, D. B. 1995: *Class Stratification: A Comparative Perspective*. Harvester Wheatsheaf: London.

Brown, R. and Brannen, P. 1970: Social relations and social perspectives amongst ship-building workers, I & II. *Sociology*, 4 (1), 71–84; 197–211.

Brubaker, R. 1985: Rethinking classical theory. *Theory and Society*, 14, 745–73.

Bulmer, M. 1975: *Working-class Images of Society*. Routledge: London.

Burchardt, T., Le Grand, J. and Piachaud, D. 1999: Social exclusion in Britain 1991–1995. *Social Policy and Administration*, 33 (3), 227–44.

Burchell, B., Ladipo, D. and Wilkinson, F. (eds) 2002: *Job Insecurity and Work Intensification*. Routledge: London.

Burrows, R. and Gane, N. 2006: Geodemographics, software and class. *Sociology*, 40 (5), 793–812.

Butler, T. and Savage, M. (eds) 1996: *Social Change and the Middle Classes*. UCL Press: London.

Butler, T., Hamnett, C., Ramsden, M. and Webber, R. 2007: The best, the worst and the average: secondary school choice and education performance in East London. *Journal of Education Policy*, 22 (1), 7–29.

Calhoun, C. 2003: Pierre Bourdieu. In G. Ritzer (ed.), *Blackwell Companion to the Major Social Theorists*. Blackwell: Oxford.

Cannadine, D. 2000: *Class in Britain*. Penguin: London (1st edn 1998).

Castells, M. 1977: *The Urban Question*. Edward Arnold: London.

Castells, M. 2000: Materials for an exploratory theory of the network society. *British Journal of Sociology*, 51 (1), 4–24.

Chan, T. W. and Goldthorpe, J. H. 2004: Is there a status order in contemporary British society? *European Sociological Review*, 20 (5), 383–401.

Chan, T. W. and Goldthorpe, J. H. 2007: Social stratification and cultural consumption: music in England. *European Sociological Review*, 23 (1), 1–19.

Charlesworth, S. J. 2007: Reflection on violence and suicide in South Yorkshire: (dis)United Kingdom. *Anthropology Matters Journal*, 9 (1), www.anthropologymatters.com.

Clark, J., Modgil, C. and Modgil, S. (eds) 1990: *John H. Goldthorpe: Consensus and Controversy*. Falmer Press: Basingstoke.

Clark, T. and Lipset, S. M. 1991: Are social classes dying? *International Sociology*, 6 (4), 397–410.

Clark, T. N., Lipset, S. M. and Rempel, M. 1993: The declining political significance of social class. *International Sociology*, 8 (3), 293–316.

Collins, R. 1971: Functional and conflict theories of educational stratification. *American Sociological Review*, 36, 1002–19.

Connell, R. W. 1982: A critique of the Althusserian approach to class. In Giddens and Held 1982.

Connell, R. W., Ashendon, D. J., Kessler, S. and Dowsett, G. W. 1982: *Making the Difference: Schools, Families and Social Division*. George Allen & Unwin: Sydney.

Cox, O. C. 1959: *Caste, Class and Race*. Review Press: New York.

Crompton, R. 1979: Trade unionism and the insurance clerk. *Sociology*, 13 (3), 403–26.

Crompton, R. 1987: Gender, status and professionalism. *Sociology*, 21 (3), 413–28.

Crompton, R. 1989a: Women in banking. *Work, Employment and Society*, 3 (2), 141–56.

Crompton, R. 1989b: Class theory and gender. *British Journal of Sociology*, 40 (4), 565–87.

Crompton, R. 1990a: Professions in the current context. *Work, Employment and Society* (special issue).

Crompton, R. 1990b: Goldthorpe and Marxist theories of historical development. In Clark et al. 1990.

Crompton, R. 1991: Three varieties of class analysis: comment on R. E. Pahl. *International Journal of Urban and Regional Research*, 15 (1), 108–13.

Crompton, R. 1992: Patterns of social consciousness amongst the middle classes. In R. Burrows and C. Marsh (eds), *Consumption and Class*. Macmillan: Basingstoke.

Crompton, R. 1996a: The fragmentation of class analysis. *British Journal of Sociology*, 47 (1), 56–67.

Crompton, R. 1996b: Consumption and class analysis. In S. Edgell, K. Hetherington and A. Warde (eds), *Consumption Matters*. Blackwell: Oxford.

Crompton, R. 1996c: Gender and class analysis. In Lee and Turner 1996.

Crompton, R. 1998: *Class and Stratification*. Polity: Cambridge (2nd edn).

Crompton, R. 2006a: Class and family. *Sociological Review*, November, 658–76.

Crompton, R. 2006b: *Employment and the Family: The Reconfiguration of Work and Family Life in Contemporary Societies*. Cambridge University Press: Cambridge.

Crompton, R. and Gubbay, J. 1977: *Economy and Class Structure*. Macmillan: London.

Crompton, R. and Harris, F. 1998: Gender relations and employment: the impact of occupation. *Work, Employment and Society*, 12 (2), 297–315.

Crompton, R. and Jones, G. 1984: *White-Collar Proletariat: Deskilling and Gender in the Clerical Labour Process*. Macmillan: London.

Crompton, R. and Scott, J. 2005: Class analysis: beyond the cultural turn. In Devine et al. 2005.

Crompton, R., Dennett, J. and Wigfield, A. 2003: *Organisations, Careers and Caring*. Policy Press: Bristol.

Crompton, R., Lewis, S. and Lyonette, C. 2007a: Continuities, change and transformations. In Crompton et al. 2007.

Crompton, R., Lewis, S. and Lyonette, C. (eds) 2007b: *Women, Men, Work and Family in Europe*. Palgrave Macmillan: Basingstoke.

Crook, S., Pakulski, J. and Waters, M. 1992: *Postmodernization*. Sage: Beverly Hills, CA.

Crouch, C. 1999: *Social Change in Western Europe*. Oxford University Press: Oxford.

Crouch, C. and Streeck, W. (eds) 1997: *Political Economy of Modern Capitalism*. Sage: London.

Crowder, N. D. 1974: A critique of Duncan's stratification research. *Sociology*, 8, 19–45.

Dahrendorf, R. 1959: *Class and Class Conflict in an Industrial Society*. Routledge: London.

Dahrendorf, R. 1969: On the origin of inequality among men. In A. Beteille (ed.), *Social Inequality*. Penguin: Harmondsworth.

Dahrendorf, R. 1988: *The Modern Social Conflict*. University of California Press: Berkeley/Los Angeles.

Davis, K. and Moore, W. E. 1945; 1964: Some principles of stratification. Reprinted in L. A. Coser and B. Rosenberg (eds), *Sociological Theory*. Collier-Macmillan: London.

Dawley, A. 1979: E. P. Thompson and the peculiarities of the Americans. *Radical History Review*, 19 (Winter), 33–60.

Dean, H. 1991: In search of the underclass. In P. Brown and R. Scase (eds), *Poor Work: Disadvantage and the Division of Labour*. Open University Press: Milton Keynes.

Dench, S., Aston, J., Evans, C., Meager, N., Williams, M. and Willison, R. 2002: *Key Indicators of Women's Position in Britain*. London: Department of Trade and Industry.

Dennis, N., Henriques, F. and Slaughter, S. 1956: *Coal is our Life*. Tavistock: London (2nd edn 1969).

Devine, F. 1997: *Social Class in America and Britain*. Edinburgh University Press: Edinburgh.

Devine, F. 2004: *Class Practices: How Parents Help their Children Get Good Jobs*. Cambridge University Press: Cambridge.

Devine, F. and Savage, M. 2005: The cultural turn: Sociology and class analysis. In Devine et al. 2005.

Devine, F., Crompton, R., Savage, M. and Scott, J. (eds) 2005: *Rethinking Class: Culture, Identities and Lifestyles*. Palgrave: Basingstoke.

Du Gay, P. 1993: Numbers and souls: retailing and the de-differentiation of economy and culture. *British Journal of Sociology*, 44 (4), 563–87.

Du Gay, P. 1996: *Consumption and Identity at Work*. Sage: London.

Du Gay, P. and Pryke, M. 2002: *Cultural Economy*. Sage: London.

Duke, V. and Edgell, S. 1987: The operationalisation of class in British sociology: theoretical and empirical considerations. *British Journal of Sociology*, 38 (4), 445–63.

Durkheim, E. 1968: *The Division of Labour in Society*. Free Press: New York.

Edwards, P. 2000: Late twentieth century workplace relations: class struggle without classes. In R. Crompton, F. Devine, M. Savage and J. Scott (eds), *Renewing Class Analysis*. Blackwell: Oxford.

Ehrenreich, B. and Hochschild, A. R. 2003: *Global Woman*. Granta Books: London.

Emmison, M. 1991: Wright and Goldthorpe: constructing the agenda of class analysis. In J. Baxter, M. Emmison and J. Western, *Class Analysis and Contemporary Australia*. Macmillan: Melbourne.

Erikson, R. and Goldthorpe, J. H. 1988: Women at class crossroads: a critical note. *Sociology*, 22, 545–53.

Erikson, R. and Goldthorpe, J. H. 1993: *The Constant Flux*. Clarendon Press: Oxford.

Ermisch, J., Francesconi, M. and Seidler, T. 2006: Intergenerational mobility and marital sorting. *Economic Journal*, July, 659–79.

Esping-Andersen, G. 1990: *The Three Worlds of Welfare Capitalism*. Polity: Cambridge.

Esping-Andersen, G. (ed.) 1993: *Changing Classes: Stratification and Mobility in Post-Industrial Societies*. Sage: London.

Evans, G. 2006: *Educational Failure and White Working Class Children in Britain*. Palgrave Macmillan: Basingstoke.

Fagnani, J. 2007: Fertility rates and mothers employment behaviour in comparative perspective: similarities and differences in six European countries. In Crompton et al. 2007.

Featherman, D. L., Jones, L. and Hauser, R. M. 1975: Assumptions of mobility research in the U. S.: the case of occupational status. *Social Science Research*, 4, 329–60.

Featherstone, M. 1987: Lifestyle and consumer culture. *Theory, Culture and Society*, 4 (1), 55–70.

Featherstone, M. 1991: *Consumer Culture and Postmodernism*. Sage: London.

Finch, J. and Mason, J. 1993: *Negotiating Family Responsibilities*. Tavistock/Routledge: London.

Foucault, M. 1972: *The Archaeology of Knowledge*. Tavistock: London.

Foucault, M. 1977: *Madness and Civilization*. Tavistock: London.

Frank, T. 2000: *One Market under God*. New York: Doubleday.

Frankenberg, R. 1966: *Communities in Britain*. Penguin: Harmondsworth.

Fraser, N. 1995: From redistribution to recognition? Dilemmas of justice in a 'post socialist' age. *New Left Review*, 212, 68–94.

Fraser, N. 1998: Heterosexism, misrecognition and capitalism: a response to Judith Butler. *New Left Review*, 228, 140–9.

Fraser, N. 2000: Rethinking recognition. *New Left Review*, May/June, 107–20.

Freidson, E. 1986: *Professional Powers*. University of Chicago Press: Chicago and London.

Friedland, R. and Mohr, J. (eds) 2004: *Matters of Culture: Cultural Sociology in Practice.* Cambridge University Press: Cambridge.

Fulcher, J. and Scott, J. 1999: *Sociology.* Oxford University Press: Oxford.

Gallie, D. 1994: Are the unemployed an underclass? *Sociology,* 26, 737–57.

Gallie, D. and Vogler, C. 1993: Unemployment and attitudes to work. In D. Gallie et al. (eds), *Social Change and the Experience of Unemployment.* Oxford University Press: Oxford.

Garfinkel, H. 1967: *Studies in Ethnomethodology.* Prentice-Hall: Englewood Cliffs, NJ.

Gershuny, J. 2005: Busyness as the badge of honour for the new superordinate working class. *Working Paper of the Institute for Social and Economic Research, paper 2005-9.* Colchester: University of Essex.

Gerth, H. and Mills, C. W. (eds) 1948: *From Max Weber.* Routledge: London.

Gewirtz, S., Ball, S. J. and Rowe, R. 1995: *Markets, Choice and Equity in Education.* Open University Press: Buckingham.

Giddens, A. 1973: *The Class Structure of the Advanced Societies.* Hutchinson: London (2nd edn 1981).

Giddens, A. 1982: Hermeneutics and social theory. In *Profiles and Critiques in Social Theory.* Macmillan: London/Basingstoke.

Giddens, A. 1984: *The Constitution of Society.* Polity: Cambridge.

Giddens, A. 1987: *Social Theory and Modern Sociology.* Polity: Cambridge.

Giddens, A. 1990: Structuration theory and sociological analysis. In J. Clark, C. Mogdil and S. Mogdil (eds), *Anthony Giddens: Consensus and Controversy.* Falmer Press: Basingstoke.

Giddens, A. 1991: *Modernity and Self Identity.* Polity: Cambridge.

Giddens, A. (ed.) 2001: *The Global Third Way Debate.* Polity: Cambridge.

Giddens, A. and Held, D. (eds) 1982: *Classes, Power and Conflict.* Macmillan: London/Basingstoke.

Glass, D. V. (ed.) 1954: *Social Mobility in Britain.* Routledge: London.

Glucksmann, M. 1995: Why 'work'? Gender and the 'total social organization of labour'. *Gender, Work and Organization,* 2 (2), 63–75.

Goldthorpe, J. H. 1967: Social stratification in industrial society. In Bendix and Lipset 1967a.

Goldthorpe, J. H. 1973: A revolution in sociology? *Sociology,* 7, 449–62.

Goldthorpe, J. H. 1978: The current inflation: towards a sociological account. In F. Hirsch and J. H. Goldthorpe (eds), *The Political Economy of Inflation.* Martin Robertson: London.

Goldthorpe, J. H. 1983: Women and class analysis: in defence of the conventional view. *Sociology,* 17 (4), 465–88.

Goldthorpe, J. H. 1984a: The end of convergence: corporatist and dualist tendencies in modern Western societies. In J. H. Goldthorpe (ed.), *Order and Conflict in Contemporary Capitalism.* Clarendon Press: Oxford.

Goldthorpe, J. H. 1984b: Women and class analysis: a reply to the replies. *Sociology,* 18 (4), 491–9.

Goldthorpe, J. H. 2000: *On Sociology: Numbers, Narratives and the Integration of Research and Theory.* Oxford University Press: Oxford.

Goldthorpe, J. H. 2004: Trends in intergenerational class mobility in Britain in the late twentieth century. In R. Breen (ed.), *Social Mobility in Europe,* www.oxfordscholarshiponline.com.

Goldthorpe, J. H. and Hope, K. 1974: *The Social Grading of Occupations: A New Approach and Scale*. Clarendon Press: Oxford.

Goldthorpe, J. H. and Llewellyn, C. 1977: Class mobility in modern Britain: three theses examined. *Sociology*, 11 (2), 257–87.

Goldthorpe, J. H. and Marshall, G. 1992: The promising future of class analysis: a response to recent critiques. *Sociology*, 26 (3), 381–400.

Goldthorpe, J. H. (with C. Llewellyn and C. Payne) 1980: *Social Mobility and Class Structure in Modern Britain*. Clarendon Press: Oxford (2nd edn 1987).

Goldthorpe, J. H., Lockwood, D., Bechhofer, F. and Platt, J. 1968: *The Affluent Worker: Industrial Attitudes and Behaviour*. Cambridge University Press: Cambridge.

Goldthorpe, J. H., Lockwood, D., Bechhofer, F. and Platt, J. 1969: *The Affluent Worker in the Class Structure*. Cambridge University Press: Cambridge.

Goldthorpe, J. H., Lockwood, D., Bechhofer, F. and Platt, J. 1970: *The Affluent Worker: Political Attitudes and Behaviour*. Cambridge University Press: Cambridge.

Goodman, A., Johnson, P. and Webb, S. 1997: *Inequality in the UK*. Oxford University Press: Oxford.

Gornick, J. C. and Meyers, M. K. 2003: *Families that Work*. Russell Sage Foundation: New York.

Gouldner, A. 1954: *Patterns of Industrial Bureaucracy*. Free Press: New York.

Gouldner, A. 1979: *The Future of Intellectuals*. Macmillan: London.

Granovetter, M. S. 1985: Economic action and social structure: the problem of embeddedness. *American Journal of Sociology*, 91 (3), 481–510.

Granovetter, M. and Swedberg, R. (eds) 1992: *The Sociology of Economic Life*. Westview Press: Boulder, CO.

Gregg, P. and Wadsworth, J. 2001: Everything you ever wanted to know about measuring worklessness and polarization at the household level but were afraid to ask. *Oxford Bulletin of Economics and Statistics*, 63, 777–806.

Gregory, D. 1982: *Regional Transformation and Industrial Revolution*. Macmillan: London.

Grimshaw, D., Ward, K. G., Rubery, J. and Beynon, H. 2001: Organisations and the transformation of the internal labour market in the UK. *Work, Employment and Society*, 15 (1), 25–54.

Grimshaw, D., Beynon, H., Rubery, J. and Ward, K. 2002: The restructuring of career paths in large service sector organisations: 'delayering', upskilling and polarisation. *Sociological Review*, 50, 89–115.

Grusky, D. B. and Sorensen, J. B. 1998: Can class analysis be salvaged? *American Journal of Sociology*, 103 (5), 1187–234.

Gubbay, J. 1997: A Marxist critique of Weberian class analysis. *Sociology*, 31 (1), 143–52.

Hakim, C. 1980: Census reports as documentary evidence: the Census commentaries 1801–1951. *Sociological Review*, 28 (3), 551–80.

Halford, S. and Savage, M. 1995: Restructuring organizations, changing people. *Work, Employment and Society*, 9 (1), 97–122.

Halford, S., Savage, M. and Witz, A. 1997: *Gender, Careers and Organisations*. Macmillan: Basingstoke/London.

Hall, S. 1981: Cultural studies: two paradigms. In T. Bennett, G. Martin, C. Mercer and J. Woollacott (eds), *Culture, Ideology and Social Process*. Batsford Academic and Educational: London.

Hall, S. and Jaques, M. (eds) 1989: *New Times: The Changing Face of Politics in the 1990s.* Lawrence & Wishart: London.

Halsey, A. H. (ed.) 1988: *British Social Trends since 1900.* Macmillan: Basingstoke and London.

Halsey, A. H., Health, A. F. and Ridge, J. M. 1980: *Origins and Destinations.* Clarendon Press: Oxford.

Halsey, A. H., Lauder, H., Brown, P. and Wells, A. S. (eds) 1997: *Education: Culture, Economy, Society.* Oxford University Press: Oxford/New York.

Hamnett, C. 1989: Consumption and class in contemporary Britain. In Hamnett et al. 1989.

Hamnett, C., McDowell, L. and Sarre, P. (eds) 1989: *Restructuring Britain: The Changing Social Structure.* Sage: London.

Harvey, D. 1990: *The Condition of Postmodernity.* Blackwell: Oxford.

Harvey, D. 2005: *A Brief History of Neoliberalism.* Oxford University Press: Oxford.

Hatcher, R. 1998: Class differentiation in education: rational choices? *British Journal of Sociology of Education,* 19 (1), 5–24.

Hayek, F. 2001: *The Road to Serfdom.* Institute of Economic Affairs: London.

Heath, A. 1981: *Social Mobility.* Fontana: London.

Heath, A. and Britten, N. 1984: Women's jobs do make a difference. *Sociology,* 18 (4), 475–90.

Heath, A., Curtice, J., Jowell, R., Evans, G., Field, J. and Witherspoon, S. 1991: *Understanding Political Change: The British Voter 1964–1987.* Pergamon: Oxford.

Hebdige, D. 1979: *Subculture: The Meaning of Style.* Methuen/Routledge: London.

Herrnstein, R. J. and Murray, C. 1994: *The Bell Curve.* Free Press: New York.

Hills, J. 2004: *Inequality and the State.* Oxford University Press: Oxford.

Hindess, B. 1973: *The Use of Official Statistics in Sociology.* Macmillan: London.

Hirsch, F. 1977: *Social Limits to Growth.* Routledge: London.

HMSO 1966: *Census 1961: Occupation Tables.* HMSO: London.

HMSO 2007: *Fairness and Freedom.* HMSO: London.

Hochschild, A. 2000: Global care chains and emotional surplus value. In W. Hutton and A. Giddens (eds), *On the Edge: Living with Global Capitalism.* Jonathan Cape: London.

Hodge, R. W., Siegel, P. M. and Rossi, P. H. 1964: Occupational prestige in the United States: 1925–1963. *American Journal of Sociology,* 70, 286–302.

Hodge, R. W., Treiman, D. J. and Rossi, P. H. 1967: A comparative study of occupational prestige. In Bendix and Lipset 1967a.

Holmwood, J. and Stewart, A. 1983: The role of contradictions in modern theories of social stratification. *Sociology,* 17 (2), 239–54.

Hout, M., Brooks, C. and Manza, J. 1993: The persistence of classes in post-industrial societies. *International Sociology,* 8 (3), 259–77.

Ingham, G. K. 1970: Social stratification: individual attributes and social relationships. *Sociology,* 4 (1), 105–13.

Ingham, G. K. 1974: *Strikes and Industrial Conflict.* Macmillan: London.

Jenkins, R. 1992: *Pierre Bourdieu.* Routledge: London.

Johnson, R. 1979: Culture and the historians. In J. Clarke, C. Critcher and R. Johnson (eds), *Working-Class Culture: Studies in History and Theory.* Hutchinson: London.

Jones, F. L. 1988: Stratification approaches to class measurement. *Australian and New Zealand Journal of Sociology,* 24 (2), 279–84.

Jones, F. L. and McMillan, J. 2001: Scoring occupational categories for social research. *Work, Employment and Society*, 15 (1), 539–63.

Joseph Rowntree Foundation 1995: *Inquiry into Income and Wealth*. Joseph Rowntree Foundation: York.

Joyce, P. (ed.) 1995: *Class*. Oxford University Press: Oxford.

Kaye, H. J. 1984: *The British Marxist Historians*. Polity: Cambridge.

Keat, R. and Urry, J. 1975: *Social Theory as Science*. Routledge: London (2nd edn 1981).

Kelly, G., Kelly, D. and Gamble, A. (eds) 1997: *Stakeholder Capitalism*. Macmillan: Basingstoke.

Kerr, C., Dunlop, J. T., Harbison, F. and Myers, C. A. 1973: *Industrialism and Industrial Man*. Penguin: Harmondsworth (1st edn 1963).

Kumar, K. 1995: *From Post-Industrial to Postmodern Society*. Blackwell: Oxford.

Laclau, E. and Mouffe, C. 1985: *Hegemony and Socialist Strategy*. Verso: London.

Lamont, M. 1992: *Money, Morals and Manners: The Culture of the French and American Upper-Middle Class*. Chicago University Press: Chicago.

Lamont, M. 2000: *The Dignity of Working Men: Morality and the Boundaries of Race, Class and Imagination*. Russell Sage Foundation/Harvard University Press: New York.

Lareau, A. 1997: Social class differences in family–school relationships: the importance of cultural capital. In Halsey et al. 1997.

Lash, S. 1994: Reflexity and its doubles. In U. Beck, A. Giddens and S. Lash (eds), *Reflexive Modernization, Politics, Tradition and Aesthetics in the Modern Social Order*. Polity: Cambridge.

Lash, S. and Urry, J. 1987: *The End of Organized Capitalism*. Polity: Cambridge.

Lash, S. and Urry, J. 1994: *Economies of Signs and Space*. Sage: London.

Layder, D. 1990: *The Realist Image in Social Science*. Macmillan: Basingstoke.

Le Roux, B., Rouanet, H., Savage, M. and Warde, A. 2007: Class and cultural division in the UK. CRESC working paper, University of Manchester.

Lee, D. and Turner, B. 1996: *Conflicts about Class*. Longman: London.

Lenski, G. E. 1966: *Power and Privilege: A Theory of Social Stratification*. McGraw-Hill: New York.

Lewis, J. 1992: Gender and the development of welfare regimes. *Journal of European Social Policy*, 2 (3), 159–73.

Lewis, O. 1959: *Five Families: Mexican Case Studies in the Culture of Poverty*. Basic Books: New York.

Lipset, S. M. and Bendix, R. (eds) 1959: *Social Mobility in Industrial Society*. Heinemann: London.

Lipset, S. M. and Rokkan, S. (eds) 1967: *Party Systems and Voter Alignments*. Free Press: New York.

Lipset, S. M. and Zetterberg, H. L. 1959: Social mobility in industrial societies. In Lipset and Bendix 1959.

Littlejohn, J. 1963: *Westrigg: The Sociology of a Cheviot Parish*. London: Routledge and Kegan Paul.

Lockwood, D. 1958: *The Blackcoated Worker*. Allen & Unwin: London (2nd edn 1989).

Lockwood, D. 1964: Social integration and system integration. In G. K. Zollschan and W. Hirsch (eds), *Explorations in Social Change*. Houghton Mifflin: Boston.

Lockwood, D. 1966: Sources of variation in working-class images of society. *Sociological Review*, 14 (3), 244–67.

Lockwood, D. 1974: For T. H. Marshall. *Sociology*, 8 (3), 363–7.

Lockwood, D. 1981: The weakest link in the chain? In S. Simpson and I. Simpson (eds), *Research in the Sociology of Work: 1*. JAI Press: Greenwich, CT; reprinted (1988) in D. Rose (ed.), *Social Stratification and Economic Change*. Unwin Hyman: London.

Lyonette, C., Crompton, R. and Wall, K. 2007: Gender, occupational class and work–life conflict: a comparison of Britain and Portugal. *Community, Work and Family*, 10 (3), 283–308.

Machin, S. and Vignoles, A. 2004: Educational inequality: the widening socio-economic gap. *Fiscal Studies*, 25 (2), 107–28.

Mann, M. 1973: *Consciousness and Action among the Western Working Class*. Macmillan: London.

Marsh, C. 1986: Social class and occupation. In R. Burgess (ed.), *Key Variables in Social Investigation*. Routledge: London.

Marshall, G. 1982: *In Search of the Spirit of Capitalism*. Hutchinson: London.

Marshall, G. 1988: The politics of the new middle class: history and predictions. Paper presented at the annual conference of the British Sociological Association.

Marshall, G. 1991: In defence of class analysis: a comment on R. E. Pahl. *International Journal of Urban and Regional Research*, 15 (1), 114–18.

Marshall, G. 1997: *Repositioning Class*. Sage: London.

Marshall, G. and Rose, D. 1990: Out-classed by our critics. *Sociology*, 24 (2), 255–67.

Marshall, G. and Swift, A. 1993: Social class and social justice. *British Journal of Sociology*, 44 (2), 187–211.

Marshall, G., Newby, H., Rose, D. and Vogler, C. 1988: *Social Class in Modern Britain*. Hutchinson: London.

Marshall, G., Roberts, R. and Burgoyne, C. 1996: Social class and underclass in Britain and the United States. *British Journal of Sociology*, 47 (1), 22–44.

Marshall, G., Swift, A. and Roberts, S. 1997: *Against the Odds?* Clarendon Press: Oxford.

Marshall, T. H. 1963: Citizenship and social class. In *Sociology at the Crossroads*. Heinemann: London.

Marx, K. 1955: *The Poverty of Philosophy*. Progress Publishing: Moscow.

Marx, K. 1962a: The Eighteenth Brumaire of Louis Bonaparte. In K. Marx and F. Engels, *Selected Works*, vol. 1. Foreign Languages Publishing House: Moscow.

Marx, K. 1962b: Preface to *A Contribution to the Critique of Political Economy*. In K. Marx and F. Engels, *Selected Works*, vol. 1. Foreign Languages Publishing House: Moscow.

Marx, K. 1974: *Capital*, vol. 3. Lawrence & Wishart: London.

Marx, K. and Engels, F. 1962: *Manifesto of the Communist Party*. In K. Marx and F. Engels, *Selected Works*, vol. 1. Foreign Languages Publishing House: Moscow.

Marx, K. and Engels, F. 1970: *The German Ideology*. Lawrence & Wishart: London.

Massey, D. 1984: *Spatial Divisions of Labour*. Macmillan: London/Basingstoke.

Mayer, K. 1963: The changing shape of the American class structure. *Social Research*, 30, 458–68.

McDowell, L. 2003: *Redundant Masculinities?* Blackwell: Oxford.

McLennan, G. 2000: The new positivity. In J. Eldridge, J. MacInnes, S. Scott, C. Warhurst and A. Witz (eds), *For Sociology: Legacies and Prospects*. Sociologypress: Durham.

McNall, S. G., Levine, R. F. and Fantasia, R. 1991: *Bringing Class Back In*. Westview Press and Praeger: New York.

Meillassoux, C. 1973: Are there castes in India? *Economy and Society*, 2 (1), 89–111.

Merton, R. K. 1959: Notes on problem-finding in sociology. In R. K. Merton, L. Broom and L. S. Cottrell (eds), *Sociology Today*. Harper & Row: New York.

Merton, R. K. 1965: Social structure and anomie. In *Social Theory and Social Structure*. Free Press: New York.

Mitchell, J. C. 1983: Case and situation analysis. *Sociological Review*, 31, 187–211.

Morris, L. 1994: *Dangerous Classes*. Routledge: London.

Morris, L. 1995: *Social Divisions*. UCL Press: London.

Morris, L. 1996: Classes, underclasses and the labour market. In Lee and Turner 1996.

Morris, L. and Scott, J. 1996: The attenuation of class analysis. *British Journal of Sociology*, 47 (1), 45–55.

Muller, W. 1990: Social mobility in industrial nations. In Clark et al. 1990.

Mullins, P. 1991: The identification of social forces in development as a general problem in sociology: a comment on Pahl's remarks on class and consumption relations as forces in urban and regional development. *International Journal of Urban and Regional Research*, 15 (1), 119–26.

Murphy, J. (ed.) 2006: *Social Mobility and Public Service Reform*. Policy Network, www.policy-network.net.

Murray, C. A. 1984: *Losing Ground*. Basic Books: New York.

Murray, C. A. (ed.) 1990: *The Emerging British Underclass*. IEA Health and Welfare Unit: London.

Murray, C. A. 1994: *Underclass: The Crisis Deepens*. IEA: London.

Murray, R. 1989: Fordism and post-Fordism. In Hall and Jaques 1989.

Neale, R. S. (ed.) 1983: *History and Class*. Blackwell: Oxford.

Newby, H. 1977: *The Deferential Worker*. Allen Lane: London.

Nichols, T. 1979: Social class: official, sociological and Marxist. In J. Irvine, I. Miles and J. Evans (eds), *Demystifying Social Statistics*. Pluto: London.

Nolan, P. 2003: Reconnecting with history. *Work, Employment and Society*, 17 (3), 473–80.

Nyberg, A. 2006: Economic crisis and the sustainability of the dual earner, dual carer model. In D. Perrons, C. Fagan, L. McDowell, K. Ray and K. Ward (eds), *Gender Divisions and Working Time in the New Economy*. Edward Elgar: Cheltenham.

O'Neill, J. 1999: Economy, equality and recognition. In L. Ray and A. Sayer (eds), *Culture and Economy after the Cultural Turn*. Sage: London.

O'Neill, J. 2001: Oh! My others, there is no Other: capital culture, class and Other-wiseness. *Theory, Culture and Society*, 18, 2 April.

Offe, C. 1985a: 'Work' – a central sociological category? In *Disorganized Capitalism*. Polity: Cambridge.

Offe, C. 1985b: New social movements: challenging the boundaries of institutional politics. *Social Research*, 52 (4), 817–68.

ONS/HMSO 2002: *The National Statistics Socio-Economic Classification User Manual*. HMSO: London.

Ossowski, S. 1963: *Class Structure in the Social Consciousness*. Routledge and Kegan Paul: London.

Pahl, R. E. 1989: Is the emperor naked? Some questions on the adequacy of sociological theory in urban and regional research. *International Journal of Urban and Regional Research*, 13 (4), 709–20.

Pahl, R. E. 1996: A reply to Goldthorpe and Marshall. In Lee and Turner 1996.

Pakulski, J. and Waters, M. 1996: *The Death of Class.* Sage: London.

Parkin, F. 1972: *Class Inequality and Political Order.* Paladin: London.

Pateman, C. 1988: *The Sexual Contract.* Polity: Cambridge.

Pateman, C. 1989: *The Disorder of Women.* Polity: Cambridge.

Pawson, R. 1989: *A Measure for Measures.* Routledge: London.

Payne, G. 1987: *Mobility and Change in Modern Society.* Macmillan: Basingstoke/ London.

Peacock, A. 1991: Welfare philosophies and welfare finance. In T. Wilson and D. Wilson (eds), *The State and Social Welfare.* Longman: London/New York.

Peterson, R. A. and Kern, R. M. 1996: Changing highbrow taste: from snob to omnivore. *American Sociological Review*, 61, 900–7.

Pfau-Effinger, B. 1993: Modernisation, culture and part-time employment. *Work, Employment and Society*, 7 (3), 383–410.

Phillips, T. and Western, M. 2005: Social change and social identity: postmodernity, reflexive modernisation and the transformation of social identities in Australia. In Devine et al. 2005.

Pickvance, C. G. 1992: Comparative analysis, causality and case studies. In A. Rogers and S. Vertovec (eds), *The Urban Context: Ethnicity, Social Networks and Situational Analysis.* Berg: London.

Pirenne, H. 1936: *Economic and Social History of Medieval Europe*, trans. I. E. Clegg. Routledge: London.

Plant, R. 1991: Welfare and the enterprise society. In T. Wilson and D. Wilson (eds), *The State and Social Welfare.* Longman: London/New York.

Polanyi, K. 1957: *The Great Transformation.* Beacon Press: Boston.

Poulantzas, N. 1975: *Classes in Contemporary Capitalism.* New Left Books: London.

Prandy, K. 1991: The revised Cambridge scale of occupations. *Sociology*, 24 (4), 629–56.

Prandy, K. 1998: Deconstructing classes: critical comments on the revised social classification. *Work, Employment and Society*, 12 (4), 743–54.

Prandy, K. and Blackburn, R. M. 1997: Putting men and women into classes. *Sociology*, 31 (1), 143–52.

Price, R. and Bain, G. S. 1988: The labour force. In Halsey 1988.

Przeworski, A. 1985: *Capitalism and Social Democracy.* Cambridge University Press: Cambridge.

Reay, D. 1998: Rethinking social class: qualitative perspectives on class and gender. *Sociology*, 32 (2), 259–75.

Reay, D. and Ball, S. J. 1997: Spoilt for choice: the working classes and education markets. *Oxford Review of Education*, 23 (1), 89–101.

Reay, D. and Ball, S. J. 1998: Making their minds up: family dynamics of school choice. *Educational Research Journal*, 24 (4), 431–48.

Reay, D. and Lucey, H. 2003: The limits of 'choice': children and inner city schooling. *Sociology*, 37 (1), 121–42.

Reay, D., Davies, J., David, M. and Ball, S. J. 2001: Choices of degree or degrees of choice? Class, 'race' and the higher education choice process. *Sociology*, 35 (4), 855–74.

Reid, I. 1981: *Social Class Differences in Britain.* Grant McIntyre: London.

Reid, I. 1998: *Class in Britain.* Polity: Cambridge.

Reiss, A. J. 1961: *Occupations and Social Status.* Free Press: New York.

Rex, J. 1961: *Key Problems of Sociological Theory.* Routledge: London.

Rex, J. 1986: *Race and Ethnicity*. Open University Press: Milton Keynes.

Ringen, S. 2000: Inequality and its measurement. *Acta Sociologica*, 43 (1), 84.

Ritzer, G. 1996: *The McDonaldization of Society*. Pine Forge Press: Thousand Oaks, CA.

Ronay, B. 2007: Anyone want to play on the left? *Guardian*, Wednesday 25 April.

Rose, D. and Elias, P. 1995: The revision of OPCS social classifications. *Work, Employment and Society*, 9 (3), 583–92.

Rose, D. and Marshall, G. 1986: Constructing the (W)right classes. *Sociology*, 20 (3), 440–55.

Rose, D. and O'Reilly, K. 1997: *Constructing Classes: Towards a New Social Classification for the UK*. ESRC/ONS: Swindon and London.

Rose, D., Marshall, G., Newby, H. and Vogler, C. 1987: Goodbye to supervisors? *Work, Employment and Society*, 1 (1), 7–24.

Rose, N. 1989: *Governing the Soul*. Routledge: London.

Rubin, L. B. 1976: *Worlds of Pain*. Basic Books: New York.

Runciman, W. G. 1990: How many classes are there in contemporary British society? *Sociology*, 24 (3), 377–96.

Rutter, M. and Madge, N. 1976: *Cycles of Disadvantage*. Heinemann: London.

Sabel, C. F. 1982: *Work and Politics*. Cambridge University Press: Cambridge.

Sainsbury, D. (ed.) 1994: *Gendering Welfare States*. Sage: London.

Sarlvik, B. and Crewe, I. 1983: *Decade of Dealignment: The Conservative Victory of 1979 and Electoral Trends in the 1970s*. Cambridge University Press: Cambridge.

Sarre, P. 1989: Recomposition of the class structure. In Hamnett et al. 1989.

Saunders, P. 1987: *Social Theory and the Urban Question*. Unwin Hyman: London.

Saunders, P. 1990a: *Social Class and Stratification*. Routledge: London.

Saunders, P. 1990b: *A Nation of Home Owners*. Unwin Hyman: London.

Saunders, P. 1996: *Unequal but Fair? A Study of Class Barriers in Britain*. Institute of Economic Affairs: London.

Saunders, P. 1997: Social mobility in Britain. *Sociology*, 31 (2), 261–88.

Savage, M. 2000: *Class Analysis and Social Transformation*. Open University Press: Buckingham.

Savage, M., Dickens, P. and Fielding, T. 1988: Some social and political implications of the contemporary fragmentation of 'service class' in Britain. *International Journal of Urban and Regional Research*, 12 (3), 455–76.

Savage, M., Barlow, J., Dickens, A. and Fielding, T. 1992: *Property, Bureaucracy and Culture: Middle Class Formation in Contemporary Britain*. Routledge: London.

Savage, M., Bagnall, G. and Longhurst, B. 2001: Ordinary, ambivalent and defensive: class identities in the Northwest of England. *Sociology*, 35 (4), 875–92.

Savage, M., Warde, A. and Devine, F. 2005: Capitals, assets and resources: some critical issues. *British Journal of Sociology*, 56 (1), 31–47.

Sayer, A. 1984: *Method in Social Science: A Realist Approach*. Hutchinson: London.

Sayer, A. 2005: *The Moral Significance of Class*. Cambridge University Press: Cambridge.

Sayer, A. and Walker, R. 1992: *The New Social Economy*. Blackwell: Oxford.

Scott, J. 1982: *The Upper Classes*. Macmillan: London.

Scott, J. 1991: *Who Rules Britain?* Polity: Cambridge.

Scott, J. 1996: *Stratification and Power*. Polity: Cambridge.

Seccombe, W. 1993: *Weathering the Storm*. Verso: London/New York.

Sen, A. 1999: *Development as Freedom*. Oxford University Press: Oxford.

Sennett, R. 1998: *The Corrosion of Character*. W. W. Norton: New York/London.

Sennett, R. and Cobb, J. 1973: *The Hidden Injuries of Class*. Vintage Books: New York.

Skeggs, B. 1997: *Formations of Class and Gender*. Sage: London.

Skeggs, B. 2004: *Class, Self, Culture*. Routledge: London.

Skeggs, B. 2005: The re-branding of class: propertising culture. In Devine et al. 2005.

Smelser, N. J. 1959: *Social Change in the Industrial Revolution: An Application of Theory to the Lancashire Cotton Industry 1770–1840*. Routledge: London.

Smelser, N. J. (ed.) 1988: *Handbook of Sociology*. Sage: Beverly Hills, CA.

Smelser, N. J. and Swedberg, R. (eds) 2005: *The Handbook of Economic Sociology*. Princeton University Press: Princeton, NJ.

Smiles, S. 1859: *Self-Help: With Illustrations of Conduct and Perseverance* (4th edn). Murray: London.

Smith, C. 1987: *Technical Workers, Class, Labour and Trade Unionism*. Macmillan: London.

Stacey, M. 1960: *Tradition and Change: A Study of Banbury*. Oxford University Press: London.

Stacey, M. 1969: The myth of community studies. *British Journal of Sociology*, 20 (2), 134–47.

Stacey, M. 1981: The division of labour revisited or overcoming the two Adams. In P. Abrams, R. Deem, J. Finch and P. Rock (eds), *Practice and Progress: British Sociology 1950–1980*. Allen & Unwin: London.

Stanworth, M. 1984: Women and class analysis: a reply to Goldthorpe. *Sociology*, 18 (2), 159–70.

Stark, D. 1980: Class struggle and the transformation of the labor process. *Theory and Society*, 9 (1), 89–130.

Stedman Jones, G. 1976: From historical sociology to theoretical history. *British Journal of Sociology*, 27 (3), 295–305.

Stedman Jones, G. 1983: *Languages of Class: Studies in English Working-Class History*. Cambridge University Press: Cambridge.

Steedman, H. 2001: *Benchmarking Apprenticeship: UK and Continental Europe Compared*. Centre for Economic Performance, London School of Economics: London.

Sullivan, A. 2001: Cultural capital and educational attainment. *Sociology*, 35 (4), 893–912.

Szreter, S. R. S. 1984: The genesis of the Registrar-General's social classification of occupations. *British Journal of Sociology*, 35, 522–46.

Taylor, R. 2002: *Britain's World of Work: Myths and Realities*. Economic and Social Research Council: Swindon.

Therborn, G. 1983: Why some classes are more successful than others. *New Left Review*, 138 (March–April), 37–55.

Thomas, R. and Elias, P. 1989: Development of the standard occupational classification. *Population Trends*, 55, 16–21.

Thompson, E. P. 1968: *The Making of the English Working Class*. Penguin: Harmondsworth.

Thompson, P. and Warhurst, C. (eds) 1998: *Workplaces of the Future*. Macmillan: Basingstoke.

Thrift, N. and Williams, P. (eds) 1987: *Class and Space*. Routledge: London.

Tumin, M. 1964: Some principles of stratification: a critical analysis. In L. A. Coser and B. Rosenberg (eds), *Sociological Theory*. Collier-Macmillan: London.

Turner, B. S. 1988: *Status*. Open University Press: Milton Keynes.

Urry, J. 1981: *The Anatomy of Capitalist Societies*. Macmillan: London/Basingstoke.

Urry, J. 2000a: Mobile sociology. *British Journal of Sociology*, 51 (1), 185–203.

Urry, J. 2000b: *Sociology beyond Societies*. Routledge: London.

Vincent, C. and Ball, S. J. 2006: *Childcare Choice and Class Practices*. Routledge: London/ New York.

Walker, A. 1990: Blaming the victims. In Murray 1990.

Walker, P. 1979: *Between Capital and Labor*. Monthly Review Press: New York.

Walvin, J. 2001: *The Only Game*. Pearson Education: London.

Warner, L. 1963: *Yankee City*. Yale University Press: New Haven, CT.

Waters, M. 1996: Succession in the stratification system. In Lee and Turner 1996.

Weber, M. 1948: Class, status, party. In Gerth and Mills 1948.

Weber, M. 1976: *The Protestant Ethic and the Spirit of Capitalism*, trans. T. Parsons. Allen & Unwin: London.

Weber, M. 1978: *Economy and Society* (eds), G. Roth and C. Wittich. University of California Press: Berkeley and Los Angeles.

Weininger, E. B. 2005: Foundations of Pierre Bourdieu's class analysis. In Wright 2005.

Westergaard, J. 1995: *Who Gets What?* Polity: Cambridge.

Westergaard, J. and Resler, H. 1975: *Class in a Capitalist Society*. Heinemann: London.

Wilkinson, F. and Ladipo, D. 2002: What can governments do? In Burchell et al. 2002.

Wilkinson, R. G. 2005: *The Impact of Inequality*. Routledge: Abingdon.

Willis, P. 1977: *Learning to Labour: How Working Class Kids Get Working Class Jobs*. Saxon House: London.

Wilson, W. J. 1987: *The Truly Disadvantaged: Inner City Woes and Public Policy*. University of Chicago Press: Chicago.

Wilson, W. J. 1991: Studying inner-city social dislocation: the challenge of public agenda research. *American Sociological Review*, 56, 1–14.

Wilson, W. J. (ed.) 1993: *The Ghetto Underclass*. Sage: London.

Womack, J. P., Jones, D. T. and Roos, D. 1990: *The Machine that Changed the World*. Macmillan: New York.

Wood, E. M. 1986: *The Retreat from Class*. Verso: London.

Wootton, B. 1955: *The Social Foundations of Wage Policy*. Allen & Unwin: London.

Wright, E. O. 1976: Class boundaries in advanced capitalist societies. *New Left Review*, 98, 3–41.

Wright, E. O. 1979: *Class Structure and Income Determination*. Academic Press: New York.

Wright, E. O. 1980: Class and occupation. *Theory and Society*, 9, 177–214.

Wright, E. O. 1985: *Classes*. Verso: London.

Wright, E. O. (ed.) 1989: *The Debate on Classes*. Verso: London.

Wright, E. O. 1997: *Class Counts*. Cambridge University Press: Cambridge.

Wright, E. O. (ed.) 2005: *Approaches to Class Analysis*. Cambridge University Press: Cambridge.

Wright, E. O. and Martin, B. 1987: The transformation of the American class structure, 1960–1980. *American Journal of Sociology*, 93 (1), 1–29.

Wright, E. O. and Singlemann, J. 1982: Proletarianization in the changing American class structure. *American Journal of Sociology*, 88 (Supplement), 176–209.

Wrong, D. 1966: The oversocialized conception of man in modern sociology. Reprinted in L. A. Coser and B. Rosenberg (eds), *Sociological Theory*. Collier-Macmillan: London.

Wynne, D. 1990: Leisure, lifestyle and the construction of social position. *Leisure Studies*, 9, 21–34.

Young, M. and Wilmott, P. 1957: *Family and Kinship in East London*. Routledge: London.

INDEX